Relationship Marketing

PEARSON
Education

We work with leading authors to develop the strongest
educational materials in marketing, bringing cutting-edge
thinking and best learning practice to a global market.

Under a range of well-known imprints, including
Financial Times Prentice Hall, we craft high quality
print and electronic publications which help
readers to understand and apply their content,
whether studying or at work.

To find out more about the complete range of our
publishing please visit us on the World Wide Web at:
www.pearsoneduc.com

Relationship Marketing

Exploring relational strategies in marketing

John Egan

 Prentice Hall
FINANCIAL TIMES

An imprint of Pearson Education
Harlow, England • London • New York • Boston • San Francisco • Toronto • Sydney • Singapore • Hong Kong
Tokyo • Seoul • Taipei • New Delhi • Cape Town • Madrid • Mexico City • Amsterdam • Munich • Paris • Milan

For Alison, Thomas and Alice

Pearson Education Limited
Edinburgh Gate
Harlow
Essex CM20 2JE
England

and Associated Companies throughout the world

Visit us on the World Wide Web at:
www.pearsoneduc.com

First published 2001

ISBN 0273-64612-5

British Library Cataloguing-in-Publication Data
A catalogue record for this book is available from the British Library

Library of Congess Cataloging-in-Publication Data
Egan, John.
   Relationship marketing : exploring relationship strategies in marketing / John Egan.--
1st ed.
     p. cm.
  Includes bibliographical references and index.
  ISBN 0-273-64612-5
   1. Relationship marketing. I. Title.

  HF5415.55 .E34 2001
  658.8'12--dc21

                                  2001023168

10 9 8 7 6 5 4
07 06 05 04 03

Typeset by 30 in 9.5/13pt Stone Serif
Produced by Pearson Education Malaysia Sdn Bhd
Printed in Malaysia, LSP

Contents

Preface

Although the main title *'Relationship Marketing'* sets out the parameters of this text it is (as is frequently the case) the subtitle that may prove more enlightening. The emphasis in this book is on acknowledging the role that relationship marketing (RM) is playing in modern management and, perhaps more importantly, establishing the contexts in which RM is most beneficially exercised. This is not, however, a 'how to do it' type text on 'relationship marketing', 'customer relationship management' or any of the various 'relational business' subject areas (complete with prescriptive solutions). Rather this book seeks to generate questions and debate and encourage individual responses to particular marketing situations.

This does not mean that this book is without bias. It is most definitely written from the viewpoint of marketing as an art rather than a science, and my concerns regarding the mathematical manipulation of (sometimes spurious) data no doubt come through in the text. I concur with that body of opinion that sees marketing as constructed of a 'messy set of rules, tools and guidelines that produce (results) according to the expertise and sensitivity of the craftsman (or craftswoman), not the empirical accuracy of the rules, tools and guidelines' (Damarest, 1997, p. 375). This may (understandably) annoy some of my more mathematically and statistically minded colleagues.

Despite this one, albeit fundamental, bias the author has tried as far as possible to be objective. This does not negate, however, the responsibility of the reader to make up his or her own mind as to whether to accept or refute any of the positions taken in the text. By way of advice it is suggested that a healthy scepticism is maintained. The reader is encouraged to question conclusions and research findings in whatever way they see fit. I would welcome comments with the proviso that, whether or not critical, they are non-abusive. Please don't shoot the messenger even if you believe he comes from an alien camp.

RM has, recently experienced a (perhaps justified) backlash. This text should *not* be regarded as a fight-back by relational marketers but rather as a contribution to the ongoing debate. I do, however, take the view that just because a concept may be flawed does not necessarily mean it should be wholly abandoned, as has been implied in some quarters. This potential for 'throwing the baby out with the bath water' incidentally, in my view, applies to *both* relationship and traditional marketing.

Although RM is usually associated with services marketing I would like to think that many of the ideas hold resonance for product manufacturers. In the same way I trust that it will be of interest to both consumer and business-to-business marketers. Indeed, I hope that the text may offer help in establishing how these areas of business are associated with one another within a relational context.

The book is (rather unevenly) divided into three parts. In the first the ideas surrounding relational strategies in general and relationship marketing in particular are discussed. In the second the central RM tenet of the 'core firm and its partnerships' is analysed over a series of chapters. In the final part the place of technology in relational strategy management and the management process itself are discussed.

This book would never have seen the light of day without the help of a number of people. I would like to thank wholeheartedly Liz Sproat, Marie Osman and Anita Atkinson for all their help and support. Penelope Wolf should also be thanked for her sane and sensible advice prior to going to print. The anonymous reviewers deserve considerable praise for their attention to detail and the very constructive suggestions and occasional admonishments. My colleagues at Middlesex University deserve a mention for putting up with me since I joined the Business School. Last (but very definitely not least) my family for putting up with the trials and tribulations of the past few months and to whom this book is dedicated.

There is an Instructor's Manual to accompany this title, available for download on www.booksites.net/Egan.

Reference

Damerest, M. (1997) 'Understanding knowledge management', *Long Range Planning* 30(3), 374–84.

Acknowledgements

We are grateful to the following for permission to reproduce copyright material:

Figures 1.1, 1.6, 6.1, 6.2 and 7.1 adapted from *Relationship Marketing* (Christopher, Payne and Ballantyne, 1991), Figure 3.3 adapted from *Relationship Marketing for Competitive Advantage: Winning and Keeping Customers* (Payne, Christopher and Peck (eds) 1995), Figure 6.7 from *Total Relationship Marketing; Rethinking Marketing Management from 4Ps to 30Rs* (Gummesson, 1999) and material in 10-step strategic marketing planning process in Figure 11.2 from (McDonald, M., 1999) 'Strategic marketing planning: theory and practice', in Baker, M. (ed.) *The CIM Marketing Book*, 4th edn, all Oxford: Butterworth Heinemann; Figure 3.4 from *Principles of Direct and Database Marketing* published by Pearson Education, © A. Tapp (Tapp, 1998); Figure 2.1 adapted from 'Developing buyer–seller relationships', *Journal of Marketing*, published by the American Marketing Association, (Dwyer, Schurr and Oh, 1987), 51 (April) 14; Figure 2.2 adapted from 'What does your customer really want?', *Quality Progress* (Fredericks and Salter, 1998, p. 64) © 1998 American Society for Quality, reprinted with permission; Figures 2.3 and 5.3 adapted from 'Customer loyalty: towards an integrated framework', *Journal of the Academy of Marketing Science*, reprinted with permission of The American Marketing Association/Sage Publications, Inc (Dick and Basu), Vol. 22, pp. 99–113 © 1994 The American Marketing Association; Figure 3.5 reprinted by permission of Harvard Business School Press, from *The Loyalty Effect: The Hidden Force Behind Growth, Profits and Lasting Value* by F.F. Reichheld and T.A. Teal, Boston, MA 1996, p. 43, copyright © 1996 Harvard Business School Publishing Corporation; Figure 3.6 adapted from 'Adopting share of wallet as a basis for communications and customer relationship management', *Interactive Marketing*, 2 (1), 29–40 (Pompa, Berry, Reid and Webber, 2000) © Henry Stewart Publications 2000, Interactive Marketing, www.henrystewart.com; Figure 4.3 adapted from 'Towards a paradigm shift in marketing: an examination of current marketing practises', reproduced with permission from the *Journal of Marketing Management*, Vol 13 (5), pp. 383–406 (Brodie, Coviello, Brookes and Little, 1997) © Westburn Publishers Ltd. (1997) www.westburn.co.uk; Figure 6.8 adapted from 'Managing customer relations for profit: the dynamics of relationship quality', *International Journal of Service Industry Management*, 5, 21–38 (Storbacka, K., Strandvik, T. and Grönroos, C. 1994) and Figure 9.2 adapted from 'Knowledge and relationship marketing: where, what and how?', in 2nd WWW Conference on Relationship Marketing, 15 November 1999–15 February 2000, paper 4 (www.mcb.co.uk/ services/conferen/nov99/rm) (Tzokas, N. and Saren, M. 2000) both Bradford: MCB University Press Ltd; Figure 10.1 from 'In one-to-one marketing, which one comes first?', *Interactive Marketing*, 1 (4) 354–67 (Mitchell, 2000), reproduced with permission of the author.

Material on p.6 adapted from 'Relationship marketing and imaginary organisations: a synthesis', *European Journal of Marketing*, 30 (2) 31–44 (Gummesson, 1996) and material in Box 11.1 Transactional versus relationship marketing, adapted from 'Commentary: princely thoughts on Machiavelli, marketing and management', *European Journal of Marketing*, 34 (5/6), 524–37 (Thomas, 2000) both Bradford: MCB University Press Ltd; material on p. 23 adapted with permission of the Publisher and Author from *Relationship Marketing* Ontario: John Wiley & Sons (Gordon, 1998) © 1998 by Ian H. Gordon c/o John Wiley and Sons Canada, Ltd. All Rights Reserved; material in Box 1.2 TM and RM compared, adapted from *Relationship Marketing for Competitive Advantage: Winning and Keeping Customers* (Payne, Christopher and Peck (eds) 1995) and material in Box 9.2 The British Airways 'Oneworld Alliance' adapted from *Tales from the Marketplace; Stories of Revolution, Reinvention and Renewal*, (Piercy, 1999) both from Oxford: Butterworth Heinemann; Case study from Now that's really radical, *Marketing Business*, November 1999 (Laura Mazur), Editorial from *Marketing Business*, December 1998/January 1999 issue (Jane Simms), Case study from A question of trust, *Marketing Business*, July/August 2000 (David Murphy), Box 10.2 Technology is no substitute for thought when it comes to customer care, *Marketing Business*, May 1999 (John Edmund), Box 10.6 Fact, fiction or fad?, from 'On the right track', *Marketing Business* April 2000 (M. McDonald), Case study from A difficult age, *Marketing Business*, December 1999/January 2000 (Laura Mazur) all © Chartered Institute of Marketing; Case study Ikea has to look out for retailer's friendly touch, reproduced from an article by Laura Mazur, in the 29 June 2000 edition of *Marketing*, Case study The value of complaints, reproduced from an article by Laura Mazur, in the 27 July 2000 edition of *Marketing*, Case study Mr.Clean: biography of Toffael Rashid, head of marketing, myhome, reproduced from an article by Paul Whitfield in the 8 June 2000 edition of *Marketing*, Case study Employees hold key to thwarting the competition, reproduced from an article by Peter Bell, in the 24 August 2000 edition of *Marketing*, Box 10.5 Customer relationship management, reproduced from an article by Julian Dodds, in the 29 June 2000 edition of *Marketing*, all reproduced with the permission of the copyright owner, Haymarket Business Publications Ltd; material in Box 6.2 Special characteristics of services, from *Principles of Services Marketing*, (Palmer, 1998), reproduced with the kind permission of McGraw-Hill Publishing Company; extract on p. 157 and material in Box 8.1 Company organisation cultures, both from 'Buyer/supplier partnering in British industry: the automotive and telecommunications sectors' (Brennan, 1997) reproduced with permission from *The Journal of Marketing Management*, Vol 13, 8, p. 767 © Westburn Publishers Ltd (1997) *www.westburn.co.uk*; Case Study from PR Newswire, Chicago, 24th August, 2000; Case study End of the line for loyalty? *Incentives Today*, June 2000, London: Trades Exhibitions (Joel Harrison).

We are grateful to the Financial Times Limited for permission to reprint the following material:

Case Study from Manchester United plans to establish fans' forum, © *Financial Times*, 21 August 2000; Case Study from Inside Track, © *Financial Times*, 5 November 1999; Case Study from What to Buy, © *Financial Times*, 21 October 1999; Box 9.4 from Supermarket group in joint venture with US internet company, © *Financial Times*, 20 July 2000.

Whilst every effort has been made to trace the owners of copyright material, in a few cases this has proved impossible and we take this opportunity to offer our apologies to any copyright holders whose rights we may have unwittingly infringed.

List of abbreviations

B2B	business-to-business/industrial marketing
B2C	business-to-consumer marketing or consumer marketing
CIM	Chartered Insitutute of Marketing
CPT	cost-per-thousand (media audience measurement)
CRM	customer relationship management
DbM	database marketing
DM	direct marketing
DMA	Direct Marketing Association
EDI	electronic data interchange
ERP	enterprise resource planning
FMCG	fast moving consumer goods
IDM	Institute of Direct Marketing
IMP	Industrial Marketing & Purchasing Group
ISP	Institute of Sales Promotion
IT	information technology
NPD	new product development
PMP	process management perspective
PTM	part-time marketers
R&D	research and development
RFV	recency, frequency, monetary value model
RM	relationship marketing
ROI	return on investment
ROR	return on relationships
SME	small-medium sized enterprises
SRC	supplier/retailer collaboration
TM	transactional (or transaction-based) marketing
TQM	total quality management
WWW	World Wide Web

Part I

Relationships

This first part describes and analyses the market phenomenon that has become generally known as relationship marketing (RM). RM is itself 'shorthand' for quite a wide range of 'relationship-type' strategies that have developed over the past few decades in product as well as service markets and in consumer as well as business-to-business sectors although not necessarily with the same intensity or success.

As Chapter 1 develops it may become apparent that agreement on a definition of RM is far from generally accepted. The chapter does, however, build up (or construct) a working definition that may be a starting point for analysis. Those readers who prefer to 'deconstruct' are invited to jump ahead to page 23 where they will find the definition upon which the chapter is based.

Chapter 2 investigates the concept of relationships, both actual and metaphoric. It examines whether relationships with constructs as nebulous as 'organisations' are possible and whether they are a result, a prelude and/or a mediating factor in the establishment of interpersonal and non-personal relationships. It examines various forms and types of relationship (including so-called customer loyalty) and examines these in the perspective of the RM debate.

Chapter 3 looks at the economic arguments that are seen to underpin RM. As Francis Buttle (1996, p. 5) notes, RM strategies (or any of RM's 'relational' variants) are certainly not designed to be philanthropic but are based on the perceived profitability of relationship retention and longevity. The acceptance of relationship economics as a 'given' is, however, questionable in certain industry situations.

Chapter 4 investigates the potential for a 'marketing strategy continuum', which, it is hoped, will be fully explained in the text. Chapter 5 looks at those drivers to relational strategies that are perceived to exist and tests whether these are apparent in different industries or along the continuum.

References
Buttle, F.B. (1996) *Relationship Marketing Theory and Practice*. London: Paul Chapman.

1 Relationships in marketing

Key issues
➤ The current state of marketing
➤ Antecedents to relationship marketing (RM)
➤ The development of RM
➤ Defining RM

Introduction

Relationship marketing (RM) has been a topic of serious discussion among academics and marketing practitioners for the best part of 20 years. It was, however, during the last decade of the 20th century that relational strategies gained a wider following and that debate on RM began to dominate the marketing agenda. During this period RM was probably *the* major trend in marketing and certainly *the* major (and arguably *the* most controversial) talking point in business management. RM in the 1990s became the leading topic of discussion at academic conferences in Europe, North America, Australia and elsewhere around the globe. RM was frequently the subject of dedicated practitioner conferences, academic journal articles (as a general topic, in RM editions of major publications as well as in at least one dedicated RM journal, the *International Journal of Consumer Relationship Management*) and specialist marketing magazines. RM was the basis of academic and practitioner texts by major marketing writers (e.g. McKenna, 1991; Christopher *et al.*, 1991; Payne *et al.*, 1995; Buttle, 1996; Gordon, 1998; Gummesson, 1999), and such was RM's perceived importance that few, if any, marketing books failed to include at least one section dedicated to the concept.

RM's rise to prominence was rapid. As the last decade of the 20th century passed into history, the number of devotees to the concept continued to grow fast. Indeed, RM had, according to one prominent marketing writer, managed to get up a real 'head of steam', with academics seemingly leaping aboard with 'lemming like abandon' (Brown, 1998, p. 171). If this was true of marketing academics then marketing practitioners were just as enthusiastic. Indeed, practitioner interest became the driving force behind RM's growth (O'Malley and Tynan, 2000, p. 809), with innumerable case studies reported at conferences, in magazines and in texts supporting and justifying the relational approach.

Claims for the benefits of relational strategies abounded not least that RM was becoming a unifying force within marketing. Mattsson (1997b, p. 448) suggested that

3

here at last there was a concept within marketing research that served as the generic context for all marketing transactions, whether products or services, consumer or industrial. Grönroos (1996, pp. 12–13) believed, that RM represented the biggest change in 50 years, in effect 'taking marketing back to its roots'. RM, it was being suggested, was a (or *the*) 'new marketing paradigm' (e.g. Kotler, 1992; Grönroos, 1994a; Gummesson, 1999) and a 'paradigm shift' (e.g. Sheth and Parvatiyar, 1993; Grönroos, 1994a; Morgan and Hunt, 1994; Gummesson, 1997; Buttle, 1997) was taking place in marketing practice and thought. Major companies (e.g. British Airways, Boots, Tesco etc.) were confident enough about RM's capabilities to appoint RM managers and directors whose principal function was to operationalise the concept. At around the same time Safeway became the first UK supermarket chain to set up a dedicated RM team (Whalley, 1999). RM was in vogue among contemporary marketing academics and practitioners, not only in service and inter-organisational contexts, from where it had developed, but even in consumer markets, where it had initially been overtly shunned (O'Malley and Tynan, 1999, p. 587).

While most marketers approached the concept with some level of rationality, there were some claims that were almost messianic in nature. Reichheld (1996, p. 24) suggested that the relational concept[1] represented a 'shift in business thinking as fundamental as the shift to a Copernican sun-centred system was for astronomers'. Elsewhere (p. 33) he suggested that the benefits of loyalty-based marketing represented 'a kind of miracle of loaves and fishes'. According to Mattsson (1997a, p. 37) relationship marketing was the 'battle cry' of the 1990s. The 'marketing mix' and other aspects of 'traditional marketing' were, it was suggested, dying: 'Long live Relationship Marketing'.

Influences on relational strategy development

The assumption is sometimes made that RM was the first major new development in marketing for many years. This is not strictly the case. During the 20th century there had been a number of major developments, often associated with differences in research emphasis. According to Christopher *et al.* (1991, pp. 8–9) the 1950s were the age of consumer marketing when corporate manufacturers and brand marketing concepts dominated the marketing agenda. In the 1960s marketing was characterised by industrial marketing research. The 1970s were a decade when attention started to be paid to the non-profit sector and the 1980s the period where the service sector came to prominence for the first time. Each of these research concentrations (see Figure 1.1) led to new ideas being developed and a general expansion of marketing's influence in the commercial world.

All of these prior developments were to have an influence on 'relational research' in the 1990s and beyond. In addition, RM mirrored (and to a certain extent borrowed from) events taking place in other areas of business research, including trends in organisational structures (Gummesson, 1999, p. 7), distribution management and total quality concepts.

---

[1] Reichheld uses the term 'loyalty-based management' although the term embodies what most scholars would recognise as relationship marketing concepts.

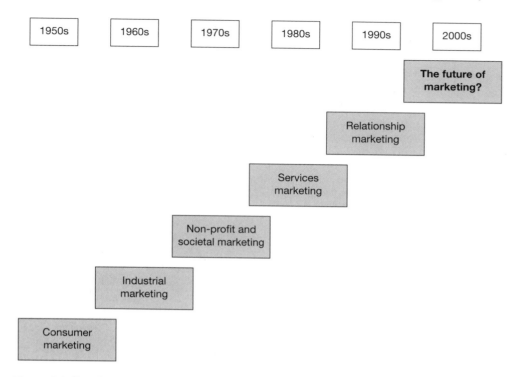

Figure 1.1 Development in marketing
(*Source*: Adapted from Christopher *et al.* 1991)

This diversity of influences was to lead to several different academic perspectives from which RM theory (or, more correctly, theories) was to develop (Figure 1.2). Grönroos and Strandvik (1997, p. 342) note that these perspectives included contributions from the Nordic School of Service Management, the network approach to industrial (or business-to-business) marketing, the Anglo-Australian approach to integrating quality, customer service and marketing, 'strategic alliances and partnerships' research and, more generally, investigation into the nature of relationships in marketing. One factor which may be noted was that, although North American researchers made a significant contribution to the development of RM, their influence over this area of research was not as dominant as had been the case in the past. RM was to become a global research concept.

Among the various centres of research, the Nordic School in particular was to be highly influential in RM development. According to Gummesson (1996, p. 32), this School was originally conceived for services marketing research in the early 1980s and was characterised by a shift in focus from those ideas associated with traditional marketing concepts. These included:

- Stressing the importance and relevance of services marketing and industrial marketing more than consumer goods marketing.
- A gradual shift away from an emphasis on goods and services to an emphasis on customer value.

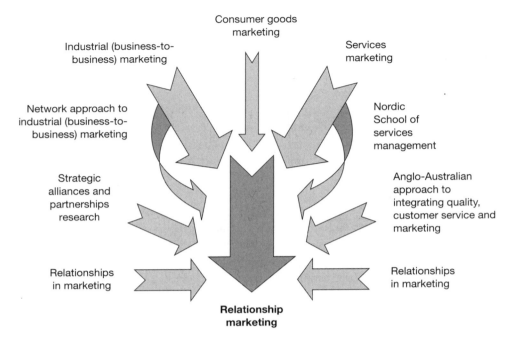

Figure 1.2 Influences on relationship marketing

■ The integration of the marketing department function with other organisational functions and with general management.

■ Less emphasis on quantitative research than that suggested by management research traditions in other countries.

■ More theory generation than theory testing and, consequently, more inductive and abductive than deductive research (see Box 1.1).

■ Research output that was empirical, theoretical and holistic.

(Adapted from Gummesson, 1996, p. 32)

Box 1.1

Research terms defined

Deductive: Argument from general principals to particular conclusions, thus analytical and certain. Deduced, or capable of being deduced, from premises. Deductive research is associated with a 'scientific' view of research.

Inductive: Making empirical (i.e. founded on experience and observation and not theory) generalisations by observing particular instances. The conclusions go beyond the facts so they can never be more than strong possibilities. Inductive research is associated with qualitative research methods.

Abductive: Reasoning for the purposes of discovery as opposed to the justification of scientific hypotheses or theories.

It is probably not surprising that, with these various inputs from different countries and research traditions, different approaches to what had generally become known as 'relationship marketing' appeared to be developing. By the middle of the 1990s Palmer (1996, p. 19) was suggesting that research into RM could be classified in three broad ways:

- At a tactical level where RM is used principally as a sales promotion tool (e.g. loyalty schemes).
- At a strategic level where long-term relationships with customers are created by 'detention rather than retention' with the aid of legal, economic, technological, geographical and other 'barriers to exit' (see page 64).
- At a philosophical level where RM was seen to go to the heart of marketing philosophy, refocusing marketing strategy away from products and their life cycles towards customer relationship life cycles and the integration of customer orientation and inter-functional coordination.

The suggestion made in Palmer's research was that some marketers, rather than embracing the philosophy, were using the term 'relationship marketing' as a smokescreen for largely traditional (if updated) 'transactional' strategies and tactics.

Brodie *et al.* (1997, pp. 384–5) also noted multiple uses of the term (see Figure 1.3). They suggested that RM was being applied at four levels. At the first level it was seen as an elaborate form of database marketing. This represented RM as a technology-based tool used by firms to facilitate the acquisition and management of customers. Again, the implication was that, rather than employing ideas and concepts new to marketing, this form of RM was simply utilising new and updated 'tools' to manage largely traditional customer transactions, albeit in a more efficient way, a charge that has been levelled against some direct marketers (see Chapter 11).

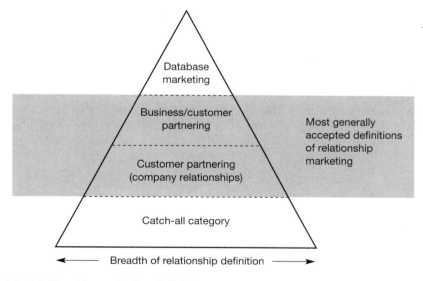

Figure 1.3 Relationship marketing definitions
(*Source*: Based on Brodie *et al.* 1997)

At a second, broader, level Brodie *et al.* saw RM as a focus on actual or potential relationships between the business and its customer base with a concentration on customer retention. On a third (even broader) level, RM was seen as a form of 'customer partnering' with buyers cooperatively involved in the design of the product or service offering. Working relationships on this level implied true interaction between the buyer and seller. At a fourth (and broadest) level RM was seen as incorporating 'everything from databases to personalised service, loyalty programmes, brand loyalty, internal marketing, personal/social relationships and strategic alliances'. When used in this way the term becomes a 'catch-all' phrase for a variety of relational (and perhaps some strictly non-relational) concepts.

This last, very broad, definition could be said to have helped create difficulties in establishing the parameters of RM from more traditional marketing approaches. As O'Malley and Tynan (2000, p. 809) note, with 'the diversity in operational approaches employed, and the lack of accepted definitions', it became 'impossible to delimit the [RM] domain'. The boundaries were 'completely permeable and elastic' and this resulted in 'difficulties in identifying appropriate contexts for empirical research and exacerbated conceptual problems within the emerging discipline'.

RM development

Although RM undoubtedly emerged as a strong concept on the back of prior research, its dramatic growth has been strongly associated with the perceived crises in marketing that took place during the latter part of the 20th century. To get a fuller picture of the drivers to relational strategy development, a brief look at the history and perceived weaknesses of traditional marketing may be appropriate.

Twentieth-century marketing

Marketing is, as most textbooks will tell you, not a modern phenomenon. From ancient times producers have traded their goods, retailers have sold their wares, theatre managers promoted events and 'professionals' advertised their services utilising the marketing skills and marketing communications tools available to them at that time. That these 'marketers' did not recognise these skills or techniques as anything more than part and parcel of their trade says more for the structured scientific nature of the 20th century than for the lack or perversity of marketing expertise by those who went before us.

Marketing as a recognisable commercial activity, however, came to prominence as the 20th century developed. The turn of that century coincided with a period in history when, for the first time, products and services not strictly required for human survival became generally available to large numbers of consumers in Europe and North America. In the UK, as elsewhere, an industrialised working class emerged living mainly in towns and cities who had steady jobs and a regular wage and who were to create a regular demand for mass consumer goods (Seth and Randall, 1999, p. 8). As mass production dramatically increased the range and complexity of the goods and services available, producers (and to a more limited extent service providers) sought larger markets. As competition grew in these wider, more diverse, markets the need both to publicise and differentiate brands became evident.

The golden age of marketing

If the 20th century can be called the 'century of marketing' then the period between 1950 and 1970 could be said to have been its heyday. During this 'golden age' the public appetite for new goods and services appeared insatiable. In western markets consumption rose substantially as prices, in real terms, fell. The period coincided with the launch of independent commercial television, which was, ultimately, to become the marketer's most powerful mass-market communications medium. Consumer spending (conservatively) doubled during this time and much of this increase was attributed to the power and influence of marketing. Modern marketing, it appeared, could do no wrong.

As the contribution of marketing came to be regarded as more and more important so the demand for marketing education and research grew. It was during this period that many of the marketing concepts still taught in business schools around Europe, North America and the rest of the world today were first developed. In the 1960s Borden (1964) produced his 12 elements of a marketing programme (see Figure 1.4), which were later simplified further to what became known as the '4Ps of marketing' (see Figure 1.5) or the 'marketing mix' (McCarthy, 1978). The traditional marketing framework that developed during this period viewed marketing as a strategic and managerial matching process. This matching process sought to ensure that the marketing mix and internal policies of the company were appropriate to the market forces (opportunities and threats) operating within the company's competitive environment.

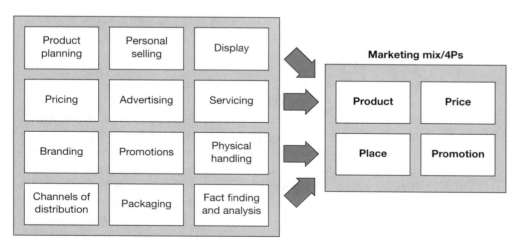

Figure 1.4 Borden's (1964) 12 elements of a marketing programme and McCarthy's (1978) marketing mix

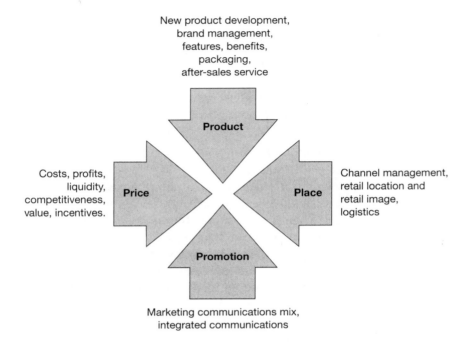

New product development,
brand management,
features, benefits,
packaging,
after-sales service

Costs, profits,
liquidity,
competitiveness,
value, incentives.

Channel management,
retail location and
retail image,
logistics

Marketing communications mix,
integrated communications

Figure 1.5 Marketing mix

This traditional marketing framework was quickly adopted, by students, teachers and practitioners alike, as a straightforward, easy to remember and intuitively rational marketing model. In this era of high consumer trust, effective mass advertising, growing prosperity, homogeneous demand, poorly developed distribution channels and, above all, dominant manufacturing power (O'Driscoll and Murray, 1998, p. 396), the 'brand management model' and the 'toolbox' approach (Grönroos, 1994b, p. 5) of the marketing mix appeared to be working very effectively indeed.

Market changes

In the 1960s the favourable conditions that had seen the growth of marketing began to change dramatically. During this decade the UK, US and other developed consumer markets became saturated. Population growth, a feature and major driver behind the rise in consumer purchasing, was declining. Most brands showed very little growth and markets became dominated by oligopolies. Branding, originally conceived to provide customers with quality assurance and little else, had, over time, evolved into a segmentation tool with different brands for each segment. As segments proliferated so did brands, contributing further to marketing's productivity problems (Sheth and Sisodia, 1999, p. 78).

As Christopher (1996, p. 55) notes, 'mature markets', such as those that developed in the UK and US in the 1960s, exhibit certain characteristics that differentiate them from 'growth markets' and that were to contribute significantly to marketing's perceived decline in effectiveness. In particular, consumers, faced with a surfeit of goods and services, were becoming much more demanding. In this 'buyer's market' customers began to realise the attractiveness of their spending power and began taking advantage of it. Customers were also growing more sophisticated and less easily persuaded by marketing messages.

At the same time as this greater consumer power and sophistication became evident, the perceived benefits (relative to costs) of advertising were seen to be in decline as the market fragmented and the 'cost-per-thousand'[2] targets rose substantially. In addition 'premium brand' dominance was declining as consumers perceived little difference between rival products, leading to a decline in market share and profitability for manufacturers' brands largely in favour of retail store equivalents ('own brands'). Many of the top fast-moving consumer goods (FMCG) brands were, by now, over 40 years old and the failure rate for new brands was reaching very high levels despite often substantial marketing support. There was an erosion of margins caused by a decline in brand premiums as manufacturers' brands fought for market share. There was a subsequent increase in 'below the line' expenditure as brand owners vied for shelf space from increasingly powerful retailers. The combined effect of these changes was the downward pressure on pricing and ultimately profitability.

Despite the growing complexity and competitiveness of the marketplace at the end of the 1980s, marketers were still persevering with the tools and concepts of the more predictable 'golden age' that had evidently now passed. According to McKenna (1991, p. viii) the homogeneity marketers continued to seek was a myth advanced by those who were still using the American market model circa 1950/1960. By this time consumers, politics and even religions were growing more diverse as each year passed. The world was changing but marketing appeared stuck in a rut.

Marketing in crisis

As marketing entered the 1990s things appeared to be going from bad to worse. Companies were beginning to question the large expenditure on marketing without a measurable return on investment that had been assumed in past decades. Accountants, looking to reduce costs and increase rates of return, asked for justification of expenditure and were not pleased with the vague responses they were receiving from marketing departments. Brand-building exercises with largely immeasurable outcomes were no longer seen as justifiable.

The last decade of the 20th century was also to see the marketing function being marginalised in many organisations (Sheth and Sisodia 1999, p. 84). Even marketing pioneers such as Proctor & Gamble and Unilever were abolishing the position of marketing director (Doyle, 1995, p. 23) to concentrate on other functional activities. Marketing was being openly criticised for lack of innovation in the face of hostile markets and for largely adopting defensive strategies to cope. As Doyle (1995, p. 24) noted, marketers of the period generally made the mistake of seeing marketing as a functional discipline rather than an integrated business process. This led to the

---

[2] Cost-per-thousand (CPT) is a frequently used comparative ratio of cost to audience or circulation.

belief that 'the discipline was about tactical and generally superficial segmentation and positioning rather than real innovation and the creation of sustainable competitive advantage'. This functional defensiveness was to further harden attitudes against marketers.

Marketing education

Despite the obvious problems that existed, little was changing in marketing education. Marketing theory remained mired in a futile search for laws, regularities and predictability (Brown, 1995, p. 159). The marketing mix approach was still (and arguably still is) the dominant marketing model although it was beginning to be seen as offering a too 'seductive sense of simplicity' (Christopher *et al.*, 1991, p. 8) which, despite its pedagogical virtues, was prone to misguide academic and practitioner alike (Grönroos, 1990, p. 3). The 'toolbox' approach (Grönroos, 1994b, p. 5) of science-orientated marketing was criticised as a 'neglect of process in favour of structure', leading to a consequent 'lack of study into other key variables' (Christopher *et al.*, 1991, p. 8) not suggested by the marketing mix concept. Marketers were suffering from difficulties of their own creation by applying, unmodified, the principals they had learned in past decades (Gordon, 1998, p. 1) despite the fact that the commercial world was changing all around them. It seemed that the problem was no longer 'marketing myopia'[3] but the myopia of marketing (Brown, 1995, p. 179).

So it appeared that marketing, the leading department of the first three-quarters of the century, was losing its primacy to other organisational disciplines (Doyle, 1995, p. 23) and doing little to resolve the problem. According to Gordon (1998, p. 1) marketers were so busy attending to the practice of marketing they may not have noticed that it was, for all practical purposes, dead. If not dead, it certainly was in crisis.

Antecedents of RM

The marketing discipline had, from its very beginning, been dominated by consumer goods marketing and in particular American consumer goods practice of the 1950s (O'Driscoll and Murray, 1998, p. 409). In most marketing texts prior to 1990, concepts, models and strategies concentrated primarily on corporate manufacturers and their consumer brands. Services and industrial (business-to-business) marketing, despite their growing recognition as important components of the overall business environment, continued to be largely treated as separate disciplines. To many marketers of the period the traditional principals of marketing did not quite 'fit' these different marketing types. Rather than question the validity of the existing model, non-consumer goods were treated as anomalies or afterthoughts usually found in separate chapters invariably towards the end of marketing texts.

---

[3] A term coined by Levitt (1960) in his seminal article of the same title.

A number of marketers were, however, beginning to recognise that 'gaps' existed between marketing textbooks and analysis, on the one hand, and practical implementation on the other (Gummesson, 1998, p. 242). They hypothesised that the disparity suggested by researchers into industrial (business-to-business) and services marketing, rather than being an argument for continued separation of the disciplines, should be considered as a basis for inclusive research. It was these researchers who were to begin the search for a more holistic view of marketing and whose radical ideas were to revolutionise marketing thought.

Industrial marketing research

Industrial marketing had always been treated as mainstream marketing's unglamorous 'poor relation'. The emphasis in this business seemed to be on raw materials, bulk shipments, pricing mechanisms and rational buying models where marketing played only a marginal role. What part it did play relied on extending the prevailing view of consumer marketing while acknowledging certain perceived differences (e.g. order size and frequency).

It was becoming apparent, however, largely through the work of the Industrial Marketing and Purchasing Group (IMP), that this approach did not reflect the complexities of how industrial markets operated (Naudé and Holland, 1996, p. 40). As Baker (1999, p. 211) notes, industrial marketers had learnt that if you could not offer a 'better' product at the same price or equivalent product at a lower price then the only way to stay in business was to foster relationships and add value through important, but usually intangible, service elements. Research suggested industrial marketing involved not just managing exchanges between companies but much more complex human interactions. This theory of network-interaction marketing was to be defined as all activities undertaken by the firm to build, maintain and develop customer relations (Christopher *et al.*, 1991, p. 10). The IMP literature argued that it was the ongoing nature of exchange episodes that led to the formalisation of relationships between buying and selling firms (Naudé and Holland, 1996, p. 40).

It is interesting to note that this industrial or 'business-to-business' research into interaction, relationships and networks predated RM research by at least a decade and maybe two (Mattsson, 1997b, p. 37). It stressed the importance of the understanding of the complex relationships that exist within and between industries (Naudé and Holland, 1996, p. 44) and served as a platform upon which relationship marketers were to develop their ideas.

Services marketing

If industrial (or business-to-business) marketing was the poor relation then 'services marketing' was the black sheep. This second-class view of services *vis-à-vis* consumer goods was despite the fact that the importance of services was growing rapidly. Indeed, development in most western countries was such that they were becoming largely service-led as opposed to production-led economies. In the early

1990s, for example, the UK became the first country to export more services than physical goods. By the middle of the decade over 75% of the working populations of the UK and USA were employed in service industries. This rapidly changing situation both emphasised the importance of services and underlined the requirement for further research.

The intangible nature of service industries had always posed a problem to traditional marketers whose models (e.g. the BCG matrix) had always proved to be an ineffectual fit. Pure service characteristics, often described as intangibility, inseparability, variability, perishability and inability to 'own' the service (Palmer, 1998, p. 11) coupled with the importance of people and processes, was providing challenges that traditional marketing concepts were having difficulty rationalising. Above all, it was the potential advantages that the building of relationships might create where service differential was low which drove research in this area.

Impetus for RM research

It was, therefore, to be the relationship issues surfacing in industrial and service marketing that exposed the problems of the traditional marketing model in a more explicit way than with consumer goods (Christopher et al., 1991, p. 10). The stimulation from this research into industrial and service marketing was to prove key in bringing 'relationships' onto the marketing agenda.

The development of RM

With the difficulties that marketers were experiencing and the ideas emanating from industrial and service research, questions were being asked. In particular, could marketing theories and practice, designed for a bygone era, be developed to cope with the multiplicity and complexity of products and services now available, or did the whole structure require rebuilding?

The marketing mix

Research was beginning to show that the 4Ps model of marketing was evidently too restrictive for business-to-business and services marketing. Gummesson (1987) went so far as to suggest that application of the marketing mix to areas other than consumer goods could be destructive as it failed to recognise the unique features of these areas. To a growing extent the marketing mix was also becoming an outdated concept for consumer goods marketing as the importance of intangible service characteristics and customer service considerations became a prime differentiation factor between products.

The first attempts to extend beyond the restrictive nature of marketing were, however, through the adaptation of the marketing mix model. According to Grönroos (1996, p. 8) the marketing mix could still be useful but other elements, not normally regarded as part of the marketing function, needed to be added (e.g.

delivering, installing, repairing, servicing and maintenance, billing, complaints, customer education etc.). Gummesson (1994b, p. 9) too, believed that the marketing mix would always be needed, but that it had become peripheral in comparison to relationships. Other authors tried to retain the 'mix' as an easy-to-remember framework that incorporated the new marketing ideas coming through. Further Ps were added such as People, Physical Evidence, Processes (Booms and Bitner, 1981), Political Power and Public Opinion. Other adaptations (see Gummesson, 1994b, p. 8) were suggested to fill the credibility gap. Indeed, early models of RM (e.g. Christopher *et al.*, 1991, p. 13) adopted this approach by incorporating the notion of 'customer service' (and by implication an endless list of sub-functions) as additional and central to the 'updated' marketing mix (see Figure 1.6).

Kotler *et al.* (1999, p. 110) took a marginally different approach. They suggested that the marketing mix represented the seller's view of marketing and proposed that marketers should view the 4Ps from a customer-orientated perspective. Thus the 4Ps became 4Cs (see Figure 1.7) where companies met customer needs economically, conveniently and with effective communication. Thus price became the cost to the customer, place was substituted with convenience, products and services become customer needs and wants and promotion was transformed into communication

Valuable as these contributions were for some marketers, they were not radical enough for others. This latter group saw the attempts to update the marketing mix

Figure 1.6 Customer service and the marketing mix
(*Source*: Adapted from Christopher *et al.*, 1991, p. 13)

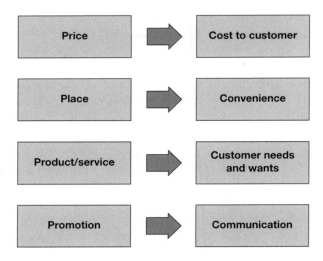

Figure 1.7 From 4Ps to 4Cs
(*Source*: Based on Kotler *et al.*, 1999, p. 110)

as the commercial equivalent of rearranging the deckchairs on the *Titanic*. They suggested that the 'marketing toolbox' approach to marketing education had, for too long, restricted discussion of the meaning and consequences of the marketing concept. In catering for the real needs and desires of the consumers, marketing had become, in effect, the sterile management of this toolbox (Grönroos, 1994b, p. 5). To these marketers the marketing mix concept theoretically had no foundation, pedagogically no longer served a useful purpose and practically was being surpassed by more dynamic approaches (O'Malley and Patterson 1998, p. 840). Rather than tinkering with the 'mix' they believed a more fundamental change was required.

Customer supremacy

The marketing mix was not the only traditional marketing practice being challenged. It was frequently acknowledged that 'customer supremacy', the central tenet of marketing, although rational in principle was flawed in practice. What in effect was happening was that marketers attributed 'need' to individuals as a *post hoc* rationalisation to account for, and render rationality and meaning to some recurrent behaviour observed rather than as a 'driver' (Knights *et al.*, 1994, p. 48). Despite the claims to the contrary the actual needs, wants and expectations of the customer were not perceived in reality as of paramount importance (Buttle, 1996, p. 7).

Thus, while lip-service was paid to customer supremacy in principle, in practice marketers all too frequently ignored it. Indeed marketers appeared to view their customers in one (or both) of two ways: the first as near-passive recipients of messages and prompts from marketers, and the second as one half of a confrontational or adversarial relationship (Buttle, 1996, p. 8). Neither perception sat comfortably with the traditional marketing doctrine of 'customer supremacy' yet they largely dictated strategy development.

Market segmentation, positioning, market share and marketing research

A number of other established marketing concepts were under attack. Market segmentation and positioning strategies were proving particularly vulnerable (Doyle, 1995, p. 27). Market segmentation, a central marketing concept, no longer appeared to be operating effectively. While markets were still being presented demographically, psychologically, attitudinally or by lifestyle, the realisation was beginning to dawn on marketers that the only category that was really meaningful was 'actual', as opposed to 'speculative', buyer behaviour (Gordon, 1998, p. 3).

Market share, widely regarded as a principal performance measure, was also under fire. It was becoming apparent that it was ambiguous and subjective (Doyle, 1995, p. 27) and largely manipulated by marketers to serve whatever arguments they sought to promote. Market (or marketing) research too was showing its limitations. It was being used by marketers to identify issues and assess customer responses to hypothetical solutions (Gordon, 1998, p. 6) based on a frequently outdated historical basis. It was also, in fast-changing markets, taking more time than marketers generally had available and was proving a barrier to swift competitive response.

The fall of TM

The traditional transactional marketing (TM) model was, it appeared, unsuited to complex modern marketing reality and rapidly becoming outdated. TM was seen as overly scientific, relying heavily on quantitative research, and based solely on short-term economic transactions. Vividly described by one author as 'hit and run' marketing (Buttle, 1996, p. vii), it looked to each transaction as an opportunity to 'get one over' on the gullible customer without any consideration of future contact. At the extreme it was regarded as manipulative and exploitative of the customer's ignorance (Gummesson, 1994b, p. 9).

The recognition of the problems associated with the TM model suggested a functional and theoretical 'mid-life crisis' in marketing which demanded attention. Under siege from all sides, not only were specific components of marketing being challenged but so also was the validity of the whole. It was openly debated that a 'paradigm shift' was needed if marketing was going to survive as a discipline (Grönroos, 1994b, p. 4). The apparent success of a relational approach in the service and business-to-business sectors (which were themselves beginning to receive proper recognition) began to attract the attention of other marketers, who hypothesised the emergence of a new generic marketing paradigm to possibly replace, but certainly augment, the transactional model.

The early days of RM

It was into this growing theoretical void that the concept of RM began to take shape across all areas of marketing and to excite the marketing fraternity. RM found ready acceptance in a marketing world where it had become patently obvious that strategic competitive advantage could no longer be delivered on the basis of product characteristics alone and where corporate profitability was beginning to become associated with satisfying existing customers (Barnes, 1994, pp. 651–2). In industrial marketing, services marketing, managing distribution channels and even packaged goods marketing itself, a shift was clearly taking place from marketing to anonymous masses of customers to developing and managing relationships with more or less well known, or at least somehow identifiable, customers (Grönroos, 1994b, p. 14).

The need for market-driven business was as strong as ever but was now perceived, more realistically, as an iterative process in which marketing strategy shapes as well as responds to buyer behaviour (Sheth and Sisodia, 1999, p. 81). It became evident that there was a need to transform marketing from a narrow set of functional skills based on the conventional marketing mix to a broader business orientation where delivery of 'superior customer value' was a key objective. (Christopher, 1996, p. 64). What was needed was a form of marketing that was orientated to creating rather than controlling a market and based on developmental education, incremental improvement and ongoing process rather than simple market share tactics and raw sales data (McKenna, 1991, pp. 2–3). A clear shift would also be needed away from the adversarial mind-set implied by the bargaining power perspective towards a cooperative stance focused on mutual gain.

Towards a definition of RM

Although a clearer picture of RM will, it is hoped, become evident it may be beneficial to determine, more specifically, what is meant by the term 'relationship marketing'. One thing that will become clear very early on is that RM is not an easy concept to define in a form which is acceptable to even a majority of 'relational marketers'.

Despite considerable academic research and practitioner interest, RM may still be regarded more as a general 'umbrella philosophy' with numerous relational variations rather than as a wholly unified concept with strongly developed objectives and strategies. To confuse matters further other terms have been frequently used either as substitutes for relationship marketing, or to describe similar concepts (Buttle, 1996, p. 2). These include direct marketing, database marketing, customer relationship management, data-driven marketing, micromarketing, one-to-one marketing, loyalty (or loyalty-based) marketing, 'segment-of-one' marketing, wraparound marketing, customer partnering, symbiotic marketing, individual marketing, relevance marketing, bonding, frequency marketing, integrated marketing, dialogue marketing and interactive marketing (Vavra, 1992; Buttle, 1996; Tapp, 1998), to name but a few. Many of these relational variations describe a particular or closely associated aspect of RM philosophy rather than a holistic concept and can rarely be said to 'stand alone' in any true sense. Others are associate concepts that may be seen to overlap with RM in some way. What is generally described as 'direct marketing' or 'database marketing', for example, while not fully mirroring RM concepts may include a number of recognisable relational strategies and tactics. To regard RM and database/direct marketing as synonymous, however, as is frequently claimed, may not be a wholly acceptable perspective. Customer relationship management (CRM), a concept to which we will return in Chapter 10, is another 'relational approach' that has grown in popularity particularly among direct marketers. CRM's definition is as hazy as the rest but seems to relate to management of the 'lifetime relationship with the customer' usually through the use of information technology (Ryals, 2000, p. 259), and is, as such, more tactical than strategic. As the definition of RM becomes clearer this differentiation may become more evident (see Chapter 10).

Broad church?

Perhaps differences of emphasis are to be expected as the theory (or theories) associated with RM continue to develop. One view may be to suggest that no purist definition of RM is possible or even practical. It may be wholly valid to recognise that a term such as relationship marketing, involving as it does such a vague notion as 'relationships', is bound to generate multiple definitions. Relationships are after all 'fuzzy' entities with 'fuzzy' borders and many overlapping properties (Gummesson, 1994a, p. 18).

A potentially defendable position may be to suggest that RM should continue to remain a flexible series of concepts and ideas rather than a fixed and inflexible theory if for no other reason than its application may differ considerably from industry to industry. In effect, RM should remain a 'broad church'. It may indeed be beneficial for RM development not to become 'straight-jacketed' by one position or the other (Grönroos, 1994b, p. 10). Indeed, it may be possible, within a general relational management position, for companies to develop strategies that appear contradictory to one another yet are relevant to specific industries or even individual customer types. In this way RM can make a major contribution to marketing thought and practice by challenging the embedded strategies of the past and by encouraging marketers to constantly review their business strategies in the light of changing relationships.

Common ground?

Despite the undoubted problems in coming to a consensus on the meaning and application of RM, the marketing literature on the subject can be examined to establish whether research suggests some common ground. What is clear is that the current divergence of views suggests no agreement as to a single definition of RM (one reason why its claim to 'paradigm status' may be premature). It is, however, equally evident that many definitions have common denominators. As such and despite the evident difficulties we can try to establish a 'best fit' definition from where RM can be further investigated.

RM's roots

RM, according to Gordon (1998, p. 9) is not a wholly independent philosophy but draws on traditional marketing principals. This view suggests that the basic focus upon customer needs still applies but that it is the way marketing is practised that requires changing fundamentally (Christopher, 1996, p. 55). If RM is indeed a descendent of traditional marketing then a good starting point in developing a definition of RM would be to look at how marketing has traditionally been perceived. This traditional view might be summed up succinctly using the Chartered Institute of Marketing's (CIM) definition of marketing as:

the management process of identifying, anticipating and satisfying customer requirements profitably.

This definition includes a number of assumptions that are important in the discussion of relational strategy development. 'Process' assumes that traditional marketing is a series of activities carried out as part (only) of a company's other functions. It implies a functional marketing department responsible for a fixed number of responsibilities presumably closely associated with the 'marketing mix'. It also implicitly suggests that 'identifying, anticipating and satisfying customer requirements' is the singular responsibility of the marketing department. 'Profitably' is assumed to mean that these responsibilities are carried out in a competitively superior manner (Gordon, 1998, p. 9), although there is no indication of the time scale over which this profitability should be measured.

This description of traditional marketing and others of a similar nature emphasise, above all, the functional and process nature of traditional marketing and make no explicit recognition of the long-term value of the customer (Buttle, 1996, p. 2). The focus of traditional or mass marketing also implies that whatever the status of the customer (non-customers, current customers and past customers) they are all treated in the same way and are of comparable worth status to the organisation.

Early definition

Berry (1983, p. 25) was among the first to introduce the term 'relationship marketing' as a modern concept in marketing. He suggested that this 'new' approach should be defined as:

attracting, maintaining and . . . enhancing customer relationships.

While recognising that customer acquisition was, and would remain, part of a marketer's responsibilities, this viewpoint emphasised that a 'relationship view of marketing' implied that retention and development were of equal (or perhaps even greater) importance to the company in the longer term than customer acquisition. It further implied, by differentiating between customer types, that not all customers ·or potential customers should be treated in the same way.

Cooperative marketing

The concept was taken a stage further by, among others, Grönroos (1996, p. 6), who challenged the traditional notion that marketing need be an adversarial contest between the company and the customer. Certainly in the past markets had been frequently conceived as 'battlefields' and marketing practice dominated by combative battle metaphors (fight, competition, capture, take-over etc.). The general view of the traditional marketing model was of businesses vying to be winners over not only their competition but their customers as well. RM, in contrast, implied a focus on building 'value-laden relationships' and 'marketing networks' (Grönroos, 1994b, p. 9) rather than such confrontation.

A change in attitude away from the traditional 'winner and loser' philosophy was becoming apparent. Sheth and Sisodia (1999, p. 82) noted the clear evidence of a shift away from the adversarial mind-set implied by the 'bargaining power' perspective towards a cooperative stance focused on mutual gain. Gummerson (1997, p. 56) suggested that the RM approach resulted in both parties deriving value from the transaction, and Voss and Voss (1997, p. 293) that shared value was a key objective in the design and implementation of an RM programme. In effect 'relational marketers' were seeking strategies that produced 'win–win' situations (Gummerson, 1997, p. 56) with both parties gaining value from the buyer–seller partnership. The result was to be achieved through mutual exchange and fulfilment of promises (Grönroos, 1994b, p. 9) by *both parties* in a series of interactions over the lifetime of their relationship.

This view of marketing also implied that suppliers were not alone in creating or benefiting from the value created by the company. Rather RM was seen as an ongoing process of identifying and *creating new value* with individual customers and then *sharing the value benefits* with them over the lifetime of the association (Gordon, 1998, p. 9). A 'relationship', in these terms, was definable as the sum total of 'meaning-filled episodes' where relational partners co-produce value (Buttle, 1997, p. 148).

Relationship burdens

One important aspect of the original Berry definition required attention. The seeming philanthropy of the altruistic sentiments implied by RM might be seen to contradict the fact that the profit motive was still a principal business driver. The difference between RM and traditional marketing was that RM was seen to achieve this profitability through co-production and cooperation rather than through manipulation. RM would, it was suggested, potentially benefit both parties: the buyer, through reduced transaction costs, and the seller, through better under-standing of customers' circumstances and requirements (Tynan, 1997, p. 992).

Not all relationships, however, are (or have the potential to be) profitable. Although, as a rule of thumb, customer retention was seen as the path to prosperity some buyer–seller relationships were definite 'burdens' to a company (Håkansson and Snohota, 1995, p. 522). Indeed, situations can develop where a small number of highly profitable customers, in essence, subsidise a larger number of customers where the company actually loses money (Sheth and Sisodia, 1999, p. 83).

Such is the likely scale of this problem that Storbacka *et al.* (1994, pp. 31–32) suggest that it is not uncommon for 50% of a retail bank's customers to be unprofitable. In later research concentrating on the Scandinavian banking system, Storbacka (1997, p. 488) reported that approximately 1% of customers were responsible for the erosion of the profits from the top 25% of the bank's customer base. Other researchers have made similar observations. In certain industrial markets, for example, Cooper and Kaplan (1991, p. 134) reported that 20% of customers represented 225% of total customer base profitability. Around 70% of these customers hovered around the break-even point while 10% of the customer base represented a loss equivalent to 125% of the firm's eventual profit! Allowing this situation to continue over any length of time is particularly dangerous for larger companies that may be vulnerable to entry into the market of smaller companies that systematically target their most profitable customers (Sheth and Sisodia, 1999, p. 83).

This recognition of the potential loss-making capability of some relationships suggested that marketing management from a relationship perspective must pay attention to three key objectives rather than the two areas originally suggested (Strandvik and Storbacka 1996, p. 72):

■ The management of the initiation of customer relationships.
■ The maintenance and enhancement of existing relationships.
■ The handling of the termination of relationships.

This termination may be interpreted in two ways. In the first marketing may be seen to be moving towards accepting 'customer de-selection' or 'adverse selection' (Smith 1998, p. 4) as part of the marketing process. This might be operationalised, according to Smith, by 'dumping unprofitable customers while selectively seeking and keeping the more profitable ones'. The implication here is that cost–benefit ratios needed to be constantly monitored (Tynan, 1997, p. 992) to minimise, and where possible remove, the effect of loss-making customers. Although this perspective appears intuitively counter to a relationship philosophy, it represents commercial realism that required incorporation into the RM definition.

A second interpretation of the requirement to manage the 'burden of relationships' (Håkansson and Snohota, 1995, p. 552) is to regard loss-making customers as part and parcel of the business. In this respect marketing needs to develop a theory of subsidisation (Sheth and Sisodia, 1999, p. 83): in effect, a strategic understanding of when and how to subsidise. This view suggests that subsidies are not always bad for business and that if used strategically can turn competitive vulnerability into competitive advantage. It also challenges marketers to accept the burden of loss making in the short term in the hope of long-term profitability.

Relationships, networks and interactions.

A further feature of 'older' definitions and writings on the subject of relationship marketing was that they focused wholly on the supplier–customer relationship (the 'supplier–customer dyad'). Later contributions, however, were seen to widen RM's scope (Buttle, 1996, p. 3). According to Gummesson (1999, p. 1), marketing is more than just the dyadic relationship between the buyer and the seller; rather, it represents the whole series of 'relationships, networks and interactions' which the company (or more strictly the company's employees or representatives) undertakes as part of its commercial dealings. As marketing activities are subsets or properties of society, it is suggested (Gummesson, 1999, p. 6) that these relationships, networks and interactions have been at the core of business since time immemorial.

As will become apparent in later chapters, RM thinking was developing away from the strictly 'two-way dialogue' between the supplier and the customer towards the synonymous development of other company relationships.[4] Among the relationships (the simple dyad as well as the complex networks) the parties enter into active contact with each other. This Gummesson (1999, p. 1) calls 'interaction'. Thus RM was seen to represent 'all marketing activities directed towards establishing, developing and maintaining successful relational exchanges' (Morgan and Hunt, 1994, p. 22).

RM definition

Most of the concepts, ideas and developments discussed above are present in Grönroos' (1994b, p. 9) refined definition of RM, in which he described the objectives of RM as to:

> **identify and establish, maintain and enhance and, when necessary, terminate relationships with customers and other stakeholders, at a profit so that the objectives of all parties involved are met; and this is done by mutual exchange and fulfilment of promises.**

No definition will ever be perfect and it may well be that other ideas and concepts may in time also require inclusion. For the purposes of introducing RM, however, this definition will, for the moment, suffice. In later chapters we will investigate more closely how these concepts were translated into strategies and tactics and their perceived benefits. In particular we will look at the claims that are implicit in this definition. These may be seen to include six dimensions that differ significantly from the historical definition of marketing (Gordon 1998, p. 9). These are that:

- RM seeks to create new value for customers and then share it with these customers.
- RM recognises the key role that customers have both as purchasers *and* in defining the value they wish to achieve.
- RM businesses are seen to design and align processes, communication, technology and people in support of customer value.
- RM represents continuous cooperative effort between buyers and sellers.
- RM recognises the value of customers' purchasing lifetimes (i.e. lifetime value).
- That RM seeks to build a chain of relationships within the organisation, to create the value customers want, and between the organisation and its main stakeholders, including suppliers, distribution channels, intermediaries and shareholders.

(Adapted from Gordon, 1998, p. 9)

---

[4] Research into business-to-business marketing RM was of particular influence in the development of these external relationship theories.

On the tactical side comparisons have been suggested (Payne *et al.*, 1995, p. viii) between the different approaches to customers that TM and RM take (see Box 1.2). These elements too will be expanded upon in later chapters.

Box 1.2

TM and RM compared

Transactional marketing	**Relationship marketing**
■ Orientation to single sales	■ Orientation to customer retention
■ Discontinuous customer contact	■ Continuous customer contact
■ Focus on product features	■ Focus on customer value
■ Short time scale	■ Long time scale
■ Little emphasis on customer service	■ High emphasis on customer service
■ Limited commitment to meeting customer expectations	■ High commitment to meeting customer expectations
■ Quality as the concern of production staff	■ Quality as the concern of all staff

(*Source*: Adapted from Payne *et al.*, 1995)

As Sheth and Sisodia (1999, p. 84) note, we should always bear in mind that marketing is context driven, and that the context has changed, is changing and will no doubt change in the future. Marketers need to question and challenge what these authors call the well-accepted 'law-like generalisations' (or in-bedded concepts) that have grown up around marketing. Over the following chapters RM ideas, concepts, claims and perceptions will be tested as we try to establish the importance of relationship marketing.

Summary

This chapter has looked at the development of relationship marketing and the considerable interest it has created among academics, consultants and practitioners alike. Although there are different perspectives evident there are also a number of common denominators beginning to develop. It looked at the roots of RM. It reviewed the perceived problems with traditional marketing in the light of fast-changing and complex markets. It examined RM's growth in popularity, acknowledging that there is no generally accepted definition. In an attempt to clarify thinking on RM different perceptions (from simple to catch-all) were explored.

The earliest definitions of RM were analysed and found somewhat wanting. Not only was customer acquisition and retention important but ways had to be found to eliminate (or otherwise accommodate) loss-making customers. In addition RM theory was developing to include other relationships with key stakeholders. A broad definition of RM was, therefore, presented that, it is suggested, could act as a reference point from where to begin our investigation. It will not all be plain sailing, however. We should not, for example, expect anything as complex as 'relationships' to be anything other than complex and paradoxical. Indeed marketing reality requires that we learn to live with this complexity, these paradoxes, and the uncertainty, ambiguity and instability generated (Gummesson, 1997, p. 58) if we are to develop further the marketing discipline.

1 What were recognised, towards the end of the 20th century, as the perceived weaknesses of traditional marketing?

2 What were the influences that led to the development of relationship marketing?

3 What part did (a) business-to-business and (b) services marketing play in this development?

4 What are the major differences between traditional and relationship marketing?

Case study

Now that's really radical

What do the following recent events have in common?

- Sir Stuart Hampson, the usually-reticent chairman of the venerable institution that is John Lewis goes on the offensive against staff rumblings about dissolving the partnership and going public as earnings plummet.
- Marks & Spencer hires an outside marketing director for the first time in the midst of hurriedly pushing through store redesigns, advertising and a vetting of the staff for 'customer-focused' qualities.
- British Airways decides to concentrate far more of its marketing effort on business customers at the expense of those at the back of the plane while performing an embarrassing turnaround on the controversial tail fins.
- Procter & Gamble, having seen revenues rise last year by only 3%, shakes up the ad world by announcing that instead of commission it will pay agencies only for results.

On the surface, not that much. But look a little deeper and a disturbing thought emerges: what were once hailed as stars of the marketing firmament can now be seen instead as prominent examples of what can only be called desperation marketing.

It's not a pretty sight. The fact that the companies that seemed to write the rules of successful marketing are falling on their swords should send shivers down the spine of any marketer struggling to make sense of the chaos that is the marketplace. Shouldn't it?

Well, not really. Because desperate marketers have been steadily sowing the seeds of their own downfall by becoming obsessed with corporate navel-gazing and forgetting the basics of marketing. For them the principles of the four Ps that set them on the road to such success, whether by intent or instinct, have became obscured as market dominance has bred rigidity, bureaucracy and, worst of all, complacency.

▶

They also give marketing a bad name. And that's a shame, because there are lots of companies who, in their own quiet way, have kept the marketing faith. They could, in fact, be called radical marketers, according to a book published earlier this year (*Radical Marketing: From Harvard to Harley, Lessons From Ten That Broke the Rules and Made it Big*; Sam Hill and Glenn Rifkin, Harper Business). Radical marketers have a visceral tie to their customers. Everything else works from that.

The authors give mainly US examples, like Harley-Davidson and Harvard Business School, with the ubiquitous Richard Branson and Virgin Atlantic the exception. But the UK has its own, often unsung, players in the radical marketing revolution. Take Ken Morrison. He is the 67-year-old founder of the Morrison supermarket chain now worth £2.3 billion, and which in September reported a 15% jump in half-year profits.

The mainly North-of-England chain operates on basic, market-stall principles, with a vertically-integrated infrastructure which means it doesn't have to over-rely on sub-contractors. It also disdains loyalty cards. For Morrison – a hands-on operator – as with other radical marketers, success lies in the details. That – along with a big chunk of the shares – helps to give him the strength to stand up to retail megaliths like Wal-Mart.

Then there is Sir Michael Bishop and the airline British Midland. Richard Branson might get all the attention. But British Midland, despite the dominant position British Airways has on so many routes, has managed to thrive. Why? In part because Bishop is a canny business operator. That is hardly the whole picture, however. Even more critically, he has successfully instilled in his frontline staff a sense of real customer service, not the begrudging service-by-numbers attitude displayed by the employees of some of his bigger rivals. Another example of radical marketing is the Unipart Group of Companies, one of Europe's leading automotive parts and logistics companies. It started life as part of the old British Leyland, but became independent after a 1987 buy-out by a team led by John Neill.

Neill has become a byword in enlightened management: not only do management and employees own nearly half the company, but Unipart was probably one of the first companies to establish a corporate university, Unipart 'U', to spread leading-edge thinking. Unipart now has sales of more than £1 billion.

What distinguishes these radical marketers from their less-agile counterparts is that the chief executives 'own' the marketing function, they seek growth and expansion over profits, and they respect their customers in that they not only listen to them but often lead them in directions they hadn't known they wanted to go. They fight against the creeping rigidity that size can bring, where too often bureaucracy takes over from flexibility, and the enemy is no longer the competition but the department next door. In other words, they don't forget just how fragile the tie with customers can be – and what they need to do to keep it from breaking. Now that really is radical.

(*Source*: Laura Mazur, *Marketing Business*, November 1999)

Case study questions

1 What, according to this case study, separates the 'winners' from the 'losers'?

2 Discuss how/whether these companies have improved their marketing since this article was written.

References

Baker, M.J. (1999) 'Editorial', *Journal of Marketing Management*, 15, 211–14.

Barnes, J.G. (1994) 'Close to the customer: but is it really a relationship?', *Journal of Marketing Management*, 10, 561–70.

Berry, L.L. (1983) 'Relationship marketing', in Berry, L.L., Shostack, G.L. and Upsay, G.D. (eds) *Emerging Perspectives on Service Marketing*. Chicago, IL: American Marketing Association, pp. 25–8.

Booms, B.H. and Bitner, M. J. (1981) 'Marketing strategies and organisational structures for service firms', in Donnelly, J. and George, W.R. (eds) *Marketing of Services*. Chicago, IL: American Marketing Association.

Borden, N. (1964) 'The concept of the marketing mix', *Journal of Advertising Research*, June, 2–7.

Brodie, R.J., Coviello, N.E., Brookes, R.W. and Little, V. (1997) 'Towards a paradigm shift in marketing; an examination of current marketing practices', *Journal of Marketing Management*, 13 (5), 383–406.

Brown, S. (1995) *Postmodern Marketing*. London: Routledge.

Brown, S. (1998) *Postmodern Marketing II*. London: International Thompson Business Press.

Buttle, F.B. (1996) *Relationship Marketing Theory and Practice*. London: Paul Chapman.

Buttle, F.B. (1997) 'Exploring relationship quality', paper presented at the Academy of Marketing Conference, Manchester, UK.

Christopher, M. (1996) 'From brand values to customer values', *Journal of Marketing Practice*, 2 (1), 55–66.

Christopher, M., Payne, A. and Ballantyne, D. (1991) *Relationship Marketing*. London: Butterworth Heinemann.

Cooper, R. and Kaplan, R.S. (1991) 'Profit priorities from activity-based costing', *Harvard Business Review*, May–June, 130–35.

Doyle, P. (1995) 'Marketing in the new millennium', *European Journal of Marketing*, 29 (12), 23–41.

Gordon, I.H. (1998) *Relationship Marketing*. Etobicoke, Ontario: John Wiley & Sons.

Grönroos, C. (1990) 'Relationship approach to the marketing function in service contexts; the marketing and organization behaviour interface', *Journal of Business Research*, 20, 3–11.

Grönroos, C. (1994a) 'From marketing mix to relationship marketing: towards a paradigm shift in marketing', *Asia-Australia Marketing Journal*, 2 (1).

Grönroos, C. (1994b) 'From marketing mix to relationship marketing: towards a paradigm shift in marketing', *Management Decisions*, 32 (2), 4–20.

Grönroos, C. (1996) 'Relationship marketing: strategic and tactical implications', *Management Decisions*, 34 (3), 5–14.

Grönroos, C. and Strandvik, T. (1997) 'Editorial', *Journal of Marketing Management*, 13 (5), 342.

Gummesson, E. (1987) 'The new marketing: developing long term interactive relationships', *Long Range Planning*, 20 (4), 10–20.

Gummesson, E. (1994a) 'Broadening and specifying relationship marketing', *Asia-Australia Marketing Journal*, 2 (1), 31–43.

Gummesson, E. (1994b) 'Making relationship marketing operational', *International Journal of Service Industry Management*, 5, 5–20.

Gummesson, E. (1996) 'Relationship marketing and imaginary organisations: a synthesis', *European Journal of Marketing*, 30 (2), 31–44.

Gummesson, E. (1997) 'Relationship marketing – the emperor's new clothes or a paradigm shift?', *Marketing and Research Today*, February, 53–60.

Gummesson, E. (1998) 'Implementation requires a relationship marketing paradigm', *Journal of the Academy of Marketing Science*, 26 (3), 242–9.

Gummesson, E. (1999) *Total Relationship Marketing: Rethinking Marketing Management from 4 Ps to 30Rs*. Oxford: Butterworth Heinemann.

Håkansson, H. and Snohota, I. (1995) 'The burden of relationships or who next?', in *Proceedings of the 11th IMP International Conference*, Manchester, UK, pp. 522–36.

Knights, D., Sturdy, A. and Morgan, R.M. (1994) 'The consumer rules? An examination of the rhetoric and "reality" of marketing in financial services', *European Journal of Marketing*, 28 (3), 42–54.

Kotler, P. (1992) 'Marketing's new paradigm: what's really happening out there?', *Planning Review*, 20 (5), 50–52.

Kotler, P., Armstrong, G., Saunders, J. and Wing, V. (1999) *Principals of Marketing*, 2nd European Edition. New York: Prentice Hall.

Levitt, T. (1960) 'Marketing Myopia', *Harvard Business Review*, July/August, 45–56.

Mattsson, L.G. (1997a) 'Relationships in a network perspective', in Gemünden, H.G., Rittert, T. and Walter, A. (eds) *Relationships and Networks in International Markets*. Oxford: Elsevier, pp. 37–47.

Mattsson, L.G. (1997b) '"Relationship marketing" and the "markets as networks approach" – a comparative analysis of two evolving streams of research', *Journal of Marketing Management*, 13 (5), 447–61.

McCarthy, E.J. (1978) *Basic Marketing: A Managerial Approach*, 6th edn. Homewood, IL: Richard D. Irwin.

McKenna, R. (1991) *Relationship Marketing*. London: Addison Wesley.

Morgan, R.M. and Hunt, S.D. (1994) 'The commitment-trust theory of relationship marketing', *Journal of Marketing*, 58 (3), 20–38.

Naudé, P. and Holland, C. (1996) 'Business-to-business marketing', in Buttle, F. (ed.) *Relationship Marketing Theory and Practice*. London: Paul Chapman.

O'Driscoll, A. and Murray, J.A. (1998) 'The changing nature of theory and practice in marketing: on the value of synchrony', *Journal of Marketing Management*, 14 (5), 391–416.

O'Malley, L. and Patterson, M. (1998) 'Vanishing point: the mix management paradigm reviewed', *Journal of Marketing Management*, 14, 829–51.

O'Malley, L. and Tynan, C. (1999) 'The utility of the relationship metaphor in consumer markets: a critical evaluation', *Journal of Marketing Management*, 15, 587–602.

O'Malley, L. and Tynan, C. (2000) 'Relationship marketing in consumer markets; rhetoric or reality?', *European Journal of Marketing*, 34 (7).

Palmer, A.J. (1996) 'Relationship marketing: a universal paradigm or management fad?', *The Learning Organisation*, 3 (3), 18–25.

Palmer, A.J. (1998) *Principles of Services Marketing*. London: Kogan Page.

Payne, A., Christopher, M. and Peck, H. (eds) (1995) *Relationship Marketing for Competitive Advantage: Winning and Keeping Customers*. Oxford: Butterworth Heinemann.

Reichheld, F.F. (1996) *The Loyalty Effect: The Hidden Force behind Growth, Profits and Lasting Value.* Boston, MA: Harvard Business School Press.

Seth, A. and Randall, G. (1999) *The Grocers.* London: Kogan Page.

Sheth, J.N. and Parvatiyar, A. (1993) *Relationship Marketing: Theory, Methods and Application.* Atlanta, GA: Atlanta Centre for Relationship Marketing.

Sheth, J.N. and Sisodia, R.S. (1999) 'Revisiting marketing's lawlike generalizations', *Journal of the Academy of Marketing Sciences*, 17 (1), 71–87.

Smith, P.R. (1998) *Marketing Communications; An Integrated Approach,* 2nd edn. London: Kogan Page.

Storbacka, K. (1997) 'Segmentation based on customer profitability: retrospective analysis of retail bank customer bases', *Journal of Marketing Management*, 13 (5), 479–92.

Storbacka, K., Strandvik, T. and Grönroos, C. (1994) 'Managing customer relations for profit: the dynamics of relationship quality', *International Journal of Service Industry Management*, 5, 21–38.

Strandvik, T. and Storbacka, K. (1996) 'Managing relationship quality', in Edvardsson, B., Brown, S.W., Johnston, R. and Scheuing, E.E. (eds) *Advancing Service Quality: A Global Perspective.* New York: ISQA, pp 67–76.

Tapp, A. (1998) *Principles of Direct and Database Marketing.* London: Financial Times Management/Pitman Publishing.

Tynan, C. (1997) 'A review of the marriage analogy in relationship marketing' *Journal of Marketing Management*, 13 (7), 695–704.

Vavra, T.G. (1992) *Aftermarketing.* Homewood, IL: Richard D. Irwin.

Voss, G.B. and Voss, Z.G. (1997) 'Implementing a relationship marketing program: a case study and managerial implications', *Journal of Services Marketing*, 11 (4), 278–98.

Whalley, S. (1999) 'ABC of relationship marketing', *SuperMarketing*, 12 March, 12–13.

2 Relationships

Key issues

➤ Relationship terminology
➤ Organisational relationships
➤ Motivational investment
➤ Relationship loyalty
➤ Unrealistic relationship development

Introduction

This chapter looks in more depth at what is meant by the term 'relationship' and how the various definitions and concepts contribute to (and sometimes confuse) the relationship marketing debate.

Relationships

There is, as with so many marketing concepts, no agreement as to what is meant by the term 'relationship' within 'relationship marketing'. RM critics suggest that this lack of clarity has provided researchers with the luxury of being able to choose whatever relationship definition best suits their research agendas at any given time (O'Malley and Tynan, 1999, p. 589). A further criticism is that relationships are invariably discussed and defined from the company perspective. That consumers should be equally interested in building and sustaining relationships is often taken for granted (Carlell, 1999, p. 1). This chapter will attempt to go beyond the rhetoric and clarify what marketers mean when they talk about relationships.

Relationship terminology

The very word relationship appears to be the basis of some concern. The use of a highly emotive term to describe a commercial strategy is open to some justifiable criticism. Such language is not, however, new to marketing. Levitt (1983, p. 111) used the language of love when he declared nearly two decades ago that the sale merely consummated the relationship with the customer and that after that the marriage began. These human relationship analogies are used frequently (see Tynan, 1997; Smith and Higgins, 2000). The RM vocabulary abounds with terms such as 'stages of a love affair', 'one night stands', 'extra marital dalliances', 'comparisons with a Mills and Boon novel' (see Brown, 1998, pp. 174–5), seduction and polygamy (Tynan, 1997, p. 987). There have even been terms seen to represent the darker side of relationships, such as stalking, prostitution and rape, used to describe certain, less than ethical, business practices (Tynan, 1997, p. 987). Even the most innocent of consumers runs the risk of being described as 'flirting' with the competition or of being a 'promiscuous' shopper.

In relationship marketing, therefore, metaphors abound. The difficulties begin, however, when we start believing our own rhetoric. As O'Malley and Tynan (1999, p. 593) note:

> As a conceptual tool a metaphor must be literally false whilst simultaneously offering creative possibilities. Thus in the case of RM, it is important to understand that exchange between consumers and organisations are not interpersonal relationships *per se* but that the attributes of interpersonal relationships might be usefully employed when describing or attempting to understand that exchange.

It is evident that the language of RM misleads some organisations into assuming that all customer–supplier contacts are capable of closeness when many (if not most) are not much more than impersonal exchanges. What these marketers call intimacy some customers see as intrusion (Smith and Higgins, 2000, p. 82) and justifiably resent.

Two key questions must, therefore, be asked:

■ Can customer–supplier interactions ever be called 'relationships'?
■ Can customers ever develop relationships with companies or must relationships always be interpersonal (Buttle, 1996, p. 11)?

Needless to say, there is no straightforward answers to these questions. Over the next few pages we will look at what evidence there is to support either or both concepts and whether and in what way they may require qualification.

Relationship forming

It would seem initially safe to assume that social relationship activity *per se* can only take place between individuals. In business-to-business markets in particular relationships between the personnel of companies are explicitly recognised by both the buyer and seller organisations and individuals within those organisations (Blois, 1997, p. 53). As we will see later, these bilateral and network relationships can, at times, develop into deep friendships that may even supersede an individual's loyalty to his or her own company.

Barnes and Howlett (1998, p. 16) express the view that two characteristics must be present for an exchange situation to be described as a relationship. These are:

■ The relationship is mutually perceived to exist and is acknowledged as such by both parties.
■ The relationship goes beyond occasional contact and is recognised as having some special status.

While acknowledging that relationships involve more than these characteristics, Barnes and Howlett suggest a 'true relationship' cannot exist if these factors are absent. The one-sided and emotionless nature of most everyday commercial (and in particular consumer goods) exchanges would suggest that they would have difficulty fulfilling such criteria. Certainly if we were to further stipulate that 'relationships' must include 'status recognition' then it is doubtful that this level of relationship could ever be developed with, for example, a local supermarket. In consumer markets, therefore, the existence of personal relationships is less obvious. Indeed as Brown (1998, p. 177) notes with some feeling:

> what consumer in their right mind would ever want to establish a relationship with a commercial organisation?

There is empirical evidence to suggest that, regardless of what marketing strategies are implemented by the supplier, buyers frequently have no wish to enter into a relationship with a company (Palmer, 1996, p. 20). It is probable that situations exist where the seller may want to develop a 'relationship' whereas the customer is happier with a transactional approach (Bund-Jackson, 1985, p. 34). This may be particularly evident in the case of certain industries (see page 42).

Despite the perceived difficulties with defining the level of relationship, particularly in the consumer goods area, marketers perceive (either metaphorically or in reality) that relationships of some sort exist in commercial exchange situations.

Categorising relationships

There would appear to be a considerable number of variations in the types of relationship that are perceived to exist between a buyer and seller dependent on the industry, the company, the customer and numerous other factors. Gummesson (1999) makes a valiant attempt to classify many of them in his 30Rs model. No attempt is made here to list the innumerable types (see Box 11.1, p. 112 for a comprehensive list). Instead we will look at the various relationship criteria and how these impact upon relationship strategy development.

Organisational relationships

The question was raised earlier as to whether or not individual customers can have relationships with organisations or whether relationships must always be interpersonal. Although social relationships are always between individuals, it is interesting to observe that customer–supplier relationships (of whatever level or closeness) frequently continue despite the loss of any organisational personnel initially involved. This suggests that a relationship of sorts must exist, independent of company employees, between the customer (individual or company) and that organisation. Gummesson (2000, p. 6) calls this 'embedded knowledge'. He explains that if an employee leaves then 'human capital' is lost. Embedded knowledge, however, is part of the structural capital that does not disappear with the employee and is, in effect, 'owned' by the company.

From an RM perspective structural capital consists of relationships that have been made with the company, as an entity, in addition to (and perhaps parallel with) the relationship with the employees. As Gummesson notes, 'the more successful a company [is in tying] relationships to its structure, the less dependent it is on individual employees and the higher the value of its structural capital'. Football clubs or charities may be particularly clear examples of where organisational loyalty is not necessarily directly associated with the personnel who work for it. Relationships with these organisations may last for years without, necessarily, any close bond developing with that organisation's employees.

It is also observable that reputation matters when dealing for the first time or subsequently with an organisation. The historical trustworthiness of parties in previous interactions make reputational effects possible (Rousseau et al., 1998, p. 397) that may again supersede individual relationships. Thus a customer will continue to frequent a supplier for reputational reasons as well as (or even in spite of) their personal relationship with that company's employees.

Based on the recognition of embedded knowledge and reputational effects it may be suggested that organisational relationships are possible as a prelude to and/or as a mediating factor in, the establishment of interpersonal or non-personal business relationships. That relationships can exist with organisations, albeit at varying emotional levels, is supported by Blois (1997, p. 53), who suggests that unless a counter-intuitive definition of 'relationship' is used, it is difficult, if not impossible, to suggest that firms do not have relationships. O'Malley and Tynan (1999, p. 594), too, suggest that when viewed as an association between two or more variables then it is clear a relationship exists between consumers and organisations.

Learning relationships

Peppers and Rogers (2000, p. 244) have suggested that relationships are built on knowledge. They propose that, when customers tell a company something about themselves then it is the responsibility of the company to customise its offering to that customer. From that point the relationship has started. The more the customer tells the company, the more valuable they become *provided* the company continues to adapt its product or service to meet the more and more specific customer needs. This relationship gets 'smarter and smarter' with every interaction. Whereas traditional marketing tended to regard information as a source of power, 'learning relationships' imply that information is a valuable resource in building relationships.

Motivational investments

Dwyer et al. (1987) suggest that the type of relationship that develops between a supplier and a customer is determined by the different amounts of motivational investment that buyers and sellers are prepared to commit to the relationship. They hypothesise that there are four types of relationships (in addition to 'no exchange; Figure 2.1):

- Bilateral relationships
- Seller-maintained relationships

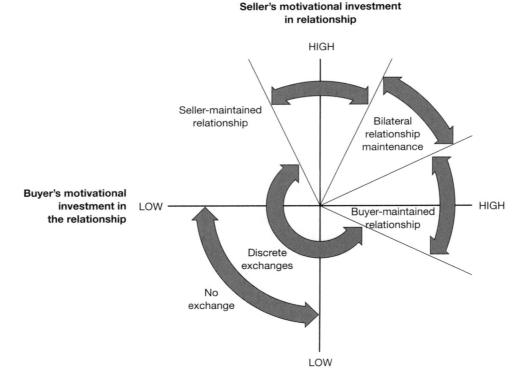

Figure 2.1 Hypothesised realm of buyer–seller relationships
(*Source*: Adapted from Dwyer *et al.*, 1987, p. 14)

■ Buyer Maintained relationships
■ Discrete exchanges.

Bilateral relationships are those where both parties are motivated highly enough to invest in a relationship. This situation reflects many of the relationship definitions and criteria discussed in Chapter 1. These bilateral relationships are particularly relevant to business-to-business markets, although some relationships of this type may be seen to exist in some consumer markets (e.g. financial services). At the other end of the scale, discrete exchanges are low-involvement, purely transactional relationships (see Chapter 4).

That relationships might exist other than bilateral (i.e. with the active involvement of both parties) or discrete (i.e. transactional) does not, according to Dwyer *et al.* (1987, p. 15), denigrate the significance of this type of relationship, albeit that it is one-sided. In Dwyer *et al.*'s conception just because one or other party has a low motivational investment does not mean it is not a relationship – rather that it is a relationship of a different type.

Examples of buyer-supported relationships may be seen in the automobile market where Toyota, Ford and other manufacturers regularly share their production information with their suppliers. Retail stores such as Tesco and Sainsbury also allow suppliers access to 'point of sale' data to facilitate distribution. It is noticeable that buyer-maintained relationships are more likely to exist when the buyer is the more dominant partner. It is, however, a significant change in attitude from past decades when such information was regarded as commercially confidential and was used to maintain an element of power and control over suppliers.

In consumer markets, although it is possible that customers may actively seek a relationship, the likelihood is that suppliers will largely manage the interaction. Relationships between buyers and sellers in these markets are generally considered to be much looser, with the bonds that tie the partners together being weaker and fewer (Möller and Halinen, 2000, p. 41). In mass-produced consumer goods markets, for example, where a large gap exists between the manufacturer and the consumer, 'relationships' are often restricted to service 'hotlines' and personalised mailings (Hennig-Thurau, 2000, p. 56). In these markets many companies are using tactics that have more in common with traditional marketing techniques (e.g. mass mailings) than RM. According to McDonald (2000, p. 31) supplier delusions about the state of their customer relationships have reached alarming proportions. Despite this, it is difficult, given that communication is taking place, not to regard them as relationships of sorts.

Higher-level relationships

Although higher-level and closer relationships may be more common in business-to-business environments (see Chapters 8 and 9) it seems possible for some consumer organisations to develop relationships that appear to be higher up the 'relationship ladder' (see Figure 3.3, p. 60).

Attachment or affinity to local football teams or voluntary organisations (e.g. a favourite charity or political party) can result in behaviour that suggests a deep and frequently emotional relationship. This may be despite the fact that many of the activities (from the perspective of the outsider) reflect commercial considerations. Thus the blatant commercialism of the football club that changes its kit design frequently in the knowledge that its fans will buy the new version has no apparent effect on that supporter's loyalty to the club although the parents of younger supporters may feel aggrieved; see Case study, p. 47).

Affinity packages (e.g. university credit cards, society or group insurance or assurance policies) arranged through companies such as MBNA, Royal Bank of Scotland, Membership Services Direct and others are prompted by the consumer's close relationship with the affiliated organisation. Whether the consumer sees this as a close relationship with the actual (as opposed to the nominal) supplier is, however, doubtful. What is more realistic is that the member sees this 'relationship' as a relatively cost-efficient way of contributing to the sponsor organisation's coffers. From the actual supplier's perspective it may be a means of targeting customers with specific needs or particular profiles associated with the membership of certain organisations. (For a fuller discussion of the implications of affinity card relationships, see Horne and Worthington 1999).

Some affinity groups may be made up of like-minded people who share a common interest and actively want a relationship not only with the supplier/organiser but also with each other. Examples of this include specialist societies (often encouraged and supported by producers), such as the Harley Davidson and Jaguar clubs.

Other affinity-type relationships include those that Foxall *et al.* (1998, p. 17) call 'frequency marketing'. Frequency marketing describes those interconnected programmes designed to link customers with brands by engaging them into clubs entitling members to special discounts, newsletters, tie-in purchases, credit cards, promotions and other privileges. Examples include collector's clubs such as those for Swatch watches and Royal Doulton bone china figurines.

Relationship loyalty

It is almost impossible to discuss relationships without discussing the concept of loyalty. Indeed the phrase 'loyalty marketing' is frequently used interchangeably with RM. Such is its perceived importance that it has been claimed that customer loyalty 'is emerging as the marketplace currency for the 21st century' (Singh and Sirdeshmukh, 2000, p. 150).

Loyalty is, however, a much used and abused term. Although it is widely utilised, most authors fail to define what they mean by the term, resulting in a lack of consistency in the marketing literature. At its most profound, the term loyalty suggests the highest possible level of relationship impinging upon the emotional not to say the irrational. Its use in commercial situations has, however, debased this higher-level meaning, although some suppliers would have us believe differently. The idea that loyalty has some special magical powers that marketers can invoke that are 'different' or 'in addition to' their normal marketing activities has been growing (Mitchell, 1998, p. 16) despite considerable evidence to the contrary.

Defining loyalty

There appear to be two main strands of thought on the essence of commercial loyalty (Javalgi and Moberg, 1997, p. 165):

■ A definition of loyalty in *behavioural* terms, usually based on the number of purchases and measured by monitoring the frequency of such purchases and any brand switching.
■ A definition of loyalty in *attitudinal* terms, incorporating consumer preferences and disposition towards brands to determine levels of loyalty.

The assumption that is frequently made is that, from whatever sources the loyalty is derived, it translates into an unspecified number of repeat purchases from the same supplier over a specified period. The problem with relying on this behavioural definition is that there may be many reasons for repeat patronage other than loyalty, among them lack of other choices, habit, low income, convenience etc. (Hart *et al.*, 1999, p. 545). Equating loyalty wholly with relationship longevity, therefore, tells us little about relationship strength (Storbacka *et al.*, 1994, p. 30).

A more comprehensive definition of loyalty may be:

> The biased (i.e. non-random) behavioural response (i.e. re-visit), expressed over time, by some decision-making unit with respect to one [supplier] out of a set of [suppliers], which is a function of psychological [decision making and evaluative] processes resulting in brand commitment.
>
> (Bloemer and de Ruyter, 1998, p. 500)

(Bloemer and de Ruyter were describing 'retail store loyalty' in this definition but it is equally applicable to suppliers in general.) Simple repatronage, therefore, is not enough. Loyalty, if it is to have any credence, must be seen as 'biased repeat purchase behaviour' or 'repeat patronage accompanied by a favourable attitude' (O'Malley, 1998, p. 50). Loyalty can originate from factors extrinsic to the relationship such as the market structure in which the relationship exists (and the possible geographic limitations) but also in intrinsic factors such as relationship strength and the handling of critical episodes during the relationship (Storbacka *et al.*, 1994, p. 29).

Antecedents to loyalty

There are two distinct viewpoints as to the antecedents to loyalty. In the first, loyalty is seen as more often built on 'hard' dimensions such as value for money, convenience, reliability, safety and functionality, and that these are the prime drivers for product or service choice (Christopher, 1996, p. 60). Fredericks and Salter's (1998, p. 64) model (Figure 2.2) shows this graphically and encompasses some of the areas that will be discussed more fully in later chapters.

This viewpoint suggests that, while a customer's positive experiences with products or services may enhance a type of temporal loyalty, it is essential to remember that 'money talks' and 'everyone has a price' (Hassan, 1996, p. 7). Such is the level and scope of price-based competition in some consumer markets (e.g. FMCG retailing) that some would even suggest that fostering 'real' loyalty in such markets is an almost impossible task (Pressey and Mathews, 1998, p. 39).

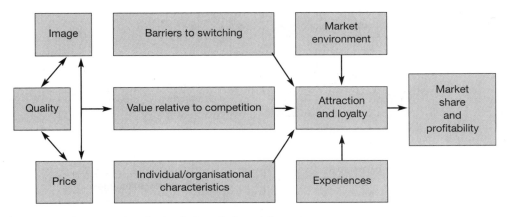

Figure 2.2 Customer loyalty: an integrated model
(*Source*: Adapted from Fredericks and Salter, 1998, p. 64)

An alternative to this view is expressed by Dick and Basu (1994, p. 99) In this model, 'softer', more intangible factors such as emotion and satisfaction are seen to affect attitude in a decisive way. This viewpoint suggests that customer loyalty is viewed principally as a result of the bond between an individual's relative attitude and repeat patronage, again mediated by social norms and situational influences or experiences (Figure 2.3).

What both models implicitly suggest is that customer satisfaction sustains loyalty. The presumption is that loyalty is built upon satisfaction derived from a positive differentiation achieved by providing superior customer service (Javalgi and Moberg, 1997, p. 165). Research (Hassan, 1996, p. 9), however, suggests that loyalty should not be confused with satisfaction (though creating more satisfaction *may* reduce the likelihood of disloyalty). Satisfaction does not always result in retention (loyalty) and it is equally apparent that dissatisfaction does not necessarily result in defection (Buttle, 1997, p. 145; O'Malley 1998, p. 48). Dick and Basu's (1994, p. 101) 'relative attitude/behaviour matrix' (see Figure 5.3, p. 103) graphically shows that 'spurious loyalty' may be caused by the lack of alternatives and numerous other variables. As Storbacka *et al.* (1994, p. 28) note:

> Customer loyalty is not always based on positive attitude, and long-term relationships do not necessarily require positive commitment from customers. The distinction is important because it challenges the idea that customer satisfaction (the attitude) leads to long-lasting relationships (the behaviour).

Indeed, research suggests that neither loyalty and satisfaction (Hassan, 1996, p. 9) nor loyalty and profitability (East, 2000, p. 7) necessarily go hand in hand.

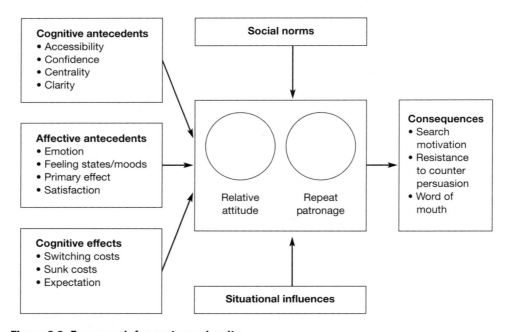

Figure 2.3 Framework for customer loyalty
(*Source*: Adapted from Dick and Basu, 1994, p. 100)

Loyalty-type behaviour

There are many ways of describing loyalty-type and non-loyal customer behaviour (see for example Brassington and Pettitt, 1997, p. 88). One example is that suggested by Uncles (1994, p. 342), who proposes three ways of considering customer repatronising behaviour:

- *Switching behaviour*: where purchasing is seen as an 'either/or' decision – either the customer stays with you (loyalty) or turns against you (switching).
- *Promiscuous behaviour*: where customers are seen as making a 'stream of purchases' but still within the context of an either/or decision – either the customer is always with you (loyalty) or flits among an array of alternatives (promiscuous).
- *Polygamous behaviour*: again, the customer makes a stream of purchases but their loyalty is divided among a number of products. They may be more or less loyal to your brand than any other.

Evidence from consumer research tends to support the view that patterns of promiscuity and polygamy are the norm (Uncles, 1994, p. 344). Barnard and Ehrenberg (1997, p. 23), for example, suggest that many or most consumers are multi-brand buyers and that only one tenth of buyers are 100% loyal. This may be because a customer's holistic requirements frequently extend beyond those capable of being effectively fulfilled by a single firm's products and services.

Consumers are, therefore, prone to 'mix and match' products and services according to their specific needs (Kandampully and Duddy, 1999, p. 316). There is also doubt over whether loyal buyers are more profitable than promiscuous or polygamous buyers. Research evidence suggests that loyalists are more often light buyers of products or services in various categories whereas multi-brand (or broad repertoire) buyers are heavier users (East, 2000, p. 7). It is not difficult to perceive a situation where the less loyal 'heavy' buyer is a more frequent purchaser of a company's products or services (and is consequently more attractive) than a buyer who is one 100% loyal (Uncles, 1994, pp. 346–7).

Loyalty schemes

There can be little doubt that we are living in the age of the loyalty scheme (Hart *et al.*, 1999, p. 544). Indeed, the perceived significance of such schemes, if claims at 'loyalty' conferences and in 'loyalty' magazines are to be believed, has reached heroic proportions. According to Uncles (1994, p. 341), the espoused view is that customers actively seek an involving relationship with 'their' brand (product manufacturer, service supplier, brand owner or retailer), which in turn offers psychological reassurances to the buyer and creates a sense of belonging. The proposed benefit of loyalty schemes, for loyal and heavy or frequent customers, is having this sense of belonging reinforced.

Hart *et al.* (1999, p. 546) offer a wider range of motives for setting up loyalty schemes:

- Building lasting relationships with customers by rewarding them for their patronage.
- Gaining higher profits through extended product usage and cross-selling.

- Gathering customer information.
- De-commodifing brands (i.e. differentiate from the crowd).
- Defending market position (against a competitor's loyalty schemes).
- Pre-empting competitive activity.

One of the principal objectives of loyalty programmes is seen to be the collection (and later qualifying) of customer data. There is little doubt that this data has the potential to be valuable and it is frequently suggested that this value balances out any costs of loyalty schemes (see Chapter 10). Views differ on customers' motives and expectations for providing this data. According to Kelly (2000, p. 263), when you hand a customer a loyalty card you immediately create the expectation in the mind of the consumer that you are now going to study their behaviour and that, in return, they expect the supplier to do something intelligent with that information. This 'cooperation' may be the basis of a future relationship. Evidence on both customer expectations and competitive advantage are, however, patchy. There is at least one school of thought that suggests data collection is over-emphasised and that the costs of data collection frequently outweigh any advantages gained (O'Malley, 1998, p. 52).

Another principal reason for developing a loyalty scheme, according to Hart *et al.*, is to build lasting relationships with customers. Although in some instances there may be a genuine desire on the part of the supplier to enter into a relationship with customers, most loyalty schemes seem to be tactical moves designed to defend short-term positions in highly competitive markets (Uncles, 1994, p. 337) rather than a relationship-building exercise. These schemes are little more than 'classic' sales promotions with short-term incentives to disloyal 'brand-switchers' (Palmer, 1998, p. 114; Uncles, 1994, p. 341).

Profitability is another proposed driver but here again the evidence is conflicting. While loyalty scheme pioneers (for example, American Airlines' Frequent Flyer Program and Tesco's Club Card) in a sector may gain additional business in the short-term, these incentives rapidly become the 'sector norm' that customers come to expect (Palmer, 1996, p. 22). All too quickly early benefits can turn into the unavoidable cost of doing business (Uncles, 1994, p. 349). When loyalty rewards become the expectation in any sector it is doubtful whether anyone is ultimately any better off (Palmer, 1998, p. 117). To exacerbate the situation, once loyalty schemes become the norm and customers come to expect rewards, then there is the costly task of 'continually ratcheting up the loyalty ladder' (Uncles, 1994, p. 348). This is likely, ultimately, to affect the relationship. Over time, customers who receive, in effect, only bribes are likely to become promiscuous and seek the highest bribe available as that is the only satisfaction they receive from the exchange (Tynan, 1997, p. 992).

If there is so much doubt about the validity of these programmes, why do 'loyalty scheme saturated sectors' continue to invest so heavily? It may simply be a case of 'follow the leader': when Tesco launched its loyalty scheme, Sainsbury was adamant that it would not follow suit; this decision was reversed within 12 months. Another reason may be that it is very difficult to measure the effectiveness of a loyalty

---

Box 2.1

Loyalty programmes

It may appear that so-called loyalty schemes are a very recent phenomenon. The technology may be more sophisticated but the principle of 'locking-in' consumers by way of 'promotions' has changed remarkably little. The Co-operative Movement has operated a loyalty scheme for decades, initially as the 'divi' (a dividend based on the amount of purchases made during a period) and later using trading stamps. Pink and Green stamps were an important incentive as early as the 1960s. Petrol retailers have been wedded to continuity programmes for many years, with 'low tech' collection devices (cards, stamps etc.) being replaced later by more technologically sophisticated mediums (e.g. Esso Tiger Cards, Mobil/BP Premier Points etc.). Airline frequent flyer programmes (e.g. Virgin Freeway, Air France Frequent Plus) have grown to the extent that very few non-cut-price airlines are without one. Store loyalty cards are but the latest ploy in marketing continuity programmes that have been around for decades (e.g. special events, discounts etc.).

---

programme. This stems from the difficulty of comparing the performance of companies that run them with companies that do not (Palmer, 1998, p. 114). In this situation it may be perceived as safer for the supplier to retain a scheme rather than chance losing custom. The risk taken by Safeway in withdrawing its loyalty programme is discussed in the Case study at the end of Chapter 10.

It is perhaps ironic that attempts to apply RM in consumer markets have concentrated on 'low-involvement' categories such as FMCG products, white and brown goods, and services such as supermarkets and petrol retailers (O'Malley and Tynan, 1999, p. 589; see Box 2.1). Indeed, many authors have pointed to these loyalty schemes as evidence of the take-up of RM in the retail sector (Pressey and Mathews, 1998, p. 39). Many such schemes would seem to have been introduced not for proactive but for defensive reasons (Khan, 1998, p. 65). As a result, customers, according to a recent Mintel report (quoted by Khan, 1998), are getting more out of loyalty schemes than retailers (see Box 2.2).

Box 2.2

Loyalty cards

Jane Simms, former editor of the Chartered Institute of Marketing magazine *Marketing Business* wrote of her frustration with loyalty schemes in an editorial in the December 1998/January 1999 issue:

'I am bombarded with press releases and phone calls from PRs enthusiastically trumpeting the benefits of relationship marketing and loyalty schemes – by which they normally mean loyalty cards. My purse is bulging with loyalty cards and they engender no sense of loyalty in me. Loyalty is an unachievable Holy Grail. The sooner marketers get their heads around a few incontrovertible facts about consumers, the sooner they will stop wasting precious marketing funds and hacking customers off. Companies seeking to "lock in" customers to their loyalty schemes are on a hiding to nothing. Loyalty is fleeting, it has to be earnt [*sic*] – it cannot be bought – and while customers may not exactly be promiscuous, they are, at best, serially loyal.'

Source: Jane Simms, *Marketing Business*, December 1998/January 1999

Loyalty in context

Features such as loyalty cards may have a part to play in relationship maintenance but they cannot realistically be taken as a proxy for the relationship marketing philosophy. Loyalty programmes are not a marketing panacea and are often not much more than sophisticated sales promotions where costs may frequently outweigh advantages (O'Malley, 1998, p. 52). At best, loyalty schemes act as reinforcing mechanisms, since it appears, on the whole, that they reward the 'already loyal' rather than anyone else (Ward *et al.*, 1998, p. 85). From a customer perspective, many loyalty schemes offer 'me too' benefits which may be nice to have (because most people like getting something for nothing) but these are no guarantee of continued loyalty and are often marginal to their brand choice decision (Uncles, 1994, p. 341). Given the evidence, it would appear to be becoming increasingly obvious that loyalty schemes have little effect on underlying affective commitment (Palmer, 1998, p. 117) or do little to directly affect the chances of account retention (Bolton *et al.*, 2000, p. 103). Loyalty schemes may, in many cases, be an expensive misnomer.

Unrealistic relational development

It is suggested in Chapter 4 that certain industries are more or less likely to benefit from relational strategy development. On a more individualistic note, it may also be the case that, even where the general indication is that a particular business may benefit from relational strategies, there are reasons why attempting to develop such relationships may be a fruitless pursuit. These 'unrealistic' RM scenarios may be determined by either the customer or the supplier

Unrealistic customer relationship development

According to Palmer (1996, p. 20) a number of unrealistic customer scenarios exist. These include:

- Where there is no reason why, or little likelihood that, a buyer will purchase again from a supplier.
- Where buyers want to avoid a relationship as it may lead to a dependency on a seller.
- Where buying processes are formalised in a way that prevents either party developing relationships based on social bonds.
- Where a buyer's confidence lowers the need for risk reduction (see Chapter 5).
- Where the costs associated with a relationship put the buyer at a cost disadvantage in a price-sensitive market.

Low likelihood of repurchase

With the growth of travel the percentage of purchases made at diverse, temporary locations (e.g. airports) increases. A buyer who is unlikely ever to repatronise a supplier will see no benefit from relationship formulation and may indeed be annoyed by the tactics associated with it (e.g. data capture).

Dependency avoidance

This situation may exist when any benefits associated with the relationship are outweighed by lost opportunities elsewhere. For example, some companies offer improved terms for exclusive agreements (e.g. estate agencies' commission rates). Customers may decide, however, that a sole-agent relationship would limit them (e.g. restrict the chances of a quick sale through a larger number of estate agents) and choose instead to open up the contract to other suppliers. They are forgoing any benefits of the relationship (e.g. reduced commission) in favour of the benefits of plurality (e.g. wider coverage).

Formalised contracts

Formalised buying situations (such as those involving government agencies) may be compromised and jeopardised by too close an association between buyer and seller. Indeed, such relationships may be contractually or legally barred. In these situations the establishment of relationships may be neither welcomed by, nor be in the long-term interest of, either party.

Low-risk situations

In many exchange situations risk (as potentially a major driver to 'relationship seeking') is minimal. As a consequence consumers are unlikely to see either the need or the justification for closer relationships (see Chapter 5).

Price-sensitive markets

It may prove more profitable for buyers in certain markets to keep their eyes open for the best deal available rather than narrow the field and commit themselves to one supplier. Indeed they may well prefer to play suppliers off against each other using an organisation's potential insecurity to gain added value.

In situations such as these, where the consumer will be unlikely to perceive any advantage from a relationship, suppliers should be looking to qualify whether costly relationship-building strategies are a viable proposition. The problem, from the perspective of the supplier, is the difficulty of knowing that some of these situations (e.g. where the customer is unlikely to repatronise) exist unless the customer volunteers the information.

Unrealistic supplier relationship development

This 'relationship avoidance' is not necessarily one way and may also be sought by the supplier in certain situations. These scenarios closely mirror Palmer's (1996, p. 20) customer list, and include:

■ Where there is no reason why a seller would ever see a buyer again.
■ Where a seller seeks to avoid a relationship in which it becomes dependent on a buyer.

- Where buying processes become formalised in a way that prevents either party developing relationships based on social bonds.
- Where the seller has little opportunity to develop relationships due to the undifferentiated nature of the market.
- Where the ethos of the industry makes relationship-building inappropriate.

Low likelihood of repurchase

Situations where a customer is unlikely to repatronise a particular supplier (perhaps because the buyer's home base is many miles from that supplier, or where, by the nature of the product or service, a second purchase is unlikely) may suggest that investment in relationship building is unlikely to provide a profitable return.

Dependency avoidance

This may reflect the supplier's desire not to 'put all of their eggs in one (or a few) basket'. This may be particularly relevant in business-to-business situations where the number of customers is, generally, lower although it may also exist in some financial services (or other potentially high-risk associations) where the level of exposure may make the organisation vulnerable to high loss. This scenario may be very difficult to manage from the supplier's perspective if the buyer is, or has the potential of being, a substantial customer and if that customer is pushing for a closer relationship. An example of where 'dependence avoidance' may be considered is where a supplier appears overly dependent on one or a few retailers, leaving it vulnerable to changes in market circumstances (as some UK suppliers of Marks & Spencer discovered to their cost when the company's buying policy changed in 1999).

Formalised contracts

This situation mirrors the buyer's dilemma. Suppliers may be at risk (particularly in public contracts) from legal action should they even attempt to build a relationship with a public body's representative as this may be construed as bribery or corrupt practice.

Undifferentiated markets

Although RM has been presented as of potential benefit in undifferentiated markets, a different interpretation may be considered. Suppliers of largely undifferentiated products or services where customers are likely at any time to switch should consider whether 'seduction' (for example, promotional discounts) rather than potentially costly relational strategies is more cost effective.

Price-sensitive markets

This situation may exist where companies rely on market opportunism. Blois (1998, p. 258) suggests that NECX Inc. in the USA is such an organisation. In a case study Blois suggests that the company exists principally to take advantage of uncertainties in both supply and demand in the computer supplies market. Blois argues that this company would feel inhibited about 'exploiting' shortage situations if it were to develop 'relationships' with its customers.

Relationships in context

There is no doubt that some companies seem to have the knack of handling relationships. Grönroos (2000, p. 4) quotes Fergal Quinn, founder and president of Superquinn stores in the Irish Republic, as saying that if the supplier handles relationships well, the customer will come back. Quinn calls this the 'boomerang principle', the beauty of which is that 'you and the customer end up on the same side . . . so that the relationship with your customer is not an adversarial one, it's a partnership'.

On the other side of the coin the danger comes when the relationship metaphor becomes accepted as truth. Many authors treat consumer–organisational relationships as though they were literally true (O'Malley and Tynan, 1999, p. 594) when realistically they will never be more than associations. As Van den Bulte (1994, p. 416) notes, after long and repeated use, a metaphor may become so hackneyed that people forget that it is a metaphor and sublimate its relationship with reality. Perhaps this is happening with RM. Indeed, when some kinds of repeat behaviour (particularly spurious loyalty) are treated as 'relationships', one may suspect that relationship as a metaphor may be rather ill suited (Carlell, 1999, p. 8).

Loyalty, as we have noted, is a very much used and abused term. Although RM and loyalty marketing have several common components (e.g. the use of information technology, customer knowledge and direct customer communications), it is questionable whether the association is any deeper (Hart *et al.*, 1999, p. 541). Loyalty programmes and other behaviour-based initiatives suggest that this view of relationships formation is more akin to a stimulus–response function (Barnes and Howlett, 1998, p. 15) than anything resembling a relationship. Rarely are loyalty programmes more than sophisticated sales promotions where the loyalty is to the programme and not the brand (O'Malley, 1998, p. 52). Whereas loyalty schemes may play a part in relationship maintenance, they cannot be realistically taken as proxy for the RM philosophy (Pressey and Mathews, 1998, p. 39).

Whatever the level of the relationship, it cannot be expected to last forever. Various terms exist for describing termination of relationships within marketing and these will be covered in more detail in the following chapters. Suffice to say at this stage that long-term relationships can carry with them the seeds of their own destruction (Grayson and Ambler 1999, p. 138). It is certainly not a foregone conclusion that relationships will mature gracefully. Whether prompted by some experience within the relationship or not, many relationships will suffer and potentially disintegrate from basic boredom or fatigue. Evident satisfaction is equally no defence as the customer, however satisfied at present, can always be more satisfied somewhere else in the future. Declining customer 'loyalty' (however it is defined) may build up in small steps that may not be discernible until it is too late (Gummesson, 1999, p. 187): Laura Ashley and Marks & Spencer may have been victims of this.

It is important, therefore, that any reference to the term 'relationship' is made in the recognition that not all relationships are close and enduring. Relationships exist at many different levels. What might be said about all relationships, however, is that they determine the type and nature of the customer–supplier interaction. As such, and at whatever level they exist, they are of interest to the marketer.

Summary

This chapter looked at the central concepts associated with 'relationships'. It examined whether customers can have relationships with organisations and whether relationships always have to be interpersonal. It suggested that, in certain situations, organisational relationships were possible and that they acted as a prelude to and/or as a mediating factor in the establishment of interpersonal and non-personal business relationships.

The chapter looked at 'learning relationships' based on 'knowing' the customer and (crucially) acting on this knowledge. It examined how 'motivational investment' affects the types of relationships that exist and how 'supplier-maintained' or 'buyer-maintained' relationships may exist in addition to bilateral and discrete exchange relationships. Higher-level relationships were discussed, including affinity, affinity packages and frequency marketing.

Loyalty as a concept close to the heart of RM was elaborated upon and the perceived antecedents to loyalty outlined. Loyalty-type behaviour was discussed and loyalty schemes put under the spotlight.

The potential for situations where relationship development is unrealistic (from either the customer or the supplier perspective) was discussed and the factors leading to such situations noted.

The chapter concluded by attempting to put relationships into perspective within the RM debate. It suggested that many levels of relationship exist, all of which are of interest to the marketer.

Discussion questions

1 In what ways are the relationship metaphor used in marketing?

2 How might relationships develop between organisations and their customers?

3 What different levels of relationship can be seen to exist between buyers and suppliers?

4 What part do loyalty schemes play in relationship development?

FT

Manchester United plans to establish fans' forum

Manchester United ushered in a new era of relations between football clubs and their fans yesterday when it unveiled plans for an independent supporters' forum, the creation of which will be monitored by the Electoral Reform Society.

Fans will be asked to put forward nominations for categories of representative – including season ticket holders, disabled fans, executive box-holders and independent supporter association members. The society will hold a draw to choose the 15 members.

The move follows last week's launch of the Premier League's 'customers' charter' aimed at improving communication between fans and clubs. It is the most high-profile example of clubs recognising the role played of supporters in the running of the business.

The society's involvement shows the club's desire for the forum to be seen as independent of the board.

Peter Kenyon, Manchester United chief executive, said: 'I think we have to work harder at communicating with our fans. We're like any other business. You have to listen to your customers – the people who use your services.' Peter Draper, its group marketing director, added: 'The consultative forum will be external to the club and we will meet it regularly during the year. What its members tell us will give us a better understanding of our fans' needs and will help us make Manchester United a better club.'

Fans welcomed the initiative. 'The supporters are an integral part of the club. It's a positive idea and an opportunity to bridge the gulf which exists between the board and the fans,' said Andy Walsh of the Independent Manchester United Supporters' Association.

Other clubs have announced plans for fan bodies. Last month, Newcastle United, which has suffered a poor relationship with supporters in the past two years, said it would establish a 300-member forum of randomly selected fans to canvass views about the club and suggest improvements.

However, Manchester United, which yesterday printed ballot forms in the match programme before the game against Newcastle, will be the first club to create a consultative body made up of nominated members.

Manchester United – which has been criticised by sections of supporters for ignoring fans' needs in favour of commercial interests – is one of the first clubs to have adopted the measures in the Premier League's customers' charter.

The charter is the result of a two-year study by the Football Taskforce into ways of improving fans' treatment by clubs. It limits the frequency with which replica kits can be changed, and sets out measures for the appointment of customer service representatives at each club to deal with complaints by supporters. Breaches could result in fines by the Premier League. However, critics argue that without an independent regulator to enforce the charter, clubs could go unpunished.

(*Source*: Matthew Garrahan, *Financial Times*, 21st August 2000)

▶

> ### Case study questions
>
> **1** Will the scheme introduced by Manchester United 'bridge the gulf which exists between the Board and the fans'?
>
> **2** What other initiatives could football clubs introduce to improve relationships with their fans?

References

Barnard, N. and Ehrenberg, A.S.C. (1997) 'Advertising: strongly persuasive or nudging?', *Journal of Advertising Research*, January/February, 21–31.

Barnes, J.G. and Howlett, D.M. (1998) 'Predictors of equity in relationships between service providers and retail customers', *International Journal of Bank Marketing*, 16 (1), 5–23.

Bloemer, J. and de Ruyter, K. (1998) 'On the relationship between store image, store satisfaction and store loyalty', *European Journal of Marketing*, 32 (5/6), 499–513.

Blois, K.J. (1997) 'When is a relationship a relationship', in Gemünden, H.G., Rittert, T. and Walter, A. (eds) *Relationships and Networks in International Markets*. Oxford: Elsevier, pp. 53–64.

Blois, K.J. (1998) 'Don't all firms have relationships?', *Journal of Business and Industrial Marketing*, 13 (3), 256–70.

Bolton, R.N., Kanna, P.K. and Bramlett, M.D. (2000) 'Implications of loyalty programme membership and service experience for customer retention and value', *Journal of Marketing Science*, 28 (1), 95–108.

Brassington, F. and Pettitt, S. (1997) *The Principles of Marketing*. London: Pitman.

Brown, S. (1998) *Postmodern Marketing II*. London: International Thompson Business Press.

Bund-Jackson, B. (1985) 'Build customer relationships that last', *Harvard Business Review*, November/December, 120–28.

Buttle, F.B. (1996) *Relationship Marketing Theory and Practice*. London: Paul Chapman.

Buttle, F.B. (1997) 'Exploring relationship quality', paper presented at the Academy of Marketing Conference, Manchester, UK.

Carlell, C. (1999) 'Relationship marketing from the consumer perspective', paper presented at the European Academy of Marketing Conference (EMAC), Berlin.

Christopher, M. (1996) 'From brand values to customer values', *Journal of Marketing Practice*, 2 (1), 55–66.

Dick, A. and Basu, K. (1994) 'Customer loyalty: towards an integrated framework', *Journal of the Academy of Marketing Science*, 22, 99–113.

Dwyer, F.R., Schurr, P.H. and Oh, S. (1987) 'Developing buyer–seller relationships', *Journal of Marketing*, 51, 11–27.

East, R. (2000) 'Fact and fallacy in retention marketing', Professorial Inaugural Lecture, 1 March, Kingston University Business School.

Foxall, G.R., Goldsmith, R.E. and Brown, S. (1998) *Consumer Psychology for Marketing*. London: International Thompson Business Press.

Fredericks, J.O. and Salter, J.M. (1998) 'What does your customer really want?', *Quality Progress*, January, 63–8.

Grayson, K. and Ambler, T. (1999) 'The dark side of long-term relationships in marketing', *Journal of Marketing Research*, 36 (1), 132–41.

Grönroos, C. (2000) 'The relationship marketing process: interaction, communication, dialogue, value', in 2nd WWW Conference on Relationship Marketing, 15 November 1999 – 15 February 2000, paper 2 (www.mcb.co.uk/services/conferen/nov99/rm).

Gummesson, E. (1999) *Total Relationship Marketing: Rethinking Marketing Management from 4Ps to 30Rs*. Oxford: Butterworth Heinemann.

Gummesson, E. (2000) 'Return on relationships (ROR): building the future with intellectual capital', in 2nd WWW Conference on Relationship Marketing, 15 November 1999 – 15 February 2000, paper 5 (www.mcb.co.uk/services/conferen/nov99/rm).

Hart, S., Smith, A., Sparks, L. and Tzokas, N. (1999) 'Are loyalty schemes a manifestation of relationship marketing?', *Journal of Marketing Management*, 15, 541–62.

Hassan, M. (1996) *Customer Loyalty in the Age of Convergence*. London: Deloitte & Touche Consulting Group (www.dttus.com).

Hennig-Thurau, T. (2000) 'Relationship quality and customer retention through strategic communication of customer skills', *Journal of Marketing Management*, 16, 55–79.

Horne, S. and Worthington, S. (1999) 'The affinity credit card relationship: can it really be mutually beneficial?', *Journal of Marketing Management*, 15, 603–16.

Javalgi, R. and Moberg, C. (1997) 'Service loyalty: implications for service providers', *Journal of Services Marketing*, 11 (3), 165–79.

Kandampully, J. and Duddy, R. (1999) 'Relationship marketing: A concept beyond the primary relationship', *Marketing Intelligence & Planning*, 17 (7) 315–23.

Kelly, S. (2000) 'Analytical CRM: the fusion of data and intelligence', *Interactive Marketing*, 1 (3), 262–7.

Khan, Y. (1998) 'Winning cards', *Marketing Business*, May, 65.

Levitt, T. (1983) 'After the sale is over', *Harvard Business Review*, November/December, 87–93.

McDonald, M. (2000) 'On the right track', *Marketing Business*, April, 28–31.

Mitchell, A. (1998) 'Evolution', *Marketing Business*, November, 16.

Möller, K. and Halinen, A. (2000) 'Relationship marketing theory: its roots and direction', *Journal of Marketing Management*, 16, 29–54.

O'Malley, L. (1998) 'Can loyalty schemes really build loyalty?', *Marketing Intelligence and Planning*, 16, (1), 47–55.

O'Malley, L. and Tynan, C. (1999) 'The utility of the relationship metaphor in consumer markets: a critical evaluation', *Journal of Marketing Management*, 15, 587–602.

Palmer, A.J. (1996) 'Relationship marketing: a universal paradigm or management fad?' *The Learning Organisation*, 3 (3), 18–25.

Palmer, A.J. (1998) *Principles of Services Marketing*. London: Kogan Page.

Peppers, D. and Rogers, M. (2000) 'Build a one-to-one learning relationship with your customers', *Interactive Marketing*, 1 (3), 243–50.

Pressey, A.D. and Mathews, B.P. (1998) 'Relationship marketing and retailing: comfortable bedfellows?', *Customer Relationship Management*, 1 (1) 39–53.

Rousseau, D.M., Sitkin, S.B., Burt, R.S. and Camerer, C. (1998) 'Not so different after all: a cross discipline view of trust', *Academy of Management Review*, 23 (3), 393–404.

Singh, J. and Sirdeshmukh, D. (2000) 'Agency and trust mechanisms in consumer satisfaction and loyalty judgements', *Journal of Marketing Science*, 28 (1), 150–67.

Smith, W. and Higgins, M. (2000) 'Reconsidering the relationship analogy', *Journal of Marketing Management*, 16, 81–94.

Storbacka, K., Strandvik, T. and Grönroos, C. (1994) 'Managing customer relations for profit: the dynamics of relationship quality', *International Journal of Service Industry Management*, 5, 21–38.

Tynan, C. (1997) 'A review of the marriage analogy in relationship marketing', *Journal of Marketing Management*, 13 (7), 695–704.

Uncles, M. (1994) 'Do you or your customer need a loyalty scheme?', *Journal of Targeting, Measurement and Analysis*, 2 (4), 335–50.

Van den Bulte, C. (1994) 'Metaphor at work' in Laurent, G., Lilien, G.L. and Pras, B. (eds) *Research Traditions in Marketing*. Boston, MA: Kluwer Academic, pp. 405–25.

Ward, P., Gardner, H. and Wright, H. (1998) 'Being smart: a critique of customer loyalty schemes in UK retailing', *Customer Relationship Management*, 1 (1), 79–86.

3 Relationship economics

Key issues
> ➤ The economic justification for relationship marketing
> ➤ Customer acquisition versus customer retention
> ➤ Stages of relationship development
> ➤ Lifetime value concepts
> ➤ Switching costs
> ➤ Relationship longevity

Introduction

As has previously been noted, there is no agreement as to a precise definition of relationship marketing, nor even yet to the philosophical, organisational or economic concepts that surround it. There are, however, a number of key ideas or concepts that have developed through relationship marketing research which, many writers claim, underpin relational marketing theory and practice.

As was noted in Chapter 1, profitability must be a driving force behind any strategy development. In this chapter, therefore, we will look at the arguments for and against relationship economics.

Relationship economics

Despite the illusion sometimes presented by the apparent philanthropic and cooperative image of RM, a principal objective behind companies adopting relational strategies must, at least ultimately, be sustainable profitability. As Grönroos (1994, p. 9) noted in his definition, relationship strategies must be exercised 'at a profit'. As Gummesson (1994, p. 17) notes, the 'language of management is money, a good question [to ask] is how the relationship portfolio pays off'. RM, is, therefore, not altruistic but based on profit-driven arguments (Buttle, 1996, p. 5) with the profitability of relationships as one of the key goals (Storbacka *et al.* 1994, p. 22). The economic arguments (sometimes referred to under the heading of 'relationship economics') used in support of RM are, therefore, a good starting point for any consideration of the benefits associated with relational strategy implementation.

Leaky bucket theory

Historically, the focus of traditional marketing has been on creating new customers. This 'offensive marketing' strategy included, in addition to acquiring wholly new customers, attempting to attract dissatisfied customers away from competitors, particularly in periods of heavy competition (Storbacka *et al.*, 1994, pp. 22–23). RM, in contrast, takes the view that, although the acquisition of customers is important, it is an intermediate step in the process (Berry and Gresham 1986, p. 43). RM, it is suggested, has the dual focus of getting and keeping customers (Christopher *et al.*, 1991, p. vii). RM highlights the proposition that, in addition to 'offensive strategies', companies need 'defensive strategies' which minimise customer turnover (Storbacka *et al.*, 1994, pp. 22–23).

The logic behind this double-headed approach is probably best illustrated using the metaphor of the leaky bucket (Figure 3.1). This emphasises the importance of keeping customers while recognising that getting customers is, of course, the basis for having any customers to keep (Grönroos, 1995, p. 253).

To succeed, a company must *both* have a flow of new customers and restrict customer exit. The aim is to keep, or where company objectives call for it, increase the number of customers available to the company. To achieve profitability the dual strategies of acquisition and retention must work in tandem.

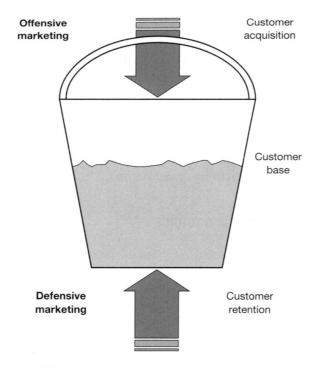

Figure 3.1 Leaky bucket theory

Customer acquisition

There is a continuous need in a business for 'new blood'. Any fall in the overall number of customers has profitability implications, particularly in service industries where fixed costs (especially staffing costs) tend to be highest. Any loss of customers has to be replaced merely for the company to stand still.

Companies in the past have tended to concentrate on the customer acquisition process as, in general, market growth provided a steady supply of new prospects. Yet even in the halcyon days of high population growth, high sector growth and/or minimal competition the possibility always existed of substitutes or new competitors entering the market and 'diverting the flow'. In the third millennium forecasters suggest low and perhaps negative population growth. This will particularly affect the number of potential customers at the freer spending, lower end of the adult age spectrum. Competition meanwhile is unlikely to fall and may, with the opening up of national borders, get worse. The likelihood is, therefore, that customer acquisition in general terms will become even more difficult.

Customer retention

Although RM has a dual focus on *both* acquisition and retention strategies it is the latter that is often given more prominence. Indeed, it has become one of the underpinning convictions of RM that it encourages *retention marketing* first and *acquisition marketing* second (Gummesson, 1999, p. 9). This bias exists because customer retention is perceived as offering significant advantages, particularly in saturated markets (Dawes and Swailes, 1999, p. 36). This is generally supported by academics, many of whom further promote the concept by suggesting that customer acquisition is between five and ten times more expensive than customer retention (e.g. Gummesson, 1999, p. 183). It has, therefore, become widely accepted by more and more companies that it makes a great deal of sense to try to keep existing customers happy rather than devote high levels of marketing effort to the stemming of customer turnover (Barnes, 1994, p. 562).

To further strengthen the argument that the principal focus should be on retention, it is proposed that the longevity of relationships also provides additional profit potential. Reichheld (1996, p. 65) for example, suggests that the benefits are cumulative and that the longer the cycle continues, the 'greater the company's financial strength'.

The dual benefits of customer retention are, therefore, that:

■ Existing customers are less expensive to retain than to recruit.
■ Securing a customer's loyalty over time produces superior profits.

These, it is proposed, are the two economic arguments that underpin RM (Buttle, 1996, p. 5). Although this is an oversimplification, there is little doubt that a major impetus for the development of RM has been a growing awareness of these *potential* long-term benefits.

Zero defections?

Despite RM's concentration on retention, no company can possibly hold on to all its customers even in monopoly situations. Although some marketing gurus call for policies leading to 'zero defections', this is neither a possible, practical nor indeed profitable objective. Total customer retention is never achievable as there is always some loss. For example, some customers will move; others will pass away. In a highly competitive market customers may switch (temporarily or permanently) to another product or service on the basis of factors that may not necessarily be within the control of the company. It is also invariably unprofitable to attempt to achieve total (or even near total) retention as the costs involved in delivering this are likely to be prohibitive. Retention strategy should not, therefore, be aimed at keeping customers at any cost (Gummesson, 1999, p. 26). The company must know when to cut and run.

Retention strategies tested

As with any generalised statements, such as those made in support of RM, there is always a danger that they become accepted truths and prescriptive remedies for all varieties of assorted ills. Although the principles may hold good in many instances, there are several inconsistencies with retention economics which should be challenged before companies consider the full application of relational strategies.

Acquisition and retention costs

It is widely suggested that an important component in calculating the benefits of customer retention is that the front-end costs of customer acquisition exceed the cost of retention. Statements such as 'it costs five to ten times as much to get a new customer as it costs to keep an existing customer' are regularly made in a wide range of general and relationship marketing texts (e.g. Christopher *et al.*, 1991, p. 157; Gummesson, 1999, p. 183). This widely accepted marketing maxim is, however, an oversimplification. It would certainly appear that some evidence supporting the proposal exists although it is highly selective. Research to date by consulting firms such as Bain and Co. (see Reichheld, 1996) has produced company-specific examples (Payne and Frow, 1997) in industries that have certain distinct and non-universal characteristics.

Front-end costs

The industries chosen most frequently as examples of the successful application of customer retention strategies appear all to have high front-end acquisition costs inherent in their make-up (e.g. banks, credit card and insurance). Important among these front-end costs are a number that occur frequently. These are:

- The high costs of personal selling.
- Commission payments.

- Direct and indirect costs of detailed information gathering.
- Supply of equipment.
- Advertising and other communications expenditure.

Personal selling

Although most businesses are involved to some degree in personal selling, it is more significant in some businesses than in others. One particular area where personal selling has always been seen as necessary is where there is a degree of complexity in the product or service. Mass marketing media does not generally handle complexity well. The salesperson has the ability to highlight and emphasise product or service features and respond to any questions that a customer may have. Personal selling is, therefore, a high-quality, marketing communications tool used in complex or high-value (for the purposes of negotiation) product sales. In the service sector it may be significant where intangibility adds to the complex nature of the offering.

The downside of personal selling is cost. Dependent on the industry, complexity, geography and other factors, salespeople who travel to visit customers can rarely meet more than a limited amount of potential new customers in a given period. Even salespeople based at fixed-site showrooms where customers do the travelling (e.g. a retail store) can only be expected to see a limited numbers of new clients in an average day. An additional variable factor is that the conversion rate (i.e. the rate at which prospects are converted into customers) may not be high. Such is the nature of personal selling that costs require constant monitoring if they are not to get out of control (see Box 3.1). All of these factors imply that the cost per customer acquisition will be high where personal selling is a major component in the customer's decision making process.

Commission

If commissions are payable (either internally or externally) on sales this may reduce the fixed costs of personal selling although the variable costs of acquisition increase. In circumstances where commissions are payable on sales it is likely that the cost of customer acquisition, relative to retention costs, will be high.

Box 3.1

Personal selling

A high-tech company I have worked with discovered that it cost them $120,000 to support a salesperson – including salary, commissions, expenses and fringe benefits. At this company, the average salesperson could make 200 calls a year. They had to attend a lot of meetings and training, and therefore could not make a call a day. Based on those numbers, it cost the company roughly $600 to make a call on a prospect. On average, it took about three calls to convert a prospect into a customer. As a result, the company's new customer acquisition cost was $1,800. Actually it was higher than that – that does not include the cost of promoting target market awareness and interest. Suppose the average new customer spends $5,000 a year and remains loyal for three years. If the profit margin is 10%, the lifetime value of the customer is $1,500. In that case the company lost money on the new customer.

(*Source:* Kotler, 1992, p. 50)

Data collection

Where the data collection required is significant and the issue of contracts or other expensive materials is involved, this may again contribute to high initial costs. In these cases (e.g. insurance) the company may not begin to make a profit on the product or service for one or more years into the lifetime of the contract.

Supply of equipment

This refers to long-term equipment hire (e.g. television rental) or supply (e.g. the free supply of digital TV receivers) where the investment is written off over the calculated lifetime of the contract. Any contract that terminates prior to the full write-off period is, therefore, loss making. In contrast, any contract which lasts beyond that point represents additional profit. The benefits of customer retention in such circumstances are obvious.

Advertising and other communication costs

Where advertising (particularly long-term brand-building) is used to promote 'front of mind awareness[1] (i.e. to ensure a brand's prominence in the marketplace) then the cost of maintaining this awareness may, justifiably, be included in the cost of customer acquisition.

High front-end-cost industries

The likelihood is that in industries where personal selling, commission, high data collection, high brand awareness investment or equipment supply expenditure are involved then new customer acquisition costs will nearly always exceed the costs of retention. Logic suggests, therefore, that industries where the greater part of expenses are up-front would benefit from writing off these costs over an extended period of time (Figure 3.2). In these instances, the longer the relationship the lower the costs relative to income and the higher the profit is likely to be (see the section on *lifetime value*, p. 63).

Low front-end-cost industries

At the other end of the acquisition costs spectrum, for example FMCG retailing, the costs of customer acquisition appear marginal as intense personal selling, commissions, detailed information gathering and/or equipment supply are not always necessary to make an individual sale. Indeed, the FMCG consumer would only seem to require one or more of a limited number of drivers such as location, perceived service quality, price competitiveness, product range and quality and/or promotional offerings to stimulate a sale. These are the same factors that influence the customer retention process.

---

[1] 'Front of mind' awareness is seen as important where infrequent buying decisions are made (e.g. life insurance). The purpose is to ensure that when the consumer is ready to make a decision, the brand is 'front of mind'.

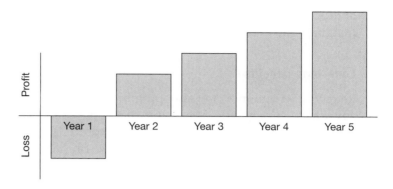

Figure 3.2 Typical profit pattern in financial services and other high acquisition cost industries
(Not to scale; for illustration only)

Advertising and other (non-personal selling) marketing communication costs, commonly included in the customer acquisition calculations, again do not fully justify the up-front cost argument. High advertising and sales promotion costs attributed to customer acquisition fail to acknowledge the part played by those same messages in the retention process. Advertising serves to remind buyers of their purchasing preferences (East, 2000, p. 96) and may, therefore, often work defensively to protect the existing customer base, rather than aggressively to bring in new buyers (Barnard and Ehrenberg, 1997, p. 38).

If drivers promoting sales to potential new customers are similar or the same as those for existing clients then the cost of acquisition must closely equal the cost of retention. Indeed, if the supplier introduces schemes that reward repeat buying over and above the single purchase (the basis of most retail and airline loyalty schemes) then the cost of retention may exceed the cost of acquisition.

Economics of retention strategies

The economics of costly relational techniques must, in circumstances where acquisition/retention cost ratios are small, be closely scrutinised. This is particularly evident in the case of many costly loyalty schemes which are, perhaps ironically, most prevalent in those sectors where validity is most highly questionable (e.g. FMCG retailing). Incentives to retention in these schemes are costs that (if profitability is to be maintained) lead ultimately to higher prices. In such markets differentials may occur in costs between the 'loyalty incentivisors' and their lower priced competition (Palmer and Beggs, 1997). The phenomenon is not new. The history of British supermarket retailing is peppered by swings between price wars and differential advantage strategies.

The evidence that exists suggests that, in industries where recognisable high front-end costs are involved, these are drivers to relational strategies that promote customer retention over customer acquisition. Where acquisition costs are low and/or where the real difference between acquisition and retention costs is marginal, the introduction of costly relational strategies may become a burden.

Long-term benefits

Retention economics are also promoted as a time-based form of competitive advantage through the suggestion that long-term relationships bring long-term advantages (Murphy, 1997, p. 1). Gummesson (1999, p. 183) has coined the phrase 'return on relationships' (ROR) to describe this concept. ROR he defines as 'the long-term net financial outcome caused by the establishment and maintenance of an organisation's network of relationships'.

Long-term benefits may be considered from two perspectives:

■ Relationship stages.
■ The lifetime value of the customer.

Relationship stages

As noted in our earlier definition, relationship marketing is seen as a means of identifying, establishing, maintaining, enhancing and, where necessary, terminating relationships (Grönroos, 1996, p. 7). This definition anticipates that, once a company starts thinking about individual customers (as opposed to mass markets), it should recognise that different customers are at different stages of relational development. Importantly, it also implies that each customer type (e.g. prospect, customer, former customer) should be handled in a different way. This may include different targeted messages (rather than mass communication) and different 'value options' (e.g. rewards) from the exchange.

The recognition of different relational stages in RM also includes the implicit assumption that the higher the stage of development the greater the profitability to the organisation and consequentially the greater the benefits to the organisation. As we will discuss later, this may be a simplification in some industries.

Stages models

Various models exist that illustrate this concept (see Figure 3.3) and that may be seen to approximately equate to both consumer and business-to-business relationships. Dwyer *et al.* (1987, p. 15) suggests a five-stage model where each phase represents a major transition in how parties in a relationship regard each other. These are:

■ Awareness
■ Exploration
■ Expansion
■ Commitment
■ Dissolution.

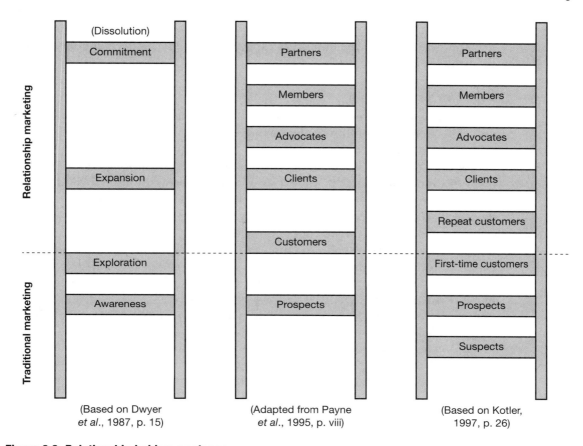

Relationship marketing	(Dissolution)	Partners	Partners
	Commitment	Members	Members
		Advocates	Advocates
	Expansion	Clients	Clients
			Repeat customers
		Customers	
Traditional marketing	Exploration		First-time customers
	Awareness	Prospects	Prospects
			Suspects
	(Based on Dwyer *et al.*, 1987, p. 15)	(Adapted from Payne *et al.*, 1995, p. viii)	(Based on Kotler, 1997, p. 26)

Figure 3.3 Relationship ladders or stages

Awareness

Awareness is where one party recognises that the other party is a 'feasible exchange partner'. Interaction has not yet taken place although there may be 'positioning' and 'posturing' by the parties to enhance their attractiveness.

Exploration

Exploration refers to the 'research and trial stage' in the exchange. At this level potential partners consider obligations, benefits and burdens of the exchange. This may well include the psychological and actual costs involved. Dwyer *et al.* suggest that this stage includes sub-phases such as attraction, communication and bargaining, development and exercise of power (see Chapter 8), norm development (e.g. contractual arrangements) and expectation development (e.g. trust and commitment; see Chapter 5).

Expansion

Expansion refers to the period where there is a continual increase in benefits obtained by exchange partners and where they become increasingly interdependent.

Commitment

Commitment relates to the implicit or explicit pledge of relational continuity between the parties.

Dissolution

The inclusion in the model of a dissolution stage reminds us that disengagement always remains a possibility in any relationship.

Dwyer *et al.* (1987, p. 25) make the important point that, although all transactions have relational properties it makes sense to consider many exchanges as 'practically discrete' (or non-relational). In other words, relationship stages, such as those described, are not automatic and can only exist where both parties recognise the potential benefits of the relationship. Although in organisational (business-to-business) markets these types of close, bilateral relationships can be seen and are explicitly recognised (Blois 1997, p. 53), doubt must remain as to whether this level of solidarity could possibly exist in consumer goods or even consumer services markets where many exchange relationships are discrete.

Other models exist which suggest relational stages of customer development. The long-established concept of a 'ladder of loyalty' was adapted by Payne *et al.* (1995, p. viii) to create a 'relationship ladder'. The metaphor of the 'ladder' and 'climbing up' to higher levels of relationship is easy to visualise. Kotler (1997, p.26) also proposes a stages model which resembles the relationship ladder. The three models noted above are compared in Figure 3.3.

In the three models illustrated, although each has a slightly different perspective, they all promote the idea of moving customers from one stage upward to another. They also illustrate the perception that, whereas traditional marketing's interest ends with the sale, RM's interest extends beyond this to the development and enhancement of the customer relationship.

In the Kotler model the process starts with the identification of suspects. In mass marketing terms this might be regarded as segmentation and targeting although the 'wastage' (media costs which are judged at a cost per thousand 'hits' invariably include an untargeted audience) would be high. In database marketing terms this may involve the rental of lists of names and addresses of suspected target groups. Either way, it is the identification of these potential customers which begins the process.

Prospects are at a higher level than suspects and have, most probably, given some indication that they are likely to purchase the goods or services on offer. Not all prospects are viewed as being of equal potential and, as such, there is a prospect hierarchy (see Figure 3.4). In this hierarchy former customers (as known users who have already had experience of the product or service) are considered most likely to revert to being customers. Next best are those customers who have made active enquiries about a product, the assumption being that, having made the effort to contact the company, they are quite probably already motivated to purchase. Referrals are seen as next best in the knowledge that referrals carry considerable weight with most customers and again, in probability, they are likely (having sought information) to be in a frame of mind to purchase. Profiled prospects are

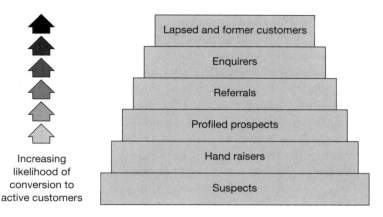

Increasing
likelihood of
conversion to
active customers

Figure 3.4 Prospect hierarchy
(*Source*: Adapted from Tapp, 1998, p. 150)

those who, based on their profile, give a strong indication that they may purchase, while 'hand raisers' have also indicated in some other way (perhaps in a consumer survey) that they also are potential customers. Finally, suspects might be indicated by demographic or lifestyle analysis. This 'prospect hierarchy' is used, particularly by direct and database marketers, to prioritise customer communication.

Kotler (unlike Payne *et al.*) differentiates between first-time and repeat customers. Certainly the decision-making process will be different in each case. With repeat purchases the consumer has actual previous experience (as opposed to hype or hearsay) to go on. It is at this point that the relational marketer is seen to diverge from the traditional marketer, whose interest is seen to be primarily in the single transaction. The prime task of the relational marketer from this point is to become skilful at moving customers to higher stages of relationship, with each stage representing a strengthening of the company's relationship with the customer (Kotler, 1997, p. 26). This is seen to be in complete contrast with the traditional marketer, who has no ambition to encourage customers to climb the loyalty ladder (Gummesson, 1999, p. 11). Traditional marketing views each transaction independently whereas with RM each further transaction is viewed in terms of its history and its anticipated future (Dwyer *et al.*, 1987, p. 12).

The Kotler stages model suggests that the company is looking to transform repeat customers into 'clients', which by definition implies a higher status and some (non-stated) form of psychological contract or 'bond' between the parties. The further jump to the status of 'advocate' implies that the customer moves from being responsive to the company to becoming actively involved in the marketing of the organisation, most commonly through word-of-mouth recommendation. 'Members' implies even greater affinity to the company while 'partnership' suggests a relationship on such a high level that, as predicted in some definitions (e.g. Gordon, 1998, p. 9) of RM (see Chapter 1, page 23), the customer becomes part of the value-creating process.

Marketing reality

As with all relational concepts, it is important with 'stages' or 'ladder of loyalty' theories to separate the reality from the rhetoric. Terms such as advocate, member or partner assume a depth of association that few consumers would recognise in relation to companies or organisations they deal with on a daily basis. It is not sufficient simply to imply an affiliation if the customer does not recognise it as such. Even if the supplier regards the process as a long-term commitment on their behalf it will be the customer who will ultimately define the relationship.

Some companies have, however, managed to introduce tactics that have successfully created membership-type relationships that assume affiliation of some sort. This does not usually include so-called 'consumer clubs', which do not normally fulfil the reciprocity conditions required in high-level relationships and are rarely regarded as more than registration or contractual devices by most consumers. Travel organisations are perhaps the furthest advanced and many (particularly airlines) have developed clubs where members are seen to enjoy privileges that ordinary consumers do not enjoy. Some organisations, for example British Airways, have taken this a stage further by openly differentiating between levels of membership dependent on the customer's commitment (determined by expenditure) to the airline. Executive Club members (who can be blue, silver or gold card holders) receive different levels of privileges dependent on their status. FMCG retailers too are trying to differentiate privileges. In 1999 Tesco introduced two levels of 'membership' above their basic card holder. 'Keyholders' and 'Premium Keyholders' openly receive better rewards (or value levels) from these enhanced levels of membership.

There are also some organisations where explicit relational bonds (or higher-level relationships) are much more evident. These include those where voluntary membership of, for example, political parties, charitable organisations etc., involves, by implication, membership commitment and, perhaps, costs or effort without monetary (but perhaps with psychological) reward. Organisations such as football clubs or arts organisations may also make explicit that a higher level of relationship can be achieved, usually with increased status potential.[2] Membership of political parties may include the member actively involved in development of the policies of that party – the political equivalent of 'value creation'. Membership of this type can even mean the member becoming involved in the management of the organisation on a part-time or even full-time basis.

Another problem with the 'ladder' or 'stages' theories is the implicit assumption that there is a linear progression from lower to higher status. It should be recognised that a consumer may, regardless of the efforts of the company, demote themselves for a multiplicity of reasons (e.g. better source of supply) or indeed cease altogether to be a customer. Remaining at any British Airways Executive Club level, for example, is determined by the points accumulated in any one membership year.

---

[2] In the Chartered Institute of Marketing, for example, you can be a student member, associate member, member or fellow. Each level of membership has different privileges and different costs.

Should customers decide to utilise another (non-affiliated) airline for a number or all of their journeys they are demoted or lose altogether their Executive Club benefits. This differential status has been retained between airlines involved with British Airways in the Oneworld alliance (see Box 3.2). Change of customer status can, therefore, be in either an upward or a downward direction.

Lifetime value

The 'lifetime value' concept suggests that a company should avoid taking a short-term view of the profit (or indeed loss) of any individual but rather should consider the income derived from that company's lifetime association with the customer. The idea is not new. Banks, for example, have traditionally offered young people attractive deals to open accounts. Although this may be costly in the short-term, these banks are prepared to do this in the knowledge that traditionally in this sector customers change infrequently to competitor organisations (although traditional allegiance may be changing, particularly with the introduction of Internet banking).

The lifetime value of a customer is an impetus to implement retention policies. Decisions concerning investment in relational strategies (to promote retention) may be made on the basis of the customer's notional lifetime value, albeit that it is

---

Box 3.2

Oneworld frequent flyer programmes (as at June 2000)

Oneworld airline programme	Oneworld emerald status	Oneworld sapphire status	Oneworld ruby status	Entry level to programme
British Airways Executive Club	Gold	Silver	*Not applicable*	Blue
American Airlines AAdvantage	Executive Platinum	Platinum	Gold	AAdvantage
Aer Lingus TAB	Gold Circle Elite	Gold Circle Prestige	Gold Circle	TAB
Cathay Pacific Marco Polo Club	Diamond	Gold	Silver	Green/Asia Miles
Finnair Finnair Plus	Platinum	Gold	Silver	Finnair Plus
Iberia Iberia Plus	Platinum	Gold	Silver	Iberia Plus Clasica
LanChile LanPass	Comodoro	Premium Silver	Premium	LanPass
Quantas Frequent Flyer	Gold	Silver	Blue	Frequent Flyer

based on historical data. These may include investments in product or service quality designed to maintain or enhance competitive advantage, or defensively to discourage defection to the competition. In the latter case the company may effectively be building 'barriers to exit' to promote retention (see the section on switching costs, below).

The downside of the lifetime value concept is that there is no guarantee that the customer will continue to patronise a supplier at the same level as previously or indeed that he or she will even stay with the company. This is particularly true in businesses with low exit barriers (e.g. retailing) and in rapidly changing, competitive markets (e.g. telecommunications). It may also be the case in industries where substantial sales promotion is used. Indeed, if customers perceive that the only difference between alternative companies is the size of the 'bribe' offered them they are likely to become increasingly promiscuous, actively seeking out the highest bribe available as the only satisfaction to be derived from the exchange (Tynan, 1997, p. 992). The merit of 'lifetime value' in situations such as these, as anything other than a broad indicator, must be doubtful. In terms of differential strategies at various levels of the relationship ladder(s) higher relationships invariably mean higher costs. It is important, therefore, for organisations to determine (on a cost–benefit basis) when it is 'worth going to the next level' (Kotler, 1992, p.52).

Switching costs

It is difficult to discuss retention strategies without referring to the subject of switching costs. Switching costs are effectively barriers to exit from the company from the perspective of the consumer. These switching costs may be created by the supplier, by the consumer or by the relationship itself. This is a controversial area within the RM debate as some costs or barriers are seen as acceptable in that they are the 'natural' barriers created in any good relationship or at the behest of the consumer. Others, however, are seen as coercive and contrary to the principles (if such principles exist) associated with relational strategies. These actual or psychological 'costs', which are not mutually exclusive, may be summarised as:

- Search costs
- Learning costs
- Emotional costs
- Inertial costs
- Risk
- Social costs
- Financial costs
- Legal barriers.

Search costs

Search costs are those based on the time and energy spent searching for alternative sources of supply.

Learning costs

Learning costs are based on the time and energy expended learning how to deal effectively and efficiently with a new supplier (e.g. learning the layout of a supermarket you have never used before).

Emotional costs

Relationships over an extended period can create emotional ties with an organisation or the personnel of that organisation. This is sometimes confused with inertia (see below).

Inertial costs

The effort involved in breaking habitual behaviour is frequently underestimated. This tendency is probably best summed up by the phrase 'I can't be bothered to go elsewhere'.

Risk

The move to a new supplier will always involve a degree of risk. Even where the risk is not immediately apparent there is still a general preference to stay with an existing supplier rather than risk a move to another of whom you have no experience. This is best summed up by the inclination of people to remain with the 'devil you know' rather than move to 'the devil you don't'.

Social costs

The existing supplier may, in some way, contribute to the social life of the customer. An exaggerated example might be the existence of 'singles shopping nights' in some supermarkets. A more commonplace example may be the opportunity to socialise with other customers and staff at a company organised event (e.g. preview evenings).

Financial cost

The break-up of a relationship may mean financial penalties (e.g. the costs frequently involved in switching mortgage providers) or the loss of rewards or status gained through relationship longevity (e.g. some loyalty schemes, no-claims insurance etc.)

Legal barriers

In some situations, a contractual arrangement ensures that the consumer stays, for a period of time, in the relationship.

Pressey and Mathews (1998, p. 43) suggest that in developed relationships efforts are made to lock-in customers using the types of barriers or costs described above. Relationship marketers generally, however, seem to have difficulty coming to terms with this. They suggest that there is more to RM than simply 'locking them in' (Barnes, 1994, p. 556) and that companies that rely on this type of retention are on a 'hiding to nothing'. Thus when 'enhancement and development of customers' is defined as 'more effective tethering and dissuasion from defection by threat of corrective action' (Worthington and Horne, 1998, p. 39) this is open to criticism. Such a view negates the conception that RM has moved away from the competitive, relatively hostile and largely transactional approach.

There does, however, appear to be a distinction between applied costs/barriers (e.g. financial penalties) and those created by the customer (e.g. emotional or social costs) or as a consequence of the relationship (e.g. search, learning or risk-associated costs). Relationships generated by companies which view RM as 'locking in' customers through penalty barriers are seen as inferior relationships to ones where the parties engaged are willing participants (Barnes, 1994, p. 565). These penalty barriers may generate dissatisfaction (Storbacka *et al.*, 1994, p. 28), which may (for example, at the end of a contractual period) lead to ultimate defection. What passes for a relationship in these situations is really a 'pseudo-relationship' in that it is one-sided with customers kept, against their will, because the cost of leaving is too high (Barnes, 1994, p. 565). According to Gummesson (1994, p. 17) this type of 'manipulative marketing' can be compared with:

> the use of artificial fertiliser and pesticides which increase short-term harvests but impoverish not only the soil where the crops grow, but the whole of nature for short-term greed. Just like ecology RM sees marketing activities as part of a larger context.

Customer-created barriers, by comparison, are usually the product of mutually recognised satisfaction (or possibly absence of dissatisfaction) created by the supplier to add value to the relationship. Those that exist as a consequence of the relationship (such as search or learning costs) may not be directly created by the supplier although it may be in that supplier's interest to illustrate the potential costs to the customer.

Relationship longevity

It has been suggested that, when used with skill, customer retention leads to enhanced revenue, reduced costs and improved financial performance. Reichheld (1996, p. 39) echoes this claim by proposing a list of accumulating benefits that contribute to an entire 'life cycle of profits' from the customer. A warning should, however, be given about the highly optimistic assumptions made, which may suggest that this analysis is of dubious universal appeal. The model (see Figure 3.5) presented assumes:

- Revenue growth over time
- Cost savings over time
- Referral income
- Price premiums.

Revenue growth

Reichheld (1996, p. 43) suggests that in most businesses customers' spending increases over time. This may indeed be the case in industries with a low turnover

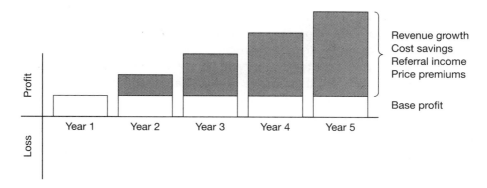

Figure 3.5 Profit growth over time

(*Source*: Reprinted by permission of Harvard Business School Press. From *The Loyalty Effect: The Hidden Force Behind Growth, Profits and Lasting Value* by F.F. Reichheld and T.A. Teal. Boston, MA 1996, p. 43. Copyright © 1996 Harvard Business School Publishing Corporation.

of customers (and possibly high exit barriers). It can reasonably be assumed, in these industries, that income will be more likely to increase than decline over time. In general, however, this is a highly optimistic assumption. In businesses with a high turnover of customers and low exit barriers it may be hypothesised that increased revenue from one customer will, most probably, be matched by those customers whose purchases decline or even cease during the same period. The likelihood is, therefore, for no net revenue growth.

Revenue growth in most businesses cannot be assumed without active intervention on the part of the supplier in expanding the offering (in terms of variety and/or value) relative to the offering of the competition. There are industries (which Reichheld acknowledges) where no customer growth is possible, such as gardening maintenance contracts, which generally involves a 'fixed' level of service. Some other product or service levels may fluctuate over a period due to external factors (such as the amount of gas consumed in cold weather, or the number of telephone calls made) but will generally level out to nil growth over a period of years. Suppliers of this type (e.g. British Gas or BT) have sought to overcome this problem through product and/or service extension (e.g. British Gas credit card, BT wake-up calls). Alternatively, promotions offering special terms may increase usage short-term. In general, however, it is difficult (particularly in the current competitive circumstances) to support the notion that longevity (without intervention) automatically leads to greater spending.

Cost savings

As has been noted the ability to amortise costs over a period brings supplier benefits. A certain naïveté, on the part of the customer, as to other opportunities available in the market may also help in this process. Reichheld (1996, p. 47) suggests that the operating cost advantages of customer loyalty are particularly strong in retailing as 'a shop selling to a constantly shifting set of customers needs a lot more inventory than a shop serving the same people year after year'. A stable set of customers, he suggests 'can help streamline inventory management, minimise mark-downs and simplify capacity forecasting'.

This type of situation *may* exist where retail inventory is relatively stable (e.g. hardware stores) or where a very close relationship is built up between the customer and a company (e.g. fashion clothes shop). In other areas, particularly the FMCG sector, it is likely to be a different scenario. In an age where customers are less naïve, more professional and more cynical (Lannon, 1993, p. 22) the costs of facilitating such customers are more likely to rise than to fall. In these markets the customer may, over time, learn to manipulate the supplier to his or her own ends (an example might be the customer who shops for bargains around a number of stores), ultimately leading to increased, not decreased, costs. With the availability of retailers and other suppliers on the Internet the ease of price comparisons may help customers to 'cherry pick' their suppliers and further exacerbate this situation.

Referral income

Again, this may be more likely in some industries than others. Referrals have always been an objective of businesses and are a valuable customer acquisition source. To depend on referrals for revenue growth, however, assumes (all other things being equal) that competitors are inactive and/or that the market is growing at a reasonably substantial rate, neither of which situation currently exists in many industry sectors. In addition, while one company may benefit from a certain number of referrals inward the competition may themselves be benefiting from referrals away from that company. The best that can be said is that those companies who are 'doing a good job' in the broadest sense of the phrase may marginally benefit from referrals over their competition.

Price premiums

Reichheld (1996, p. 39) suggests that price premiums may be obtainable from long-term, loyal customers. Such a strategy may again be determined by the naïveté of the consumer and the level of exit barriers. In many markets, however, this suggestion totally disregards the fact that widespread use of promotional schemes is helping to create a 'generation of increasingly promotion literate customers' who have become 'adept at leaping from one supplier to another' to take advantage of the best offers (Harlow, 1997). It is highly unlikely, particularly in competitive markets, that the application of price premiums to longer-term customers is a realistic strategy. Again, the visibility of Internet pricing makes this even less viable in the future.

Knowing your customer

Any discussion of the value of long-term retention must also recognise that not all customers contribute equally to the firm's profit. Indeed, as we have noted, a significant proportion of customers may, over the short or long term, be loss making.

The consequences of losing a profitable customer, therefore, may be very significant whereas the loss of a non-profitable customer may actually be beneficial. The valid assumption has been made that unless a firm has an RM focus and a subsequent knowledge of individual customer activities the loss of key customers may go unnoticed (Strandvik and Storbacka 1996, p. 72). Some UK banks, for example, work on a points system or grids (see Figure 3.6) determined by the services utilised (or indeed not utilised) by the customer to approximate that customer's value to the company. Although this is a crude measure, it allows them to differentiate between potentially profitable and less profitable customers. In most organisations the difficulty of calculating 'relationship profitability' stems from the problem in allocating costs to specific customer relationships and promotes the need to identify the cost drivers of those relationships (Storbacka *et al.*, 1994, p. 33). Not only must the individual's gross contribution to the profitability of the relationship (from the firm's perspective) be calculated but also the costs incurred when building and maintaining that relationship (Blois, 1997, p. 63; Palmer, 1998, p. 119).

Another factor in the long-term relationship calculation is whether any competitive advantage (gained through the introduction of relational strategies) can last long enough to recoup investment. With regard to financial services, the 'product' package is often designed with barriers and costs that discourage customers from defection. The advantage gained through the initial attractiveness of the offering is, therefore, sustained regardless of what products or services are introduced in the interim.

At the other end of the spectrum (again, FMCG retailing is a good example) the

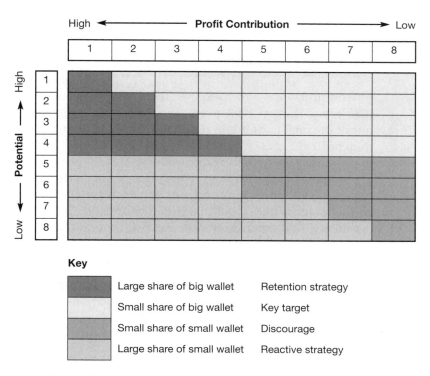

Figure 3.6 Profit/potential grid. Potential in this model is based on the MOSAIC/Pixel matrix. This evaluates potential for financial services against demographic and lifestyle data.

(*Source*: Adapted from Pompa *et al.*, 2000, p. 37)

ability to build barriers to exit is limited. Most retailers depend on some form of customer retention programme offering added value to 'loyal' customers in an attempt to sustain long-term relationships. The problem with loyalty programmes is that the potential always exists for competitors to replicate these relational programmes easily, and doubt must be expressed as to whether they can possibly give companies long-term advantage. It may be hypothesised that where differentiated advantage is perceived to be low or where a programme can be replicated easily the ability of relational strategies to develop lasting competitive advantage is minimal. It may be further hypothesised that the greater the ability to replicate differential advantage, the greater the need to constantly develop and refine RM strategies to keep 'ahead of the field'.

It has been estimated (in *Incentives Today*, February 1999) that in 1999/2000 European retailers will spend $3.5 billion on customer loyalty technology and this is before the rewards themselves are taken into account. The expense involved in such cost-escalating strategies may, as has been noted previously, ultimately lead to a divide between relational suppliers and cost competitive ones and the consequential division of an industry between RM companies and their more 'transactional' competitors. When everyone in an industry is, effectively, offering very much the same incentives (i.e. frequent flyer programmes) the net benefits are marginal. The recent assault on the airline industry (whose introduction of loyalty programmes preceded that of most retailers) by cut-price, 'no frills' airlines such as Easy Jet and Ryan Air and the introduction by British Airways of GO, may be an example of this development.

The validity of relationship economics

Interest in RM has grown exponentially, driven primarily by relationship economics (Barnes and Howlett 1998, p. 15). These economic arguments, however, revolve around one of the smallest words in the English language but the biggest word in business – If (Mitchell 1997, p. 37)! *If* the factors are right and the drivers to relational strategies are in place, the benefits will be forthcoming. The acceptance of relationship marketing as a 'good thing' because it leads to long-term profitability is, however, too simplistic and begs the question of how and with whom these relationships are to be established and what form they should take (Barnes 1994, p. 562). When it is clear, from past experience, that the average customer will continue to purchase a product or service then the benefits of relational strategies based on a lifetime value calculation may seem apparent. Examples of such claims include that:

■ 'An existing Cadillac customer is worth $332,000 over his or her lifetime.' (Gummesson, 1999, p. 183)
■ 'A Domino's Pizza customer is worth $5,000 over 10 years.' (Christopher *et al.*, 1991, p. 159)

The proviso must always be made that all such claims are based on historical data and cannot be guaranteed in the future. Estimates of 'lifetime value', therefore, can be valid from a strategy planning perspective but to rely over much on these forecasts may result in complacency.

Summary

This chapter looked at the economics of relationships. It investigated the arguments surrounding the costs of customer acquisition versus the costs of customer retention and concluded that whereas in many industries it can be stated with some certainty that the cost of acquisition exceeds that of retention, it is by no means a universal truth. The chapter also discussed the benefits of relationship longevity, including stages theories and the concept of lifetime value, and again suggested that although considerable benefits could be achieved under certain industry conditions, this could not be assumed in every case. The switching costs associated with relationship longevity were also discussed and a distinction made between costs positively associated with the relationship and coercive barriers to exit. The chapter concluded by suggesting that the notion that RM leads to long-term profitability is far too simplistic.

Discussion questions

1 What are the different cost drivers associated with (a) customer acquisition and (b) customer retention?

2 What are the potential advantages to be gained from long-term supplier–customer relationships?

3 How would you differentiate between the different stages models discussed in this chapter?

4 What effect do switching costs have on a relationship?

Case study

IKEA has to look out for retailer's friendly touch

The announcement that IKEA is planning to open 20 more stores in the UK over the next 20 years and create up to 12,000 jobs is good news for the UK economy

But it's also something of a marketing puzzle. How can a brand whose reality is so out of sync with its image survive and even thrive? And can it continue to do so?

Consider the reality of the privately-owned Swedish furniture and furnishings retailer. Its failings have been well-catalogued in the national press, the chain's unfriendly ordering, purchasing and delivery policies, including the astonishing demand that customers themselves return faulty goods; the oxymoron that is the customer service centre; the claustrophobic feelings induced by the one-way systems in the stores. One of these on its own would usually be enough to put a dent in a brand's success

Even worse is the dismissive tone of senior management. And why should they care? Customers will wait hours just to get a space in a store's car park before joining the throngs. Sales this year are predicted to rise more than £750m, up from £585m in 1999. The tills are ringing.

It's reminiscent of the attitude that Marks & Spencer had in its heyday and which it now highlights apologetically in its latest annual report. The report has a double-page spread showing a man and woman with a speech bubble which starts off with 'In the past, if shops had run out of something I needed, I thought it was my fault for getting there too late.'

It's the rest of the quote that so succinctly sums up just where M&S went wrong. 'Now I'm not so tolerant. I expect stores to rearrange themselves so they are always ready for me.' So the big question for IKEA is just how long it has before the patience of its customers finally wears just too thin.

Probably not long. And there are a number of reasons for this. First, there is the threat of competition. The furniture market in the UK has been in many ways a very underdeveloped one. That's why IKEA's formula of a Scandinavian simple style at low prices has proved so popular. But all it will take is one canny operator, perhaps exploiting the opportunities of the Internet, with good products, good prices and good customer service, to wipe the smug smile off IKEA's face.

The second reason is more fundamental and has to do with the shopper. In the 24-hour society time has ironically become even more precious, as Melame Howard of the Future Foundation pointed out at its recent conference, 'Anarchy in the UK'. If you are going to make customers wait, you have to have some powerful reasons why spending hours parking, queuing at check-outs, and finding no one to deal with complaints is not a promising recipe.

Even more so, the demographics are stacking up against IKEA's approach. By 2010, warns retail consultancy Verdict in *The Changing Face of Britain*, the well-charted decline in the 25- to 39-year-old segment and the increase by almost a fifth more of those in the 55 to 69 age group will catch out retailers who focus on selling the same product in the same environments in the same way to the mass market.

So it might profit IKEA to do some hard thinking Otherwise, its once-eager customers might decide the price of shopping there is no longer worth paying.

(*Source*: Laura Mazur, *Marketing*, 29 June 2000)

Case study questions

1 Will IKEA survive with this approach?

2 How do retailers 'draw the line' between additional customer services and the costs associated with them?

3 Discuss how/whether IKEA has improved since this article was written.

References

Barnard, N. and Ehrenberg, A.S.C. (1997) 'Advertising: strongly persuasive or nudging?', *Journal of Advertising Research*, January/February, 21–31.

Barnes, J.G. (1994) 'Close to the customer: but is it really a relationship?', *Journal of Marketing Management*, 10, 561–70.

Barnes, J.G. and Howlett, D.M. (1998) 'Predictors of equity in relationships between service providers and retail customers', *International Journal of Bank Marketing*, 16 (1), 5–23.

Berry, L.L. and Gresham, L.G. (1986) 'Relationship retailing; transforming customers into clients', *Business Horizons*, November/December, 43–7.

Blois, K.J. (1997) 'When is a relationship a relationship', in Gemünden, H.G., Rittert, T. and Walter, A. (eds) *Relationships and Networks in International Markets*. Oxford: Elsevier, pp. 53–64.

Buttle, F.B. (1996) *Relationship Marketing Theory and Practice*. London: Paul Chapman.

Christopher, M., Payne, A. and Ballantyne, D. (1991) *Relationship Marketing*. London: Butterworth Heinemann.

Dawes, J. and Swailes, S. (1999) 'Retention sans frontieres: issues for financial service retailers', *International Journal of Bank Marketing*, 17 (1), 36–43.

Dwyer, F.R., Schurr, P.H. and Oh, S. (1987) 'Developing buyer–seller relationships', *Journal of Marketing*, 51, 11–27.

East, R. (2000) 'Fact and fallacy in retention marketing', Professorial Inaugural Lecture, 1 March 2000, Kingston University Business School, UK.

Gordon, I.H. (1998) *Relationship Marketing*. Etobicoke, Ontario: John Wiley & Sons.

Grönroos, C. (1994) 'From marketing mix to relationship marketing: towards a paradigm shift in marketing', *Management Decisions*, 32 (2) 4–20.

Grönroos, C. (1995) 'Relationship marketing: the strategy continuum', *Journal of Marketing Science*, 23 (4), 252–4.

Grönroos, C. (1996) 'Relationship marketing: strategic and tactical implications', *Management Decisions*, 34 (3), 5–14.

Gummesson, E. (1994) 'Making relationship marketing operational', *International Journal of Service Industry Management*, 5, 5–20.

Gummesson, E. (1999) *Total Relationship Marketing; Rethinking Marketing Management from 4Ps to 30Rs*. Oxford: Butterworth Heinemann.

Harlow, E. (1997) 'Loyalty is for life – not just for Christmas', paper presented at the Advanced Relationship Marketing Conference, 23 October 1997. London: *Century Communications*.

Kotler, P. (1992) 'Marketing's new paradigm: what's really happening out there?', *Planning Review*, 20 (5), 50–2.

Kotler, P. (1997) 'Method for the millennium', *Marketing Business*, February, 26–7.

Lannon, J. (1993) 'Branding essentials and the new environment', *Admap*, 28 (6).

Mitchell, A. (1997) 'Evolution', *Marketing Business*, June, 37.

Murphy, J.A. (1997) 'Customer loyalty and the art of satisfaction', *FT Mastering*, London: Financial Times (www.ftmastering.com).

Palmer, A. and Beggs, R. (1997) 'Loyalty programmes: congruence of market structure and success', paper presented at the the *Academy of Marketing Conference*, Manchester, UK.

Palmer, A.J. (1998) *Principles of Services Marketing*. London: Kogan Page.

Payne, A. and Frow, P. (1997) 'Relationship marketing: key issues for the utilities sector', *Journal of Marketing Management*, 13 (5), 463–77.

Payne, A., Christopher, M. and Peck, H. (eds) (1995) *Relationship Marketing for Competitive Advantage*: *Winning and Keeping Customers*. Oxford: Butterworth Heinemann.

Pompa, N., Berry, J., Reid, J. and Webber, R. (2000) 'Adopting share of wallet as a basis for communications and customer relationship management', *Interactive Marketing*, 2 (1), 29–40.

Pressey, A.D. and Mathews, B.P. (1998) 'Relationship marketing and retailing: comfortable bedfellows?', *Customer Relationship Management*, 1 (1) 39–53.

Reichheld, F.F. and Teal, T.A. (1996) *The Loyalty Effect: The Hidden Force Behind Growth, Profits and Lasting Value.* Boston, MA: Harvard Business School Press.

Storbacka, K., Strandvik, T. and Grönroos, C. (1994) 'Managing customer relations for profit: the dynamics of relationship quality', *International Journal of Service Industry Management*, 5, 21–38.

Strandvik, T. and Storbacka, K. (1996) 'Managing relationship quality', in Edvardsson, B., Brown, S.W., Johnston, R. and Scheuing, E.E. (eds) *Advancing Service Quality: A Global Perspective.* New York: ISQA, pp. 67–76.

Tapp, A. (1998) *Principles of Direct and Database Marketing.* London: Financial Times Management/ Pitman Publishing.

Tynan, C. (1997) 'A review of the marriage analogy in relationship marketing', *Journal of Marketing Management*, 13 (7), 695–704.

Worthington, S. and Horne, S. (1998) 'A new relationship marketing model and its application in the affinity credit card market', *International Journal of Bank Marketing*, 16 (1), 39–44.

4 Strategy continuum

Key issues

Key issues
- ➤ RM's context within marketing
- ➤ The marketing continuum
- ➤ Hybrid marketing and portfolios of marketing strategies
- ➤ Continuum drivers

Introduction

The discussion concerning the economics of relationship marketing in the previous chapter suggests that, while RM may be beneficial in some instances, it is by no means certain to be beneficial in all. How do we handle a diversity of strategies? How do we decide when particular strategy types are relevant and appropriate?

RM in context

In the 1990s the debate regarding RM's place within marketing theory could be summed up as a choice between four 'alternative' philosophical viewpoints (Pels, 1999, p. 19; Brodie *et al.*, 1997, p. 389):

1 By adding a relationship dimension to the marketing management approach the 'anomalies' identified in traditional marketing could be incorporated into the existing marketing paradigm (see Chapter 1, page 14).
2 Exchange relationships (i.e. RM) should be regarded as a new marketing paradigm, suggesting that a paradigmatic shift had taken place in marketing from traditional marketing (TM) towards relationship marketing (see Chapter 1, page 4).
3 Exchange transactions (or TM) and exchange relationships (or RM) are separate paradigms and both paradigms separately coexist.
4 Traditional marketing (TM) and relationship marketing (RM) can coexist as part of the same marketing paradigm.

Put simply, RM may be considered as a concept, as the dominant theory, as one (of two) marketing perspectives or as an integral part of the overall marketing arsenal.

Early texts tended to view RM as a tactical influence on existing concepts, for example the marketing mix (e.g. Christopher *et al.*, 1991). This viewpoint has largely been eclipsed as the strategic value of relational strategies has increased. The argument about whether RM is a new dominant paradigm, however, still rages. As has been noted, many prominent writers (e.g. Sheth and Parvatiyar, 1993; Grönroos, 1994a; Morgan and Hunt, 1994; Gummesson, 1997; Buttle, 1997) believe that a paradigm shift has taken place.

Despite RM's promotion to the highest level of marketing theory, however, there still remain doubts as to whether companies would *always* (or indeed would *ever*) find it suitable and/or profitable to develop relational strategies (e.g. Palmer, 1996, p. 18; Grönroos 1997, p. 408). Kotler (1997, p. 26), for example, suggests that reports of the demise of traditional mass marketing are 'somewhat premature' and that companies such as Coca Cola, Gillette and Kodak will continue to primarily practise traditional mass-marketing techniques (e.g. mass communication using mass media) into the foreseeable future.

The logical consequence of this viewpoint is that some marketing activities may remain best handled through a transaction marketing approach (Gummesson, 1994, p. 17). As Dwyer *et al.* (1987, p. 14) note, it is possible that the real or anticipated costs (to either party) of relational strategies may outweigh the benefits of relational exchange. As Grönroos (1997, p. 408) notes, 'the main thing is . . . not whether a relational strategy is possible or not, but whether the firm finds it profitable, and in other respects suitable, to develop a relational strategy or a traditional strategy'. The suggestion is that if companies cannot justify, economically, a relational approach then they would be best advised to retain (or re-adopt) a transactional strategy.

The view that transactional marketing and relational marketing can coexist suggests that the RM should not be considered simply as a replacement for TM strategies but as another perspective in marketing. This implies that RM is not a clearly defined, delimited, phenomenon but is a 'helpful perspective' in approaching marketing (Gummesson, 1994, p. 8). The argument remains, however, whether RM and TM are exclusive relative to an individual company or industry or as part of the same paradigm (Brodie *et al.*, 1997, p. 389; Coviello *et al.*, 1997, p. 516), perhaps extremes on a 'marketing strategy continuum' (Grönroos, 1995, p. 252).

RM/TM continuum

Research conducted by Brodie *et al.* (1997, pp. 389–402) supports the marketing strategy continuum hypothesis. Their evidence suggests that, at managerial level, a combination of TM and RM approaches are used by firms and that managers maintain a 'portfolio' of strategy types. Although their case and survey results suggested that certain types of marketing (either TM or RM) are more common in some sectors than others, it did not imply exclusivity. The researchers noted that firms at the transactional end of the continuum tended to be larger and longer established businesses, but this might suggest an element of sluggishness in adopting new strategies. The researchers' analysis otherwise fails to identify clearly specific characteristics of firms dominated by one or the other practice. This may support the suggestion that 'drivers', other than strictly industry typology, may be involved.

Although, as we might expect with the level of interest in RM so high, general marketing practice does show a considerable shift towards customer orientation, Brodie *et al.*'s conclusion (p. 389) is that both transactional and relational marketing approaches can and do coexist. Pressey and Mathews (1998, p. 48) also seem to suggest a multivarious approach when they note that a customer's relationship with a supermarket cannot be classed as one that fits the characteristics of RM yet is not as 'discrete' as TM. The relationship is, therefore, between RM and TM and, as such, has parts of both. The strategies used may, therefore, be called a 'portfolio of types'.

In this marketing continuum model RM would be placed at one end. Here the general focus would be on building relationships with customers (and other stakeholders). At the other end of this continuum is TM, where the focus is short term and based on one transaction at a time (Grönroos, 1994b, p. 10). Gummesson (1999, p. 10) supports this view when he suggests that both collaboration *and* competition are essential in a functioning market economy. Whereas collaboration is the core property of RM, traditional marketing is prejudiced in favour of competition. The concept of a marketing continuum between the two perspectives allows for elements of both to be represented.

Grönroos (1994b, p. 11) suggests that industry type may influence a company's position on the continuum (see Figure 4.1). He predicts that at one extreme is the end-user, packaged consumer-goods market with a marketing mix approach based on discrete, transactional exchange and where customers are more sensitive to price

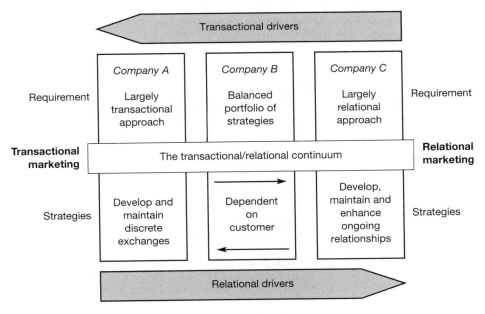

Figure 4.1 The transactional/relational continuum and drivers

than the development of any longer-term relationship. At this end of the continuum traditional measures, such as the technical quality of the output and the monitoring of market share, are used. Customer opinion is determined by *ad hoc* customer surveys as face-to-face contact is limited. Internal marketing (see Chapter 7) is not seen as a priority.

At the other end of the continuum are distribution channel, services and business-to-business marketers, who, it is proposed, would benefit from the application of relationship type strategies. The concentration here is on the long term, with the use of an interactive approach based on the development, maintenance and enhancement of ongoing relationships. Sensitivity to price is much less important at this end of the continuum as customers are seeking other benefits which are delivered via the relationship with the supplier. The dominant measurement criteria here is the quality of interactions with the consumer and the successful management of the customer base. Customer feedback is in 'real time' (i.e. feedback is part of the interaction) and continuous. As the interface with the consumer is so crucial (it is often referred to as 'the moment of truth') the role of internal marketing is of strategic importance.

Although the strict industry division may be somewhat overstated (in that it suggests that consumer goods companies would never benefit from relational strategies and that distribution channels, services and business-to-business would always benefit), it is a valuable starting point. What the concept of a marketing continuum suggests is that, although RM strategies may well be attractive for many products, services and markets, their application may be inappropriate for others (Palmer, 1996, p. 18). It also suggests that some ongoing relationships will always remain predominantly transactional with a focus on gains and losses (Rousseau *et al.*, 1998, p. 398) and never develop beyond this level.

Grönroos (1994b, p. 13) notes that the more a firm moves to the right on the marketing strategy continuum, away from the transaction-type situation, the more the market expands beyond the core product (see Figure 4.2). Barnes (1994, pp. 566–7) hypothesises that at some point on this continuum, it may be said that a transaction approach to marketing ceases to be appropriate and the possibility for the establishment of a genuine relationship begins.

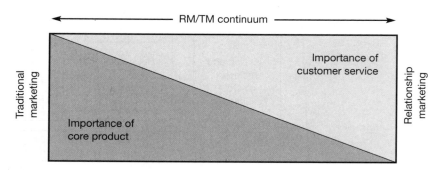

Figure 4.2 RM/TM continuum

Marketing implications

Grönroos (1995, p. 253) suggests that the marketing implications across the strategy continuum (RM versus TM) are substantially different concerning:

- The dominating marketing orientation
- The dominating quality function
- The customer information system
- Interdependency between business functions
- The role of internal marketing.

Dominating marketing orientation

RM suggests that marketing should not be restricted to 'marketing mix' activities nor should it be wholly the responsibility of the marketing department (see Chapter 7). In TM the marketing role of personnel outside of the marketing department is negligible, and elements such as advertising, campaigning and price promotions form the core. In RM these elements are there but as supporting activities to interaction and internal marketing strategies.

Dominating quality function

In TM it is normally enough if the output is of acceptable quality. In RM, although the technical quality has to be acceptable, it is no longer the only quality dimension. Rather, all the interactions within the firm (contact, information systems etc.) support the quality perceptions of the customer.

Customer information system

A firm pursuing a TM strategy will normally have little, if any, direct customer contact. TM relies instead on *ad hoc* customer satisfaction surveys and market-share statistics for information about the behaviour and attitude of customers. A firm that applies RM strategies would monitor customer satisfaction by continuous contact and by directly managing its customer base (see Chapter 10).

Interdependency between business functions

The level of interdependency between functions and departments in an organisation depends on whether the firm has chosen a TM or an RM type strategy. In TM the marketing department takes care of the marketing function. In RM the interaction between, in particular, marketing, operations and human resources becomes critical to success (see Chapter 7).

Role of internal marketing

Preparing the non-marketing employees – Gummesson (1999, p. 45) calls these 'part-time marketers' (see Chapter 7) – for their marketing tasks is an important element of RM strategy. Firms operating such strategies have to take a proactive approach towards getting the commitment required to develop marketing behaviour among all employees. The more people in the firm involved in marketing, the greater the need for active internal marketing. In TM this need is limited.

Four marketing types

Brodie *et al.*, (1997, p. 386) take the continuum concept one stage further by suggesting that there may be four main types of marketing practised. These researchers agree on the distinction between the transactional (TM) and relational (RM) forms but suggest that the latter can be further broken down into the following three types:

■ Database marketing
■ Interactive marketing
■ Network marketing.

The forms of marketing suggested by these various types together with the features associated with each are illustrated in Figure 4.3.

It may be that the three relationship types suggested by Brodie *et al. may* be described in more general terms as direct marketing, relationship marketing (consumer) and relationship marketing (business-to-business). This may be relevant as many of the descriptors seem to fit what is generally accepted to be meant by these more commonly used terms. This also suggests overlap between the terms (and, as such, the strategies) of the various types. Therefore:

■ Transactional marketing and database/direct marketing overlap, although personalised (using technology) database marketing is still distant and largely formal, with an active seller and largely passive buyer.
■ Database/direct marketing and consumer RM overlap in that both are marketing 'to the individual' as opposed to utilising mass-marketing techniques.
■ Consumer RM and business-to-business RM share a number of similarities in that they both emphasise the long-term value of continuous relationships.

Continuum drivers

A logical progression from these arguments is the suggestion that market factors determine (at any particular point in time) the value of (and thus the choice between) relational and transactional strategies. The concept of a continuum may be the basis for determining those departmental, company or industry factors, or 'drivers', that affect (or should affect) strategic decision making in a given market situation. Drivers that may affect whether the company adopts a relational or transactional strategy are shown in Box 4.1. Some of these drivers have been discussed in previous chapters while others will be referred to in more detail in subsequent chapters.

The term 'drivers' is preferred to 'antecedents' for although much RM literature describes relational factors (e.g. trust) as 'antecedents to positive relational outcomes' the empirical evidence does not always support this type of association (Grayson and Ambler, 1999, p. 132). 'Drivers', on the other hand, suggests factors that are likely to 'promote' RM rather than 'predict' it as an outcome.

	← TM perspective →	← Relationship marketing perspective →		
Type	**Transaction marketing**	**Database marketing**	**Interaction marketing**	**Network marketing**
Focus	Economic transactions	Information and economic transactions	Interactive relationship buyer and seller	Connected relationship between firms
Parties involved	Firm and buyer in the general market	Firm and buyer in the specific target market	Individual seller and buyer (a dyad)	Sellers, buyers and other firms
Communication pattern	Firm 'to' market	Firm 'to' individual	Individuals 'with' individuals	Firms 'with' firms (involves individuals)
Type of contract	Arm's length, impersonal	Personalised (yet distant)	Face-to-face interpersonal	Impersonal-interpersonal (distant–close)
Duration	Discrete, one-off (but perhaps over time)	Discrete and over time	Continuous* (ongoing and adaptive)	Continuous* (stable yet dynamic)
Formality	Formal	Formal (yet personalised by technology)	Formal and informal (social and business)	Formal and informal (social and business)
Balance of power	Active seller, passive buyer	Active seller, less passive buyer	Buyer and seller mutually active and adaptive	All firms active and adaptive
*May describe***	*Transactional marketing*	*Direct/database marketing*	*Relationship marketing (consumer)*	*Relationship marketing (business-to-business)*
Overlap				

* may be long or short term
** author's interpretation

Figure 4.3 Four marketing types

(*Source*: Adapted from Brodie *et al.*, 1997, p. 386)

Box 4.1

Drivers affecting strategic decision making

Drivers promoting relational strategies	Drivers against using relational strategies
■ High acquisition costs relative to retention costs	■ Acquisition/retention cost differential minimal
■ High exit barriers	■ Low exit barriers
■ Competitive advantage sustainable	■ Competitive advantage unsustainable
■ Buoyant/expanding market	■ Saturated market
■ High risk/high salience products or services	■ Low risk/low salience products or services
■ High emotion involved in exchange	■ Low emotion involved in exchange
■ Requirement for trust and commitment	■ Requirement for trust only
■ Perceived need for closeness	■ No perceived need for closeness
■ Satisfaction beneficial to retention	■ Repeat behaviour strategy beneficial

The concept of the strategy continuum implies that an 'optimum position' exists (whether determinable or not) and that each company's individually tailored perspective is dependent on the balance between the various transactional or relational drivers. In business as well as in life, relationships are inherently unstable (Blois, 1997, p. 367) and this balance is constantly changing as factors strengthen or weaken. These constantly changing circumstances suggests a permanent 'danger area' either side of the optimum position owing to the difficulty (if not impossibility) of calculating the outcome of particular TM and RM strategies at any given point in time (see Figure 4.4). The two biggest dangers are:

■ At the transactional end of the spectrum not recognising the desire of customer for an increased level of 'customer service' (*see the IKEA Case study, page 72*).
■ At the relational end of the spectrum overestimating the level of service expected by the customer, resulting in defection to lower cost (and lower service) competitors.

The nearer the middle of the hypothesised continuum, the greater the danger of misapplication of strategies is likely to be.

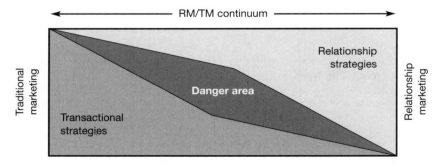

Figure 4.4 RM/TM continuum

Hybrid managerial approach

As rational and intuitively sensible as the introduction of relational strategies may appear in theory, observation of these policies, over time, will be the only real test. Observation of real-world marketing practice suggests that a hybrid managerial approach (suggested by the continuum concept) may be the most appropriate response to prevailing market circumstances (Chaston, 1998, p. 273). This would suggest the use of multiple marketing strategies (Voss and Voss, 1997, p. 279) that:

1 Develop and maintain discrete exchanges (TM).
2 Develop, maintain and enhance ongoing relationships (RM).

Developing RM concepts

The continuum/drivers hypothesis may relate to other developing RM concepts. The notion of the three forces of marketing equilibrium (elaborated by Gummesson, 1996, p. 34). suggests that even if RM puts emphasis on collaboration, it is the combination of competition, collaboration and regulatory institutions in each specific situation that creates the balance or marketing equilibrium (Gummesson, 1997). With competition (TM) and collaboration (RM) represented on the continuum and the regulatory mechanisms as a variable influence on the relevant drivers, the continuum hypothesis would seem in accord with this concept.

The concept of hybrid models may offer greater benefit than that of unswerving allegiance to a single, purist philosophy. Thus, there may exist a number of alternative marketing styles, any of which, depending on the customer–supplier relationship, may be more applicable (Chaston, 1998, p. 277). Rather than suggesting that RM is taking over as the new marketing paradigm, it may be more beneficial to accept it as part of marketing's arsenal. It is not transactional marketing versus relationship marketing, or mass marketing versus customer-specific marketing that should be the argument because all of these things are going on (Kotler, 1997, p. 27). Indeed, according to Brown (1998, p. 31) the very idea of a single, all-embracing, general theory of marketing today is 'laughingly absurd'.

Summary

This chapter investigates the arguments for a hypothesised 'strategy continuum'. It recognises that while RM may be beneficial in some instances, it may not be relevant to all. RM, the chapter proposed, should not be regarded as a dominant marketing paradigm but as a 'helpful perspective' in marketing. The suggestion is made, therefore, that a strategy continuum may exist with traditional marketing and relational marketing at either end. Any company, at any point in time, may adopt one or more of a 'hybrid' range of strategies that may be dominated by one or other end of the strategy continuum.

This idea is developed further by the suggestion that the RM end of the continuum may be segmented into database marketing interactive marketing, and network marketing, and that they may be seen as approximately equivalent to direct marketing, consumer RM and business-to-business RM. The proposal that drivers to particular strategies exist was also introduced and will be expanded upon in Chapter 5.

1 Take four companies with which you are familiar. Where would you place them on the hypothetical RM/TM continuum?

2 What factors led to your decision to place them at this point on the continuum?

3 Suggest a range of marketing strategies that might be termed a 'portfolio of strategy types'.

Case study

Inside track

Understanding the consumer and what motivates him or her to buy has long been regarded as the *raison d'être* of good marketing, but marketing companies are finding it increasingly difficult to keep up with the pace of change in society.

From the 'Glams' (greying, leisured and middle-aged) and the 'Yoofs' (young, free and single), people at both ends of the age spectrum are finding that advertising is no longer relevant in their lives. Campaigns aimed at these age groups are irritating, patronising and misleading, according to two damning reports[*] – both by marketing organisations – to be published this month.

Their common conclusion is that despite the impact of 'relationship' or 'loyalty' marketing – a 1990s sales strategy that aims to generate a lifetime's loyalty to a product or service – many top marketers are not even at the first-date stage.

The first report, by direct marketing group Brann Consulting, finds that instead of forging closer relationships with their clients, many service-oriented firms, such as retailers and banks, are pushing them away. It claims that despite the millions of pounds spent each year on 'friendlier advertising', the average shopper harbours warmer feelings towards a jar of coffee than their local supermarket.

If 1990s marketers are failing to capitalise on the emotional strength of their brands, they are also ignoring the 'profound implications of the demographic time-bomb', warns the second report, from the Chartered Institute of Marketing.

'Treating all over-55s like old farts (fearful of ageing or retiring too soon) and selling them nothing but hearing aids and unit trusts is like treating all under-21s as idiots whose sole interests are designer beer and rap music,' says Jonathan Gabay, consultant to the Chartered Institute of Marketing.

Brann's report is based on a survey of 1,000 adults. Asked to describe their relationship with products and services they used regularly, more than half said they considered their favourite tea or coffee brand to be 'a friend', while seven in 10 believed their telephone supplier was more of a 'casual acquaintance'. Rather a surprise, given the billions of pounds BT has spent on the 'It's Good To Talk' campaign, where the overriding message is that the telephone is the prime conduit for our private lives.

Brann believes that the report highlights the yawning gap between advertising fantasy and the harsh realities of shopping for food, or paying bills at a bank: 'We live in an age when marketers are making great efforts to offer far more than good prices to consumers,' says Jeremy Braune of Brann Consulting. 'Yet our research shows that however much money Tesco or Waitrose pour into creating advertising that makes us feel good, the reality of shopping in any supermarket on a Saturday morning is still horrendous.'

If advertising agencies are still living in fantasy-land when it comes to portraying the gritty realities of everyday life, then their grasp of what it is like to be over 55, or under 24, remains at best tenuous, according to the second report.

'For the over-55s or so-called "silver" market, there appear to be just two sorts of press or television adverts,' says Mr Gabay, 'and they are what I would call the false-teeth-and-stair-lifts-style or the deliriously-fit-and-enjoying-a-marvellous-sex-life approach.'

'The trouble is that not all consumers approaching retirement are racked with fears over their will, nor are all of them obsessed with hang-gliding or sex. To suggest otherwise is to disenfranchise millions of potential customers.'

In marketing to the over-55s, says Mr Gabay, it should be borne in mind that there are three groups: the 'young-old' (55 to 64), the 'mature old' (65 to 74) and the 'old-old' (75-plus). 'Once a person gets to 80,' he concedes, 'marketing people tend to give up altogether.'

Mr Gabay suggests that the over-55s prefer 'real-life' advertising to sheer fantasy – the Oxo family or even the smug Gold Blend couple being preferable to surreal beer commercials. Most car advertising appears to exclude older drivers, says Mr Gabay. as does air travel, fashion and internet-based products.

If marketers are in danger of patronising the over-50s, then their attitude towards the under-24s is 'one of sheer bewilderment', says Mr Gabay. 'Although ad agencies are stereotyped as being packed with young and beautiful people, this is far from the case,' he says. 'Most of the people who sign off ads are thirty- or forty-somethings who are desperate to be seen as young and trendy, but who continually get it wrong simply because they are out of touch.'

While advertisements for Egg, Orange, Tango and Freeserve are largely in tune with the mood of the moment, the report detects some distaste at the 'raw egocentricity' displayed in many haircare and beauty product advertisements.

Most of the UK's more successful marketers and advertising agencies claim to understand how we live and what makes us buy brand X rather than its rival. Yet if these two reports are to be believed, then today's more demanding consumer may have thrown marketing its biggest challenge yet.

*The Marketing of Ages Report: CIM, Tel.: 01628 427306. Brann Consulting Survey 1999: Tel.: 01285 644744

(*Source*: Virginia Matthews, *Financial Times*, 5 November 1999)

▶

Case study questions

1 The article suggests that consumers have different levels of 'relationships' with brands. Is this hype or reality?

2 What, if any, brands would you consider you had a casual, friendly or close relationship with?

References

Barnes, J.G. (1994) 'Close to the customer: but is it really a relationship?', *Journal of Marketing Management*, 10, 561–70.

Blois, K.J. (1997) 'Are business to business relationships inherently unstable?', *Journal of Marketing Management*, 13 (5), 367–82.

Brodie, R.J., Coviello, N.E., Brookes, R.W. and Little, V. (1997) 'Towards a paradigm shift in marketing; an examination of current marketing practices', *Journal of Marketing Management*, 13 (5), 383–406.

Brown, S. (1998) *Postmodern Marketing II*. London: International Thompson.

Buttle, F.B. (1997) 'Exploring relationship quality', paper presented at the Academy of Marketing Conference, Manchester, UK.

Chaston, I. (1998) 'Evolving "new marketing" philosophies by merging existing concepts: application of process within small high-technology firms', *Journal of Marketing Management*, 14, 273–91.

Christopher, M., Payne, A. and Ballantyne, D. (1991) *Relationship Marketing*. London: Butterworth Heinemann.

Coviello, N., Brodie, R.J. and Munro, J. (1997) 'Understanding contemporary marketing: development of a classification scheme', *Journal of Marketing Management*, 13 (6), 501–22.

Dwyer, F.R., Schurr, P.H. and Oh, S. (1987) 'Developing buyer–seller relationships', *Journal of Marketing*, 51, 11–27.

Grayson, K. and Ambler, T. (1999) 'The dark side of long-term relationships in marketing', *Journal of Marketing Research*, 36 (1), 132–41.

Grönroos, C. (1994a) 'From marketing mix to relationship marketing: towards a paradigm shift in marketing', *Asia-Australia Marketing Journal*, 2 (1).

Grönroos, C. (1994b) 'From marketing mix to relationship marketing: towards a paradigm shift in marketing', *Management Decisions*, 32 (2), 4–20.

Grönroos, C. (1995) 'Relationship marketing: the strategy continuum', *Journal of Marketing Science*, 23 (4), 252–54.

Grönroos, C. (1997) 'Value-driven relational marketing: from products to resources and competencies', *Journal of Marketing Management*, 13 (5), 407–19.

Gummesson, E. (1994) 'Making relationship marketing operational', *International Journal of Service Industry Management*, 5, 5–20.

Gummesson, E. (1996) 'Relationship marketing and imaginary organisations: A synthesis', *European Journal of Marketing*, 30 (2), 31–44.

Gummesson, E. (1997) 'Relationship marketing – the emperor's new clothes or a paradigm shift?', *Marketing and Research Today*, February, 53–60.

Gummesson, E. (1999) *Total Relationship Marketing; Rethinking Marketing Management from 4Ps to 30Rs*. Oxford: Butterworth Heinemann.

Kotler, P. (1997) 'Method for the millennium', *Marketing Business*, February, pp. 26–7.

Morgan, R.M. and Hunt, S.D. (1994) 'The commitment-trust theory of relationship marketing', *Journal of Marketing*, 58 (3), 20–38.

Palmer, A.J. (1996) 'Relationship marketing: a universal paradigm or management fad?', *The Learning Organisation*, 3 (3), 18–25.

Pels, J. (1999) 'Exchange relationships in consumer markets?' *European Journal of Marketing*, 33 (1/2), 19–37.

Pressey, A.D. and Mathews, B.P. (1998) 'Relationship marketing and retailing: comfortable bedfellows?', *Customer Relationship Management*, 1 (1), 39–53.

Rousseau, D.M., Sitkin, S.B., Burt, R.S. and Camerer, C. (1998) 'Not so different after all: a cross-discipline view of trust', *Academy of Management Review*, 23 (3), 393–404.

Sheth, J.N. and Parvatiyar, A. (1993) *Relationship Marketing: Theory, Methods and Application*. Atlanta, GA: Atlanta Center for Relationship Marketing.

Voss, G.B. and Voss, Z.G. (1997) 'Implementing a relationship marketing program: a case study and managerial implications', *Journal of Services Marketing*, 11 (4), 278–98.

5 Relationship drivers

Introduction

In the previous chapter the concept of 'drivers' towards relational strategies was introduced. Box 5.1 summarises these suggested drivers, a number of which were discussed in Chapter 3, including:

- High customer acquisition costs (*see page* 54)
- High exit barriers (*see page* 64)
- Sustainable competitive advantage (*see page* 70)
- Buoyant/expanding market (*see pages* 67–8)

In this section we will look at those other drivers that appear to have an important bearing on the decision to develop a relationship marketing approach, in particular:

- Risk, salience and emotion
- Trust and commitment
- Perceived need for closeness
- Customer satisfaction.

Risk, salience and emotion

Risk, salience and emotion are all psychological aspects involved in some way in every exchange/purchase. Although they are wholly subjective the levels of risk, degree of salience involved and the emotion generated *will* affect the choice of product or service and supplier involved, as well as the 'level' of relational involvement the customer will seek or, in some circumstances, allow.

Box 5.1

Drivers promoting/against relational strategies

Drivers promoting relational strategies	**Drivers against using relational strategies**
■ High acquisition costs relative to retention costs*	■ Acquisition/retention cost differential minimal*
■ High exit barriers*	■ Low exit barriers*
■ Competitive advantage sustainable*	■ Competitive advantage unsustainable*
■ Buoyant/expanding market*	■ Saturated market*
■ High risk/high salience products or services	■ Low risk/low salience products or services
■ High emotion involved in exchange	■ Low emotion involved in exchange
■ Perceived need for closeness	■ No perceived need for closeness
■ Requirement for trust and commitment	■ Requirement for trust only
■ Satisfaction beneficial to retention	■ Repeat behaviour strategy beneficial

* See Chapter 3

An explanation of what is meant by risk, salience and emotion in a marketing context may be appropriate:

■ Risk may be defined as 'the perceived probability of loss interpreted by the decision maker' (Rousseau *et al.*, 1998, p. 395) and presumes an element of consumer vulnerability in the exchange.

■ Salience may be regarded as the level of importance or prominence associated with the exchange.

■ Emotion is the complex series of human responses (sometimes negatively described as 'agitation of the mind' or 'cognitive dissonance') generated as a result of the exchange.

Risk, salience and emotion are separately definable concepts but are not mutually exclusive. There is a close association between the level of risk perceived in, the salience associated with, and the emotion generated by, any given exchange situation. Thus high risk is often associated with high salience products or services and with a high emotional outcome although any measures are *highly subjective* and may differ from individual to individual. It is quite possible to imagine, for example, that a particular exchange relationship will generate a perception of high levels of risk, salience and emotion with one customer yet, if the situation were to be replicated, only generate low levels with another.

High risk, salience and emotion

Case studies of companies that appear to benefit from relational strategies are frequently those involving 'high-risk purchases', either with a large single monetary outlay (e.g. vehicle purchases) or with payments over an extended period (e.g. financial services). These latter extended payments are often associated with high opportunity or actual costs as a possible consequence of incorrect decision making at the initial sale. One reason why so-called high-risk purchases may benefit from RM strategies is that a relationship, over time, is likely (but not certain) to lower the perceived risk as the consumer 'learns' more about the terms and security of the arrangement and, more generally, gets to know the supplier. Even in a situation where this long-term experience creates some doubts about the supplier, this learning exercise reduces risk by indicating those areas of the relationship where the supplier can and cannot be trusted. The existence of risk, therefore, creates an opportunity for trust that would not be needed if actions could be taken with certainty and no risk (Rousseau *et al.*, 1998, p. 395).

The case studies quoted in support of relational strategies are also generally highly salient to the consumer, either representing major and current status symbols or as affecting status or quality of life at some point in the future (e.g. pensions, investments). In situations characterised by high risk and high salience, the customer may enter the service encounter with certain specific expectations associated with rather intense emotions (Cumby and Barnes, 1998, p. 55) and may be seeking specific reassurance and reduction of cognitive dissonance. These situations appear to benefit from the closer ties and more frequent communication associated with RM strategies and tactics.

Low risk, salience and emotion

At the other end of the spectrum are those products and services that may be defined as low (actual or opportunity) cost, decidedly low risk and low salience. As a result, suppliers at this end of the spectrum, such as FMCG retailers and repetitive services (e.g. library services), are rarely involved in exchange situations that generate the emotional intensity of major purchases. In these industries there is little need for the supplier to devote time and resources to anything more than basic reassurances, guarantees and warranties and no apparent motive on the part of the customers to seek anything more than a tenuous relationship.

Personalised services

There are, however, some products and services that, seemingly, exert emotions out of proportion to their value. These tend to be highly personalised and usually associated with self-esteem. These categories include products such as clothing and services such as hairdressing or beauticians. If the benefits associated with these products and services are important emotionally to a customer then they are highly salient and the customer is likely to be risk averse. In these situations relational strategies may help secure that customer's patronage. With most consumers these personal goods or services involve a trade-off. Thus the introduction of 'personal shoppers', personal trainers or expert stylists, at an increased cost to the consumer, may be acceptable to a percentage of the population although the core value of the service is low.

This proposal is, therefore, that, in situations where there is a high level of personal risk potential and salience, *as perceived by the customer*, and a resultant high degree of emotion generated, despite the relatively low cost in monetary terms (but perhaps a high cost in psychological terms), this may promote or 'drive' RM strategies.

Trust and commitment

The requirement for trust and commitment appears to be an important indicator of when RM strategies may be potentially valuable. Equally, the existence of trust and commitment among parties is seen by some to be central to the success of relationship marketing strategies (Morgan and Hunt, 1994, p. 22) and the main means by which the affective strength of a buyer–seller relationship can be judged (Bejou and Palmer, 1998, p. 8). Trust and commitment are frequently paired together in RM literature, with few authors discussing one without the other (Pressey and Mathews, 1998, p. 41).

Trust

Trust is generally ill defined but is often taken to mean 'an acceptance of vulnerability to another's possible, but not expected, ill will or lack of good will' (Blois 1997, p. 58). Trust is, therefore, a psychological state comprising of an intention to accept this vulnerability based upon the positive expectations of the intentions or behaviour of others (Rousseau *et al.*, 1998, p. 394).

Trust is not itself a behaviour (as for example is cooperation) nor a choice (as in taking a risk) but an underlying condition that can result from such activities (Rousseau *et al.*, 1998, p. 395). Trust is seen as an important driver to both relationships and relationship enhancement in that it would appear to reduce risk perception more effectively than anything else.

Scholars have seen trust as an essential ingredient in a healthy personality, as a foundation for interpersonal relationships, as a prerequisite for cooperation and as a basis for stability in social institutions and markets (Lewicki *et al.*, 1998, p. 438). As well as generating cooperative behaviour, trust may (Rousseau *et al.*, 1998, p. 394);

- Reduce harmful conflict.
- Decrease transactional costs (e.g. negating the need for constant checks).
- Promote adaptive organisational forms (e.g. network relationships).
- Facilitate the rapid formation of *ad hoc* work groups.
- Promote effective response to a crisis.

Those suggested advantages involved with organisational groups seem, however, to assume that trust negates ambition. Given human nature and the intense political manoeuvring frequently seen within organisations, this viewpoint may be questionable.

Implicit in the above definitions and descriptions of trust is the general expectation that the word of another can be relied upon. So strong is this expectancy that in certain relationships (e.g. financial services) it is generally seen to supersede normal commercial decision making. Thus, when some UK financial advisors were seen to sell products designed to return their companies or principals a handsome profit (a notion encouraged in many sectors of industry) and themselves very satisfactory commissions, the British government decided it was 'mis-selling' and highly publicised action taken to refund customers.

The importance of trust has become central to discussions concerning Internet sales. Lack of trust in (often newly created and therefore unknown) suppliers to supply to the quality expected (or indeed at all) has been cited as one of the major suppressers of Internet sales. In response, a number of established organisations (that customers might be expected to 'trust' based on their size and/or reputation) have stepped in to offer 'seals of approval' to legitimise Internet businesses. In the UK these include BT's 'Trustwise', Barclay's 'Endorse', Royal Mail's 'Trust' and the Consumer Association's 'Which Web Trader'. The importance of this need for trust in the development of Internet sales is emphasised in the article in the Case study at the end of this chapter.

Trusting situations

Many different words or terms seem to be used to describe trusting situations. These, according to Mitchell *et al.* (1998, p. 160), may be summarised under the following headings:

■ Probity
■ Equity
■ Reliability
■ Satisfaction.

Probity

Probity focuses on honesty and integrity that may be realised in business terms as professional understanding and reputation (Mitchell *et al.*, 1998, p. 160). Reputation matters, and in particular the historical trustworthiness of parties following previous interactions. It is this social context (i.e. networks) that makes reputational effects possible (Rousseau *et al.*, 1998, p. 397). Although trust may be managed by individuals, companies can trade on their previous trustworthiness (even if the person who was responsible for generating the trust initially has gone elsewhere) because it can be 'institutionally captured' by the organisation (Shepherd and Sherman, 1998, p. 437).

Equity

Factors such as fair-mindedness, benevolence, caring, values and sincerity are in evidence here. Helpful advertising and/or cause-related sponsorship or promotions may help communicate this message to the consumer. Equity may also suggest an implied contract with mutual expectations and perceived obligations (Mitchell *et al.*, 1998, p. 160). Trust is not, however, simply cooperation (which may be coercive) but is seen to have more altruistic motivations (Rousseau *et al.*, 1998, p. 394).

Reliability

Reliability relates to the firm having the required expertise to perform its business effectively and reliably. It is emphasised through dependability, quality and consistency, and may be associated with high levels of predictability on the part of consumers as to the product or service they can expect. This may be expressed through the inherent qualities associated with the corporate name or brand or through guarantees and warranties issued by the company (Mitchell *et al.*, 1998, p. 160). It may be important to note that when customers are not able to evaluate product or service quality it is brand reputation that often drives the exchange (Selnes, 1998, p. 318).

Satisfaction

This will be covered more fully in the following section but is included here in its capacity as a predictor of trust. There would appear to be considerable overlap between trust and satisfaction as they both represent an overall evaluation, feeling or attitude about the other party in a relationship (Selnes, 1998, p. 308). Satisfaction may be developed through personal experience or, less directly, through opinion and the experience of peers. It is associated with the perceived standard of delivery and may well be dependent on the duration of the relationship. Anticipated levels of satisfaction may also have an important effect on the duration of trust (Mitchell *et al.*, 1998, p. 160).

Trust is, therefore, a belief in a person's (or organisation's) competence to perform a specific task under specific circumstances (Sitkin and Roth, 1993, p. 373). In other circumstances no such trust (or active distrust) may exist. This is because relationships are multifaceted. It is quite possible for parties to hold, simultaneously, different views of each other as to each party's trustfulness in particular situations. For example, a company may be trusted as regards quality but may not be trusted to deliver on time. Trust is almost always regarded as a beneficial force; however, excessive trust (or suppression of distrust) may be at the root of 'group-think' dynamics (Lewicki *et al.*, 1998, p. 453) or may lead to claims of naïveté.

Commitment

Relationship commitment, it is suggested, is central to relationship marketing. It is again an often ill-defined concept. In RM literature it would seem to be regarded as a situation where one or other of the party's intention is to act and their subsequent attitude towards interacting with each other (Storbacka *et al.*, 1994, p. 28). Commitment implies that both parties will be loyal, reliable and show stability in the relationship with one another (Bejou and Palmer, 1998, p. 10). It is, therefore, a desire to maintain a relationship, often indicated by an ongoing investment into activities which are expected to maintain that relationship (Blois 1997, p. 58). As it may take time to reach a point where a commitment may be made, it may also imply a certain 'maturity' in a relationship (Bejou and Palmer, 1998, p. 10).

Commitment is undoubtedly connected with the notion of trust but it is less clear which, if any, assumes precedence. Whether commitment is the outcome of growing trust or whether trust develops from the decision to commit to one or a few suppliers is not immediately clear. In addition, a breakdown in commitment may be the result of a breakdown in trust or vice versa. Commitment may also be associated (negatively) with greater competition and the availability of alternative relational parties (Bejou and Palmer, 1998, p. 10).

Trust and commitment

Notionally trust and commitment appear inseparable in the RM debate. This may well indicate that, if one or other is missing, the relationship is unlikely to be more than a 'hands off' or transient arrangement. This is because trust and commitment are invariably associated with the prerequisite that the relationship is of significantly high importance to one or both parties as to warrant maximum efforts at maintaining it (Morgan and Hunt, 1994, p. 23).

Situations which may benefit from relational strategies are, therefore, likely to be those where the consumer and/or the supplier (but not necessarily both) regard the formation of a relationship as important. Where the supplier alone recognises the importance of a relationship, relational strategies designed to 'lock-in' customers over time seem a logical development (see Chapter 3). Where the customer alone recognises the importance of a relationship (for example in situations of high risk) the supplier may use this desire to attract customers through the development of strategies perceived by the customer as satisfying this need.

What these descriptions of trust and commitment suggest is that, whatever the industry, it is important to build trust and commitment if the establishment of a relationship is the end goal (Pressey and Mathews 1998). Conversely, it may be hypothesised that if trust and commitment are generally prerequisites to a sale then relationship building is an important step towards achieving this.

There may be a number of precursors to trust and commitment, including (Morgan and Hunt, 1994, pp. 24–25):

■ Relationship termination costs
■ Relationship benefits
■ Shared values
■ Communication
■ Opportunistic behaviour.

Relationship termination costs

Relationship termination costs are *all* of the costs expected from termination, including the lack of comparable alternative partners, relationship dissolution expenses as well as other switching costs (see Chapter 3).

Relationship benefits

Relationship benefits directly influence trust and commitment (Morgan and Hunt, 1994, p. 24). RM theory suggests that partner selection may be a critical element in competitive strategy as partners deliver superior 'value benefits'. Partners that receive superior benefits are likely to be more committed to a relationship.

Shared values

Shared values also directly influence both trust and commitment. The extent to which the partners have beliefs in common about behaviours, goals and policies that are important, appropriate and right for a particular situation is likely to affect commitment to the relationship.

Communication

Communication may directly influence trust and, indirectly, commitment. The sharing of meaningful and timely information is likely to build up both trust and commitment.

Opportunistic behaviour

Opportunistic behaviour (i.e. taking advantage of the relationship partner) on the part of one of the relationship participants is likely to directly influence (negatively) trust and, indirectly, commitment. When a party engages in opportunistic behaviour such perceptions can lead to decreased trust and, as a consequence, to the lessening of commitment.

(Based on Morgan and Hunt, 1994, pp. 24–5)

Transactional marketing

At the more transactional end of the spectrum trust may also be seen to be important in that the consumer relies on the 'brand promises' of the supplier and/or the brand regarding safety, reliability and value for money for products and services. The customer, typically, must buy before 'experiencing the purchase', particularly in service situations (Berry and Parsuraman, 1991, p. 107). This implies that trust is most applicable when the outcome is unclear. The breaking of this trust may be seen to be a potential dis-satisfier and a reason for defection.

Absence of commitment to a relationship is, however, possible in workable relationships. In the FMCG sector consumers have no reason to commit themselves to one or a few suppliers because of the availability of supply in a largely undifferentiated market. At the other extreme, what at first might appear to be 'commitment' on the part of one party (e.g. the consumer) may hide the fact that they have few other exchange possibilities and are 'trapped' rather than committed to the relational exchange (Bejou and Palmer, 1998, p. 10).

The irony is that it is the FMCG sector, where commitment is low, that is the industry most heavily involved in 'loyalty schemes'. If commitment is a rarity in these businesses then loyalty is also in short supply. Indeed, most loyalty schemes, while rewarding repeat behaviour, are little more than technically advanced promotions that have little to do with retention, and may actively work against the development of long-term commitment. Exit barriers in this industry are small and the psychological costs nearly non-existent. At this end of the industry spectrum seduction is the favoured option (Tynan, 1997, p. 993). The risk is that 'promiscuous customers' will be attracted by the best deal with little regard for who supplies it. Indeed, a breakdown in commitment may well be associated with greater competition and availability of alternative relational partners (Bejou and Palmer, 1998, p. 10).

Commitment implies a state of maturity in a relationship that does not seem to exist at this end of the relational spectrum (Bejou and Palmer, 1998, p. 10). There is no need to commit oneself either to a brand or a supplier; rather, consumers seem content to work with a 'portfolio of brands' (including retailer brands) until such time as a better alternative is available (Barnard and Ehrenberg, 1997). If the requirement for the successful application of RM is both trust and commitment, and not just one or the other (Morgan and Hunt, 1994), then many such industries fail to fulfil this criterion.

Perceived need for closeness

Some relationships will always be closer than others. Closeness, therefore, is a construct that is integral to the notion of relationship in that very close and less close relationships exist in virtually all circumstances (Barnes, 1997, p. 229). Closeness can be physical, mental or emotional and can strengthen the feeling of security in a relationship. When the 'distance' between the parties is shorter, deeper relationships are likely to develop (Pels, 1999, p. 27). Conversely, when the distance is greater the relationship (if a relationship can be said to exist) is functional and at 'arm's length'. Close relationships are acknowledged to be more solid and likely to be longer lasting – precisely the characteristics relational marketers are looking for (Barnes, 1997, p. 229).

Different groups may be more or less 'prone' to the development of close relationships (Barnes and Howlett, 1998, p. 16). Not all customers want close relationships and some may only be interested in developing them with some parties and not with others (Pels, 1999, p. 27). A certain percentage may already have a moderately close relationship with a supplier and may wish that it were closer while others might wish that it were less close. A continuum of closeness may, therefore, be said to exist (Barnes, 1997, p. 229) which may, to an extent, resemble the relational–transactional continuum (see Chapter 4).

According to Barnes (1997, p. 237), degrees of closeness in a relationship may be linked, among other things, to the frequency of two-way communication with employees, and to the trust, empathy and mutuality of perceived relationship goals, and are usually associated with core products and services that involve high risk and involvement. Establishing close customer relationships in settings that are not characterised by frequent personal contact or high levels of involvement or emotion may, therefore, be a challenge. As the *sine qua non* of close relationships is two-way communication, 'unilateral communication' is deemed insufficient (Buttle, 1997,

p. 152). This concept seems to have bypassed some companies. What is seen as a relationship under the definition of most marketing programmes (e.g. customer updates) is not likely to be a relationship in the eyes of the customer in that it is mostly one-sided and lacking in two-way communication (Barnes, 1997, p. 229).

This view of the importance of 'closeness' has implications for marketers who wish to develop or otherwise exploit relationships with customers, in particular those companies utilising technology in the development of 'close relationships' (see Chapter 10). Targeted mailings, in general, fail to satisfy the criteria as the 'normal' response rate is low, with many customers rejecting the 'communication'. This applies even when the 'return on investment' on the campaign is satisfactory. Companies that rely on frequent mailings to 'keep their customers informed' are merely throwing messages at consumers, not communicating with them.

Moves to utilise technology to save staff costs (e.g. cash machines, Internet information services etc.) may also discourage the development of close relationships. By removing the human element in the process the company reverts to relying solely on the 'core product and support services' (see Chapter 10) to achieve any 'differentiation' from its competitors.

Customer satisfaction

Relationship marketing theory suggests that profitability is enhanced when customer retention is high. Retention in competitive markets is generally believed to be a product of customer satisfaction (Buttle, 1997, p. 143). In addition, customer satisfaction has been shown to be positively associated with return on investment (ROI) and market value (Sheth and Sisodia 1999, p. 80), although these are sometimes regarded as poor measures of actual company performance in the long-term.

Most researchers agree that satisfaction is a psychological process of evaluating perceived performance outcomes based on predetermined expectations (e.g. Sheth and Sisodia, 1999, p. 80). Customers are, therefore, satisfied when their 'expectations of values' are positively disconfirmed (Buttle, 1997, p. 143). In contrast, the greater the (negative) gap between the level of expectation, and the matching of such expectations, the greater the level of dissatisfaction experienced by the customer (Hutcheson and Moutinho, 1998, p. 706). Figure 5.1 illustrates these concepts.

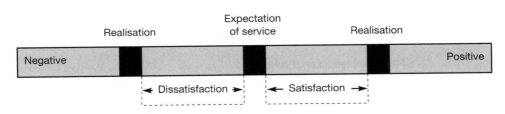

Figure 5.1 Expectation and realisation of service

Satisfaction drivers

What drives customer satisfaction? Cumby and Barnes (1998, pp. 58–60) suggest that drivers exist on five levels and that these generally involve progressively more personal contact with the service supplier:

■ Core product or service
■ Support services and systems
■ Technical performance
■ Elements of customer interaction
■ Affective dimension of services.

Core product or service

This is the basic product or service provided by the company and, probably, provides the supplier with the least opportunity to differentiate or add value. However, in the competitive marketplace the company must get the core product or service right otherwise the whole relationship is at risk.

Support services and systems

These include the peripheral and support services that enhance the provision of the core product or services (e.g. staffing levels, delivery, technical support etc.). The customer may well receive an excellent core product or service from the supplier but be dissatisfied with the supplier because of inferior support services and systems.

Technical performance

This level of the 'customer satisfaction model' deals with whether the service provider gets the core product or service *and* the support services and systems right. The emphasis is on keeping the promises made to the consumer (e.g. on-time delivery, correct billing etc.). There may be nothing wrong with the core product or service and the supplier may have the services and systems in place but they do not (perhaps because of management failings) get them right on every occasion. Customer dissatisfaction may result from this failure to deliver to the customer's expectations.

Elements of customer interaction

This level relates to the way the service provider interacts with the customer either face-to-face or through technology-based contact (e.g. telephone etc.). How do we treat customers? Are they treated with courtesy? Do we make it easy for them to do business with us? Understanding of the importance of applying this level of consideration implies that the company has thought beyond the simple provision of core products and services and support.

Affective dimensions of service

Beyond the basic interactions of the company are the messages, sometimes subtle and often unintentional, that companies send to their customers that leave them with either positive or negative feelings towards them. Cumby and Barnes (1998, p. 58) note that research evidence exists showing that a considerable amount of customer dissatisfaction has nothing to do with core products and services or with how that 'core' is delivered or provided to the customer. Indeed, the customer may be satisfied with most aspects of the interaction. The problem is with the 'little things' that may not even be noticed by staff (see Box 5.2).

(Based on Cumby and Barnes, 1998, pp. 58–60)

Cumby and Barnes (1998, p. 58) make the point that it is quite possible for the supplier to get things right on the first four levels and to dissatisfy the customer because of something that happens on the fifth level. This emphasises the importance of 'critical episodes' in the exchange process, as discussed in the following section.

Box 5.2

Frustrations

- I used to be able to telephone my bank if I had a problem and my problem would normally be sorted out then and there. Now my bank uses a 'customer care centre'. I now have to call this centre (which is frequently engaged), try to remember the fourth letter of my password (which I may have forgotten) and explain (usually from the very beginning as the call centre operator does not know me) my problem. They cannot usually answer my question because they need first to speak to my bank, who they promise to contact. I may then receive a telephone call (usually taken by my answerphone so I have no opportunity to question what I am told) a few days later either part-answering or not answering my query. I then have to call the customer care centre back and the cycle begins again. Not only was my query not answered immediately but it would seem to me that the duplication of effort on the part of the bank hardly suggests efficiency.

- A large cable telephone operator has written to me on two separate occasions urging me to join them. As I am less than happy with my current telephone provider I have called the cable company to enquire further. On both occasions the company has told me that cables have yet to be laid in my street. Discussing this with some students, I find that the same thing has happened to many of them. I am beginning to think that it is not a mistake, as I had been told, but that the company is 'mass mailing' to judge whether it would be worth laying cables in the first place.

- A well-known insurance company wrote to me last year suggesting that they could 'almost certainly' cut the cost of my home insurance. I called them only to be quoted a premium almost £200 more than my current insurer. The operator said it was because of the area in which I lived. As these rates are based almost always on post codes why did this company bother writing to me in the first place?

- Every time I go to the doctor (thankfully not often) I receive an appointment. Regardless of what time of day the appointment is it is *always* late. The reason is, I am told, that the doctor allows a certain time for each appointment and that this time allowance is *always* exceeded. It would seem too obvious that the surgery should review the time schedule on the basis of the average time the doctor spends with patients.

- I was involved for many years with a UK ceramics company for whom I was (on behalf of a large North American Department store) that company's largest customer. Towards the end of each year I would contact the company to check on the January/February shipments. Each time, without fail, I would be told there was a delay. When I asked why I would be told (each and every time) that the problem was that the factory was closing for Christmas. The fact that Christmas happened every year did not seem to influence the company's planning programmes in any way.

Episode value

One definition of relationships in RM is as 'the sum of meaning-filled episodes which relational partners co-produce' (Buttle, 1997, p. 148). Not all of these episodes have the same importance nor carry the same weight (Storbacka *et al.*, 1994, p. 30). Some are routine and others critical. Customer satisfaction can be increased, it is suggested, if episode value is improved by increasing the benefit and/or reducing the sacrifice for the buyer (Selnes, 1998, p. 305).

According to Storbacka *et al.* (1994, p. 30), the definition of a 'critical episode' is an episode that is of 'great importance to a relationship and upon which the continuation of a relationship is dependent'. Not keeping up the standard expected by the customer in an exchange may be seen to have a negative effect that may trigger a critical episode. Critical episodes are customer specific, and even a 'routine episode' can become critical if the *perceived* level of service is not met. Thus episodes indicative of high quality in one relationship may be deemed indicative of poor quality in another (Buttle, 1997, p. 153). These 'critical episodes' within the relationship are seen to have a considerable effect on customer satisfaction. The importance of episode value will be returned to in Chapter 6.

The customer satisfaction process

Jones and Sasser (1995, p. 93) suggest that at the heart of any successful strategy to 'manage' customer satisfaction is the ability to 'listen to the customer'. They suggest five categories of approach to this process:

- Customer satisfaction indices
- Feedback
- Market research
- Front-line personnel
- Strategic activities.

Customer satisfaction indices

Customer satisfaction indices are among the most popular methods of tracking or measuring customer satisfaction. Indeed, businesses of all sorts now divert considerable energies into tracking customer satisfaction in this way (Mittal and Lassar, 1998, p. 178). These studies are, however, frequently criticised for reporting overly positive results (Nowak and Washburn, 1998, p. 443). In addition, these measures are highly subjective. Fournier *et al.* (1998, p. 47) ask us to:

> consider for a moment how we measure . . . customer satisfaction. Is it simply a question of expectations versus actual performance on a given attribute of a product or service? Is it a static, context-free rating on a five-point scale?

The answer is, most probably, no. Jones and Sasser (1995, p. 91) also point out that, as important as they believe 'satisfaction surveys' to be, for a business to rely on them solely would be fatal.

Mittal and Lassar (1998, p. 178) note that many companies measure satisfaction in the hope that, if the scores are high, the customer will stay with them. They warn, however, that even a satisfied customer will leave for the lure of a competitor's offer. Their research (p. 183) suggested that, even at a satisfaction rating of five (on a five-point scale) nearly 20% of healthcare customers and over 30% of car repair customers are 'willing to switch' to another supplier. At a score of four (a level most companies would be quite happy with) the potential desertion figures reached 32.4% and 78.6% respectively. Reichheld (1993, p. 71) too recognises that customer satisfaction is not a surrogate for retention. According to his research, between 65% and 85% of customers who defected claimed they were satisfied or very satisfied before leaving. Whatever else satisfaction indices tell us, they do not fully predict loyalty.

Feedback

Feedback in this context includes comments, complaints and questions. It may be among the most effective means of establishing what the customer regards as a satisfactory level of performance and what 'dissatisfiers' exist within the operation as it is based on actual performance rather than contrived situations (e.g. market research).

Market research

In addition to research among customers and non-customers into potential 'satisfiers', 'dissatisfiers' and 'customer expectations', market research can be used at customer entrance (to establish those drivers which brought the customer to the company) and exit (to establish those factors which caused the customer to go elsewhere). Again, more valuable information may be achieved in the latter rather than the former as it is based on actual behaviour rather than perception.

Front-line personnel

Direct contact with staff can provide a good means of listening to the customer. As it is frequently suggested that many customers, rather than formally complain to a company, will simply break the relationship, front-line staff provide an opportunity for a less formal sounding board for complaints which might otherwise not be heard. The crucial factor here is how this information is fed back into the decision-making process.

Strategic activities

Actively involving the customer in company decision making may be a means of pre-empting potential 'dissatisfiers' and establishing potential 'satisfiers'. Jones and Sasser use the example of Southwestern Airlines, who invited frequent flyers to the first round of interviews with prospective flight attendants.

(Based on Jones and Sasser, 1995, p. 93)

Benefits of customer satisfaction

Much of the marketing literature takes as a 'given' the notion that customer satisfaction is a proxy for repatronising behaviour (Hutcheson and Moutinho, 1998, p. 706). As a result, many companies adopt strategies to improve customer satisfaction with the perceived objectives of strengthening bonds and achieving customer loyalty (Ravald and Grönroos, 1996, p. 19).

Great claims are made regarding higher customer satisfaction levels. It is suggested that customer satisfaction increases customer loyalty, reduces price elasticity, insulates market share from competitors, lowers transaction costs, reduces failure rates and the costs of attracting new customers, and improves the firm's reputation in the marketplace (Sheth and Sisodia, 1999, p. 80). Jones and Sasser (1995, p. 89) suggest that, except in a few rare instances, customer satisfaction is the key to securing customer loyalty and to generating superior long-term financial performance.

In simple terms, therefore, the generally accepted model suggested is as shown in Figure 5.2.

Potential flaws

As with many highly subjective concepts, these 'claims' should be treated as generalisations and even then with an element of scepticism. The simple model that justifies these arguments may be inherently flawed, particularly in industries where relationships are of more marginal importance. Although it may have an implicit logic, it is based on an oversimplification that often creates practical problems (Storbacka *et al.*, 1994, p. 23).

As Mittal and Lasson (1998, p. 178) have noted, satisfaction does always imply loyalty. They suggest two compelling reasons why not:

■ A dissatisfied customer may continue his or her patronage.
■ A satisfied customer may be willing (indeed eager) to patronise alternative suppliers in the hope of a 'more satisfying' result.

Dick and Basu (1994, p. 101) indicate graphically the first anomaly by cross-classifying the concepts of 'relative attitude' (strong or weak) to an organisation and 'repeat patronage' (high or low) as shown in Figure 5.3.

Customers who have a strong relative attitude and who are seen to frequently repatronise the supplier may be seen as loyal (at least for the time being). Those with a weak attitude (patently dissatisfied), however, may be 'spuriously loyal' as their reasons for staying with the supplier may be linked to having no other option

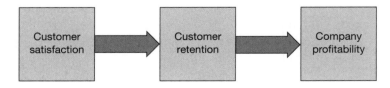

Figure 5.2 Simple 'return on relationship' model

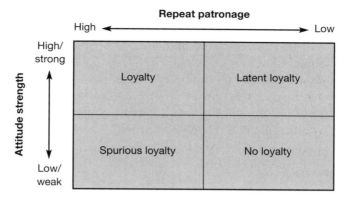

Figure 5.3 Relative attitude-behaviour relationship
(*Source*: Adapted from Dick and Basu, 1994)

but to continue the relationship. Dick and Basu also point out that 'latent' loyalists exist who hold a positive attitude but who may be prevented from patronising the supplier for reasons other than potential satisfaction (e.g. location). Customer satisfaction has been used as a proxy measure of loyalty because it has been assumed that satisfaction affects buying intentions in a positive way. Research suggests, again, that this is far too simplistic.

As regards loyal customers seeking other suppliers, this may be explained by the fact that customers always have the potential, whatever the current situation, to be *more* satisfied elsewhere. This may be particularly evident in those situations where the 'switching barriers' are low and where the benefits of developing a close relationship with a supplier are not perceived as important by the customer.

The view that customer satisfaction is the key to securing customer loyalty is, therefore, far from a fully robust concept. Satisfaction does not always result in retention and it is equally apparent that dissatisfaction does not necessarily result in defection (Buttle, 1997, p. 145; O'Malley, 1998, p. 48). Indeed, the gap that appears to exist between satisfaction and loyalty calls into question the assertions managers often make about the direct association between them (Mittal and Lassar, 1998, p. 178) (see Chapter 2).

Traditional customer satisfaction theory assumes that the customer has expectations and comparison standards (Strandvik and Storbacka, 1996, p. 73) and that these are applied on every occasion. It also presumes objectivity. This assumption of rationality is perceived to be a problem, not just in this particular scenario but generally in marketing theory, which emphasises positive decision making as being at the centre of consumer behaviour (East, 1997a, p. 41) when real-life observation suggests otherwise.

Inherent satisfaction may be the basis of one form of loyalty, particularly where the customer has exerted some effort in establishing the 'best deal' available in the marketplace. Other situational drivers (such as time and opportunity costs), however, may result in 'default loyalty' when this effort is not required and satisfaction, therefore, plays little or no part. Research by East (1997b, p. 7), for example, notes that convenience of location may be a stronger motivator in FMCG retailing than supermarket loyalty schemes. Mintel's (1996) research came to similar conclusions.

In FMCG retailing in particular, strategies designed to encourage simple repeat behaviour or to minimise disruption of consumer inertia (see the following section) may be considerably more beneficial than costly, interactive, relational strategies. In industries with lower or more complex comparability, a different need exists. Continual reassurance and frequent comparison may be required to ensure that customers remain relatively satisfied.

Inertia

One further element in the 'customer satisfaction' debate that is frequently underrated is the part played by 'inertia'. Customer satisfaction is regarded, generally, as a positive, proactive force that drives behaviour patterns. Satisfaction is not, however, always the result of positive input but may be simply the result of things not going wrong (Johnson and Mathews, 1997, p. 536). In other situations the level of 'satisfaction'[1] may be due to a lack of motivation and/or the ability of a customer to evaluate the level of service (Bloemer and de Ruyter, 1998, p. 501). In the former case this may be described not as satisfaction but as inertia. Rather than 'driving' a customer to repatronise a supplier, this non-response to other external attractions suggests habitual behaviour.

Inertia-type behaviour might be defined as behaviour that would occur anyway, assuming no external stimuli. This variety of satisfaction is passive and simply reflects the willingness of customers to stay with a supplier until they perceive (if ever) that something better is available in the market or other factors (e.g. customer moves away) cause a change. Stability in markets occur because habits may rarely change (East, 1997a, p. 40). It may be hypothesised, therefore, that in many situations it is not positive 'customer satisfaction' driving consumers to act but lack of stimulation to act otherwise. The distinction between positive and neutral satisfaction (or inertia) is important as, in certain industries, it again challenges the idea that customer satisfaction leads to long-lasting relationships (Storbacka et al., 1994, p. 28)

It is quite probable (although not a universal truth) that consumer inertia or unwillingness to change from the present behaviour may be the norm in many industries. The 'comfort zone' described is the difference between an adequate and desired level of service (Storbacka et al., 1994, p. 26), which becomes a 'zone of inertia' where customers do not act or react to increased levels of service quality. In this situation any increase in service level or quality (all other things being equal) merely helps maintain inertia or habitual behaviour rather than actually driving the competitive process (see Figure 5.4). This inertial form of routine human behaviour may help explain why aggregate responses to surveys are very weak measures (East, 1997a, p. 41). In relationship terms an analogy to marriage suggests that, whatever bond holds couples together, it is largely responsive rather than proactive,

---

[1] Bloemer and de Ruyter (1998, p. 501) call it 'latent satisfaction'.

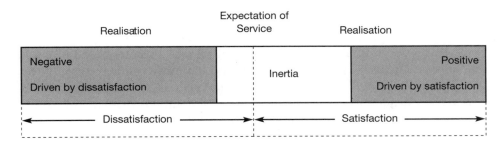

Figure 5.4 The inertia effect on expectation and realisation of service

particularly after time has elapsed. The natural tendency of relationships is toward erosion of sensitivity and attentiveness over time. Familiarity may not always breed contempt but it may well create inertia! In commercial situations it has been observed that individuals who remain 'loyal' long-term indeed show signs of this inertia (Bejou and Palmer, 1998, p. 16).

The concept of inertia in many ways runs counter to one of the main planks of the customer satisfaction paradigm, that excellent services necessarily improve profitability (e.g. Buttle, 1996, p. 9). Rather it suggests that, in certain industries, no benefit is achieved from the extra effort expended. Once resources have been allocated to the achievement of latent customer satisfaction (or more descriptively, customer inertia), up to a threshold level (and not beyond) any additional investment will not yield any return in the form of increased customer retention (Hassan, 1996, p. 9) or, ultimately, increased profitability. Indeed, if keeping up with customers' needs in a highly competitive market involves ever greater investment the potential is for ever falling, not rising, profits. This is directly contrary to another fundamental principle of RM in that its concern is to meet, or preferably exceed, customers' expectations (Buttle, 1996, p. 8).

By direct contrast, any decrease from whatever level of service the customer now expects, possibly regardless of what the market generally has to offer, may ferment switching behaviour. This view suggests that the marketing emphasis, far from being upon increasing satisfaction, should be upon retaining the *status quo*. This may be achieved not by increasing customer satisfaction but by minimising dissatisfaction as the switching costs of dissatisfaction may well outweigh the benefits of satisfaction (Hutcheson and Moutinho, 1998, p. 706).

The reason that 'inertial behaviour' seems to contradict some widely held concepts of RM may be because its application appears to coincide with more repetitive transactional exchanges at the TM end of the transactional–relational continuum' (see Chapter 4). In situations where RM is seen to be beneficial the development of customer satisfaction through differential, relational strategies may be advantageous. In repetitive, more transactional relationships, strategies that promote repetitive behaviour may be more profitable.

Satisfaction reality

The simple model (customer satisfaction→customer retention→profitability) is too simplistic and possibly misleading for many businesses. While intuitively a useful goal an increased level of satisfaction could prove counterproductive in certain industries as it may well increase expectation and, by definition, may lead to increased dissatisfaction rates (Hutcheson and Moutinho 1998, p. 718). This may simply reflect the obverse of the Buddhist principal that when you decrease your desire you increase your chances of happiness. Evidence from the US market suggests that, despite the increased focus on satisfaction and service quality among many American companies, customer satisfaction rates in that market are at an all-time low and other expressions of dissatisfaction at an all-time high (Fournier *et al.*, 1998, p. 42). Jan Lapidoth Sr, in an interview about his time at SAS (quoted by Gummesson, 1999, p. 185), describes a concept known as the 'service paradox' (Box 5.2). This suggests that less profitable customers are frequently the most satisfied while the more profitable are frequently less satisfied.

Box 5.2

The service paradox

Gummesson (1999, p. 185) introduces the notion of a 'service paradox', which suggests that the most loyal customers do not always mean the most satisfied or the most profitable. Gummesson quotes a definition of the service paradox as described to him by Jan Lapidoth Sr on his experiences at SAS. He states that 'the less profitable customers are, the more satisfied they are, while the more profitable customers are less satisfied'. Lapidoth illustrates this with the example of flights between New York and Europe. The price of fares on this route differ dramatically. Full Business Class is $3,000.00. The business traveller is highly profitable but highly demanding. Value for the business traveller is high quality, punctuality, comfort etc. The Economy Class customer contributes marginally to profits but is grateful for the low price and not so demanding. Value for the economy traveller is low prices. The likelihood is that the business traveller is less satisfied than the economy traveller despite the business traveller getting better service.

(*Source*: Based on Gummesson, 1999, p. 185)

Summary

A model was introduced at the end of Chapter 2 that suggested that there were a number of perceived 'drivers' to relational and transactional strategies. In this chapter those that had not been discussed earlier were introduced.

The existence of high risk, high salience and, consequently, high emotion in an exchange transaction appears to suggest that RM strategies would be beneficial as the customer may perceive that a close relationship is necessary in such situations. At the other end of the spectrum low risk, low salience and low emotion suggest that the customer does not perceive the benefits of staying with one or a few suppliers and is, consequently, more opportunistic.

The perceived need for trust and commitment in deep relationships provided another indicator of those situations where relational strategies may be seen as beneficial. At the transactional end of the continuum whereas there are indications that a certain level of trust is a necessary ingredient the existence of commitment is not usually observed.

The concept of closeness was also discussed. When the 'distance' between the parties is shorter, deeper relationships are likely to develop. Conversely, when the distance is greater, the relationship is functional and at arm's length. Again, observation of these characteristics in a relationship may be an indicator of whether RM strategies are likely to be beneficial.

The complexities surrounding the concept of customer satisfaction were examined and it was concluded that the widely accepted model (customer satisfaction→ customer retention→profitability) is too simplistic and may cause difficulties in certain industries. The perceived need for positive customer satisfaction in a relationship may, however, prove a reasonable indicator (or driver) to the benefits of relational strategies. At the other end of the continuum strategies which promote habitual behaviour may be more indicative of transactional marketing.

The importance of these themes is such that they will be referred to again in later chapters.

Discussion questions

1. Explain the association between risk, salience and emotion.

2. Explain the association between trust and commitment.

3. Why will close relationships be stronger than arm's length relationships?

4. Describe a situation where inertia may determine the duration of a relationship.

Case study

A question of trust

Trust is a hard-won commodity but, without it, many consumers feel anxious about buying goods over the Web. Until recently, however, UK-based websites were able to offer little in the way of independent certification of their credentials, which would give consumers the confidence to buy online. Now, however, things are changing.

The Consumers Association launched its Which Web Trader website certification scheme last summer. Since then it has signed up around 30 partner companies, of which the best known is the insurance company Direct Line. In addition, it has also recruited around another 80 companies which support the scheme as an idea but which cannot fulfil the Code of Practice because of the nature of their business.

▶

Conditions

Certification is free, but to be allowed to display the Which Web Trader logo, Web merchants must meet the CA's conditions, which ensure that if something does go wrong, the certified company will do something to put things right.

A separate certification scheme was launched a year ago in the UK by Clicksure. Companies wishing to display the Clicksure 'Quality Seal' logo must pay an initial assessment fee of between £160 and £320 depending on the size and complexity of the online operation. Thereafter, the trader pays an annual licence fee of between £600 and £1,200. So far, Clicksure has certified just six sites, but says it has another 300 or so in the pipeline. With free certification, the Which Web Trader scheme may look more attractive on paper. However, Clicksure marketing director Frank Miller questions the ability of not-for-profit schemes to adequately police the websites they certificate. 'The problem with not-for-profit certification bodies is can they actually service their clients properly?' he asks.

'For sure, they can charge little or virtually nothing for their services but, if they become popular, they just sink beneath the waves in terms of demand for their service and then the actual ability to properly maintain the credibility of the scheme goes down the pan as well. They end up with a million clients all clamouring for their service, but they've only got a certain number of people they can put on it, because the more people they put on it, the more it costs; so how do they maintain the service?

'Certification is all about trained, process-driven activity carried out on a regular basis, in other words constant monitoring. It's really tedious stuff but it has to be done professionally, systematically and on a regular basis to be of value to anyone.'

In an attempt to cut through consumer confusion – which may arise from a multitude of certification schemes, from trade associations and certificators like the Consumers Association and Clicksure – the Minister for Small Business and E-commerce, Patricia Hewitt, unveiled an accreditation system for website certification in February, in conjunction with non-profit-making organisation, TrustUK.

TrustUK is a joint venture between the Consumers Association, the Direct Marketing Association and the Alliance for Electronic Business. It hopes to persuade trade associations and operators of web certification schemes – such as Clicksure and Which Web Trader – to have them accredited by Trust. Any association applying for TrustUK accreditation must have a code of practice which applies to online activity, and accredited sites will be entitled to display the TrustUK e-hallmark.

Founder members

As founder members of TrustUK, the Consumers Association and the Direct Marketing Association have agreed to bring their schemes under the TrustUK umbrella, and according to Trust, four more organisations, including Clicksure, have stated their intention to apply for accreditation.

Organisations will pay an annual fee of between £1,000–£5,000 for accreditation, depending on the size of the organisation, the number of members and the level of membership. It will then be up to the trade association or website certification company to ensure that its members comply with Trust's criteria.

Some may question whether a trade association has the relevant skills and experience to certify websites, but as associations covering every industry under the sun look at their approach to the Web, a scheme such as TrustUK, which pulls their disparate efforts into one recognisable standard, would seem to have considerable appeal.

(*Source*: David Murphy, *Marketing Business*, July/August 2000)

Case study questions

1 What are the advantages to Internet retailers of certification schemes?

2 Which, in your opinion, are likely to prove to be successful schemes and why?

3 What other factors might assist the development of 'trust' on the Internet?

References

Barnard, N. and Ehrenberg, A.S.C. (1997) 'Advertising: strongly persuasive or nudging?', *Journal of Advertising Research*, January/February, 21–31.

Barnes, J.G. (1997) 'Exploring the importance of closeness in customer relationships', American Marketing Association Conference, Dublin, June, pp. 227–38.

Barnes, J.G. and Howlett, D.M. (1998) 'Predictors of equity in relationships between service providers and retail customers', *International Journal of Bank Marketing*, 16 (1), 5–23.

Bejou, D. and Palmer, A. (1998) 'Service failure and loyalty: an exploratory empirical study of airline customers', *Journal of Services Marketing*, 12 (1), 7–22.

Berry, L.L. and Parsuraman, A. (1991). *Marketing Services*, New York: The Free Press.

Bloemer, J. and de Ruyter, K. (1998) 'On the relationship between store image, store satisfaction and store loyalty', *European Journal of Marketing*, 32 (5/6), 499–513.

Blois, K.J. (1997) 'When is a relationship a relationship?' in Gemünden, H.G., Rittert, T. and Walter, A. (eds) *Relationships and Networks in International Markets*. Oxford: Elsevier, pp. 53–64.

Buttle, F.B. (1996) *Relationship Marketing Theory and Practice*. London: Paul Chapman.

Buttle, F.B. (1997) 'Exploring relationship quality', paper presented at the Academy of Marketing Conference, Manchester, UK.

Cumby, J.A. and Barnes, J. (1998) 'How customers are made to feel: the role of affective reactions in driving customer satisfaction', *Customer Relationship Management*, 1 (1), 54–63.

Dick, A. and Basu, K. (1994) 'Customer loyalty: towards an integrated framework', *Journal of the Academy of Marketing Science*, 22, 99–113.

East, R. (1997a) 'Inertia rules', *Marketing Business*, November.

East, R. (1997b) 'The anatomy of conquest: Tesco versus Sainsbury', working paper, Kingston Business School, UK.

Fournier, S., Dobscha, S. and Mick, D.G. (1998) 'Preventing the premature death of relationship marketing', *Harvard Business Review*, 76 (1), 42–9.

Gummesson, E. (1999) *Total Relationship Marketing: Rethinking Marketing Management from 4Ps to 30Rs*. Oxford: Butterworth Heinemann.

Hassan, M. (1996) *Customer Loyalty in the Age of Convergence*. London: Deloitte & Touche Consulting Group (www.dttus.com).

Hutcheson, G.D. and Moutinho, L. (1998) 'Measuring preferred store satisfaction using consumer choice criteria as a mediating factor', *Journal of Marketing Management*, 14, 705–20.

Johnson, C. and Mathews, B.P. (1997) 'An evaluation of consumers' interpretation of satisfaction', paper presented at the Academy of Marketing Conference, Manchester, UK, pp. 527–38.

Jones, T.O. and Sasser, W.E. (1995) 'Why satisfied customers defect', *Harvard Business Review*, November/December, 88–99.

Lewicki, R.J., McAllister, D.J. and Bies, R.J. (1998) 'Trust and distrust: new relationships and realities', *Academy of Management Review*, 23 (3), 438–58.

Mintel (1996) *Customer Loyalty in Retailing*. London: Mintel.

Mitchell, P., Reast, J. and Lynch, J. (1998) 'Exploring the foundations of trust', *Journal of Marketing Management*, 14, 159–72.

Mittal, B. and Lassar, W.M. (1998) 'Why do customers switch? The dynamics of satisfaction versus loyalty', *Journal of Services Marketing*, 12 (3), 177–94.

Morgan, R.M. and Hunt, S.D. (1994) 'The commitment–trust theory of relationship marketing', *Journal of Marketing*, 58 (3), 20–38.

Nowak, L.I. and Washburn, J.H. (1998) 'Antecedents to client satisfaction in business services', *Journal of Services Marketing*, 12 (6), 441–52.

O'Malley, L. (1998) 'Can loyalty schemes really build loyalty?', *Marketing Intelligence and Planning*, 16 (1), 47–55.

Pels, J. (1999) 'Exchange relationships in consumer markets?', *European Journal of Marketing*, 33 (1/2), 19–37.

Pressey, A.D. and Mathews, B.P. (1998) 'Relationship marketing and retailing: comfortable bedfellows?', *Customer Relationship Management*, 1 (1), 39–53.

Ravald, A. and Grönroos, C. (1996) 'The value concept and relationship marketing', *European Journal of Marketing*, 30 (2), 19–30.

Reichheld, F.F. (1993) 'Loyalty based management', *Harvard Business Review*, March/April, 64–73.

Rousseau, D.M., Sitkin, S.B., Burt, R.S. and Camerer, C. (1998) 'Not so different after all: a cross-discipline view of trust', *Academy of Management Review*, 23 (3), 393–404.

Selnes, F. (1998) 'Antecedents and consequences of trust and satisfaction in buyer–seller relationships', *European Journal of Marketing*, 32 (3/4), 305–22.

Shepherd, B.H. and Sherman, D.M. (1998) 'The grammars of trust: a model and general implications', *Academy of Management Review*, 23 (3), 422–37.

Sheth, J.N. and Sisodia, R.S. (1999) 'Revisiting marketing's lawlike generalizations', *Journal of the Academy of Marketing Sciences*, 17 (1), 71–87.

Sitkin, S.B. and Roth, N.L. (1993) 'Explaining the limited effect of legalistic remedies for trust/distrust', *Organisational Science*, 4, 367–92.

Storbacka, K., Strandvik, T. and Grönroos, C. (1994) 'Managing customer relations for profit: the dynamics of relationship quality', *International Journal of Service Industry Management*, 5, 21–38.

Strandvik, T. and Storbacka, K. (1996) 'Managing relationship quality', in Edvardsson, B., Brown, S.W., Johnston, R. and Scheuing, E.E. (eds) *Advancing Service Quality: A Global Perspective*. New York, ISQA, pp. 67–76.

Tynan, C. (1997) 'A review of the marriage analogy in relationship marketing', *Journal of Marketing Management*, 13 (7), 695–704.

Part II

The core firm and its relationships

As has been previously noted, a feature of 'older' definitions of relationship marketing was a concentration on the 'traditional' supplier–customer relationship. Later contributions to the RM debate were seen to widen the scope.

Although there are numerous models and no single definition surrounding these ideas, there does appear to be a growing consensus that, in addition to a customer focus, a company should be considering a range of partnerships with suppliers, internal customers, institutions and intermediaries (Clarkson *et al.*, 1997, p. 173). These 'network' or extended relationship theories, ideas and concepts have been advanced by a number of eminent marketing writers, including Christopher *et al.* (1991; 1994), Kotler (1992), Millman (1993), Hunt and Morgan (1994), Doyle (1995), Peck (1996), Buttle (1996) and Gummesson (1996). These writers adopted a view of marketing that continued to acknowledge the importance of managing customer relationships, but recognised that this is only one part of the relationship marketing equation.

As we will see in the following chapters, the focal relationship is between the buyer and the supplier. RM is first and foremost geared towards the management of this relationship. However, in order to facilitate this, other 'stakeholders' in the process have to be involved (Grönroos, 2000, p. 4). The common theme is that firms should compete through the development of relatively long-term relationships with all their stakeholders (Hunt 1997, p. 431; Reichheld, 1996, p. 3). Whether the relational model is represented as 'six markets' (Christopher *et al.*, 1991, p. 13; 1994, p. 21), 'ten players' (Kotler, 1992), 'four partnerships' (Buttle, 1996, p. 3), 'four partnerships and ten relationships' (Hunt and Morgan, 1994, p. 21), or '30Rs' (Gummesson, 1996; 1999, pp. 20–22), the common ground between these theories appears to be the concept of 'the core firm and its partnerships' (Doyle, 1995, p. 34). The move to RM is, therefore, seen as a move from a dyadic relationship to a multifaceted series of interrelationships not necessarily dominated exclusively by the supplier–customer interaction.

Different authors give varying prominence to each stakeholder group, and Gummesson (1999, p. 20–22) in particular goes into considerable detail regarding the possible relationships a company and its stakeholders can be involved within. For relative simplicity, however, these various relationships may be broken down into four principal groupings. These are customer partnerships, internal partnerships, supplier partnerships and external partnerships. In the chapters that follow each of these perspectives is addressed separately. (See the Box below)

This view of marketing represents a change of emphasis over and above traditional marketing. No longer is marketing simply about exchange (i.e. the transfer of goods and money in the marketplace). It also entails the creation and maintenance of dialogue between suppliers, sellers, customers, clients and others such that *all parties* are satisfied with the purchasing process (Uncles, 1994, p. 335).

In Part II we will look at each of the four principal groupings in turn. The Figure on page 113 shows how the relationships types suggested by the different authors are related to each other.

Box | **Core relationships**

	Customer partnerships	Supplier partnerships	Internal partnerships	External partnerships
Doyle (1995) The core firm and its partnerships	**Customer partnerships**	**Supplier partnerships**	**Internal partnerships** Employees Functional departments Other SBUs	**External partnerships** Competitors Governments External partners
Hunt and Morgan (1994) Four partnerships and ten relationships	**Buyer partnerships** Intermediate Final consumer	**Supplier partnerships** Goods suppliers Service suppliers	**Internal partnerships** Business units Employees Functional department	**Lateral partnerships** Competitors Non-profit organisations Government
Christopher et al. (1991; 1994) Six markets	**Customer markets**	**Supplier markets**	**Internal market** **Employee market**	**Referral market** **Influence market**
Gummesson (1996; 1999) 30Rs	**Classic market relationships** Classic dyad (customer/supplier) Classic triad (above + competitor) Classic network (distribution channels) **Special market relationships** Full-time/part-time marketers The service encounter Many-headed customer/supplier Customer's customer relationship Close versus distant relationship Dissatisfied customer relationship The monopoly relationship The customer as a member The electronic relationship Parasocial relationship (symbol etc.) The non-commercial relationship The green relationship The law-based relationship The criminal network		**Meta relationships** Profit centres Internal customer Quality (e.g. design manufacturing) Employee Matrix relationships Marketing services Owner/financiers	**Mega relationships** Personal/social Mega (e.g. government) Alliances Knowledge relationship Mega alliances (e.g. EU, NAFTA) Mass media

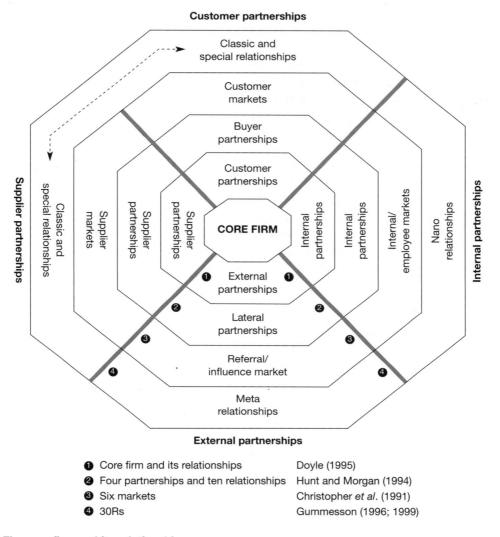

Customer partnerships

Figure: The core firm and its relationships

- ❶ Core firm and its relationships — Doyle (1995)
- ❷ Four partnerships and ten relationships — Hunt and Morgan (1994)
- ❸ Six markets — Christopher *et al.* (1991)
- ❹ 30Rs — Gummesson (1996; 1999)

References

Buttle, F.B. (1996) *Relationship Marketing Theory and Practice*. London: Paul Chapman.

Christopher, M., Payne, A. and Ballantyne, D. (1991) *Relationship Marketing*. London: Butterworth Heinemann.

Christopher, M., Payne, A. and Ballantyne, D. (1994) *Relationship Marketing*. Oxford: Butterworth Heinemann.

Clarkson, R.M., Clarke-Hill, C. and Robinson, T. (1997) 'Towards a general framework for relationship marketing; a literature review', paper presented at the Academy of Marketing Conference, Manchester, UK.

Doyle, P. (1995) 'Marketing in the new millennium', *European Journal of Marketing*, 29 (12), 23–41.

Grönroos, C. (2000) 'The relationship marketing process: interaction, communication, dialogue, value', *2nd WWW Conference on Relationship Marketing*, 15 November 1999–15 February 2000, paper 2 (www.mcb.co.uk/services/conferen/nov99/rm).

Gummesson, E. (1996) *Relationship Marketing: From 4Ps to 30Rs*. Malmö: Liber-Hermods.

Gummesson, E. (1999) *Total Relationship Marketing: Rethinking Marketing Management from 4Ps to 30Rs*. Oxford: Butterworth Heinemann.

Hunt, H.K. (1997) 'CS/D – overview and future research direction', in Hunt, H.K. (ed.) *Conceptualisation and Measurement of Customer Satisfaction and Dissatisfaction*. Cambridge, MA: Marketing Science Institute.

Hunt, S.D. and Morgan, R.M. (1994) 'Relationship marketing in the era of network competition', *Journal of Marketing Management*, 5 (5), 18–28.

Kotler, P. (1992) 'Total marketing' in *Business Week*, Advance Executive Brief no. 2.

Millman, A.F. (1993) 'The emerging concept of relationship marketing', in Proceedings of the 9th Annual IMP Conference, Bath, 23–25 September.

Peck, H. (1996) 'Towards a framework for relationship marketing: the six markets model revisited and revised', *Marketing Education Group (MEG) Conference*, University of Strathclyde, UK.

Reichheld, F.F. (1996) *The Loyalty Effect: The Hidden Force Behind Growth, Profits and Lasting Value*. Boston, MA: Harvard Business School Press.

Uncles, M. (1994) 'Do you or your customer need a loyalty scheme?', *Journal of Targeting, Measurement and Analysis*, 2 (4), 335–50.

6 Customer partnerships

Key issues

➤ Customer focus
➤ Service industries
➤ Customer service
➤ Episodes and service chains
➤ Dissolution, exit and withdrawal
➤ Profit chains

Introduction

As was discussed in the opening chapter, one of the most significant perceived differences between relationship marketing and traditional marketing is that RM is seen to extend marketing's focus beyond the single dyadic relationship of buyer and seller (Gummesson, 1999, p. 1) and to embrace other organisational relationships. Despite this overall change in emphasis, the customer–supplier relationship is still a core issue in RM and indeed across the whole marketing discipline (Möller and Halinen, 2000, p. 31). Christopher *et al.* (1991, p. 21), while acknowledging the benefits of a 'broadened view of marketing', are in no doubt that 'customer markets' should remain the primary focus and, as such, they place them firmly at the centre of their six-markets model of relationship marketing (Figure 6.1).

Customer focus

Another supposed difference between traditional marketing and RM is in the way customers are perceived and valued. Traditional marketing stands accused of treating customers as pawns in a competitive game. By its very nature, this 'market focused' approach is seen to concentrate on increasing market share and emphasising short-term profitability. The priorities of traditional marketers are seen as the 'capture' of anonymous customers, either before competitors or away from them, and manipulating these captives for short-term gain. Target segments were as personal as it got in this marketplace battlefield.

Figure 6.1 The six-markets model
(*Source*: Adapted from Christopher *et al.*, 1991, p. 21)

RM, in contrast, focuses not on what you can do *to* your customer but on what you can do *for* your customer (Worthington and Horne, 1998, p. 39) and what you can do *with* your customer, to ensure customer satisfaction.[1] The aim is to treat your customers as valued partners, to establish their needs and develop their loyalty through quality service. As the company statement quoted in Box 6.1 elegantly puts it, 'obsession with the customer should be the most vital factor in business success'.

Box 6.1

Customer focus

The following is a statement from the Burnley Building Society[2]:

'Obsession with the customer should be the most vital factor in business success. The main priority of any business must be to win and keep customers, as failure to do so results in no profits, no growth, no jobs, therefore, no business.'

This very 'modern' statement of the importance of the customer was issued by the Burnley Building Society in 1850 yet it appears as relevant today as it did a century and a half ago.

Customer focus motivation

This change of emphasis is not, as has been discussed, wholly altruistic. Company prosperity is still the long-term aim. What is different is that this is perceived, in particular circumstances, to be better achieved by focusing on the individual needs

---

[1] The distinction acknowledges the existence of one-sided relationships as discussed in Chapter 2.
[2] I am indebted to Rebecca Burrell for drawing this statement to my attention.

of the customer rather than the agglomerated marketplace. Neither is this change in attitude wholly associated with better and/or more advanced strategy development *per se*. The development of relational strategies may be seen, in part, as a recognition that the balance of power has shifted from producer to consumer and that many of the strategies of the past are no longer appropriate. The less naïve and more worldly wise buyers of today are more than ever aware that it pays to play the field (Mitchell, 1997, p. 37). In such a marketplace the supplier can no longer count on unquestioning brand loyalty and must offer something more in return for patronage than promotional bribery if sustainable advantage is to be achieved and maintained.

In today's competitive markets there are more and more undifferentiated or little differentiated products and services. If the core product or service offering leaves little scope for competitive advantage then competitive advantage must be found elsewhere. To this end the development of a 'relationship' with your customer *may* be the most effective way of building something unique and sustainable that your competitor will find difficult to replicate (Buttle, 1996, p. 1).

The realisation that marketing's focus on traditional models was insufficient in the modern marketplace was highlighted (if not driven) by the dramatic changes in national economies. The marketing priority was shifting away from products to services with the growing domination of service economies in major western markets. The realisation of the importance of the customer-focused approach in service marketing, over and above the market focus, was a major factor in further promoting the relationship marketing concept.

The importance of the reconceptualisation of both products and services in the development of RM cannot be overstated. For this reason a discussion of the nature of services and the importance of customer interaction may, at this stage, be appropriate.

Services

The word 'service' is a frequent feature in the modern marketing vocabulary and never more so than when discussing relationship marketing in general and the supplier–customer partnership in particular. The extensive use of the word and its rapid evolution and development demonstrate the importance of this sometimes elusive concept (Johns, 1999, p. 958, notes that the summer 1997 *ABI Inform* lists 279,673 articles containing the word service). Service, in marketing terms, is regarded principally in two ways. The term is used firstly to describe those businesses where the greater part of the company's central offering is intangible. These 'service industries' are generally seen to have a number of characteristics that appear to differentiate them from physical goods industries. (See Palmer 1998, p. 11, for a full discussion of the distinguishing features of service.) In addition to intangibility, these are inseparability, variability, perishability and non-ownership. These characteristics are outlined in Box 6.2.

Although these characteristics are the defining aspects of services the extent to which these features can actually be used to distinguish between goods and services has latterly been questioned by a number of writers (Palmer, 1998, p. 16) as will be discussed later in this chapter.

Box 6.2

Special characteristics of services

Intangibility: A 'pure' service cannot be assessed in the physical sense. It is an abstraction that cannot be directly examined before purchase. The intangible process characteristics that define services include such factors as reliability, personal care, attentiveness, friendliness etc. and these can only be verified once a service has been purchased and 'consumed'. Few services are wholly intangible, however, and many include a tangible element (e.g. a concert programme). Intangibility has a number of implications for the consumer, including increased uncertainty and potential risk.

Inseparability: Products may be produced in one location and sold in another. The production and consumption are, therefore, said to be separable. This is not the case for services, which are produced and consumed at one time and place. This inseparability occurs whether the producer is human (e.g. a doctor) or machine (e.g. an ATM machine). With services, marketing becomes a means of facilitating complex producer–consumer interactions, rather than being merely an exchange medium.

Variability: There are two dimensions to variability. These are the amount the production varies from the norm and the extent it needs to be varied to suit the individual customer. As the customer is usually involved in the production process of a service at the same time as they consume it, it can be difficult to carry out monitoring and control of the production to ensure consistent standards. This is exaggerated in situations where personnel are providing services on a one-to-one basis (e.g. hairdressers) where they must adapt the 'service production' to fulfil an individual customer's needs.

Perishability: Services cannot be stored. For example if a hotel fails to fill all of its rooms on a particular night, these cannot be 'carried over' to subsequent nights.

Non-ownership: The inability to 'own' a service relates to the characteristics of intangibility and perishability. Where a service is performed no ownership is transferred from the buyer to the seller. The buyer is merely buying the right to a service process (e.g. a solicitor's time).

(*Source*: Adapted from Palmer, 1998, p. 11)

The second most frequent use of the word 'service' is in connection with the phrase 'customer service'. The definition of customer service is difficult to qualify accurately but the term is generally used to describe those features of the offering or exchange that extend beyond the 'core' product or service. The phrase is further seen to imply added value (or, over time, relational benefits[3]) derived as a result of contact between buyers and sellers. Although the two concepts of 'service industries' and 'customer service' are related they are best approached, from an analytical perspective, separately.

---

[3] Gwinner *et al.* (1998, p. 102) define 'relational benefits' as 'those benefits [that a] customer receives from long-term relationships above and beyond the core service performance'.

Service industries

The intangible nature of service industries has always posed a problem for traditional marketers. Marketing research and teaching has for decades been dominated (and to an extent still is) by 'corporate product marketing'. The realisation that traditional marketing models were proving imprecise when applied to services drove some marketers to consider new approaches and concepts. Indeed, service marketers (together with their industrial marketing colleagues) can be said to have driven marketing research into new areas of research and been largely responsible for the development of the 'modern' RM approach. As Grönroos (1995, p. 252) notes:

> It is quite natural that the seeds of modern relationship marketing first started to grow in service marketing research. In fact, service marketing started to develop as a discipline because the marketing mix management paradigm and some of its key models fitted service firms' customer relations badly

Service firms have in theory always been 'relationship orientated' as the very nature of service businesses is relationship based (Grönroos, 1995, p. 252). The reasons behind this are many-fold. In service industries a process or performance takes place where the customer is seen to be heavily involved in the creation and delivery (see Box 6.2, inseparability). As most service providers compete with companies very similar to themselves (resulting in so-called 'parity offerings') they frequently counter the effect of direct competition by building relationships with their customers. In services marketing there is always some form of direct contact (although not necessarily physical) between the customer and the service firm. This 'service encounter' is so important a part of service delivery that it is frequently called the 'moment of truth' (Johns, 1999, p. 965). This phrase underlines the crucial role each service encounter plays in customer evaluation of a service (Odekerken-Schröder et al., 2000, p. 107). This customer involvement in service industries can vary considerably. It may sometimes be for a long time, sometimes for a short time, sometimes on a regular basis and sometimes as a one-off encounter (Grönroos, 1995, p. 252) but a successful outcome is invariably dependent on the result of this social contact between buyer and seller. Czepiel (1990, p. 13) sums up the importance of the social nature of services when he comments:

> Service encounters are interesting phenomena with short-run and long-run effects. In the short-run they are the social occasion of economic exchange in which society allows strangers to interact . . . . In the long-run encounters provide the social occasions in which buyer and seller can negotiate and nurture the transformation of their accumulated encounters into an exchange relationship. The concept of a marketplace-relationship, the mutual recognition of some special status between the exchange partners, is especially interesting in services marketing.

Modern service marketers, therefore, view marketing as an interactive process within a social context where relationship building and management are the vital cornerstones (Grönroos, 1994, p. 5). Indeed, service encounters can be regarded, first and foremost, as social encounters (McCallum and Harrison, 1985, p. 35) the variety of which goes a long way to explaining the problem of variability (see Box 6.2). It is this social contact that makes it feasible to envisage creating a relationship with the customer, if both (or perhaps either; see Chapter 2) parties are interested in such an association (Grönroos, 1995, p. 252).

Goods versus services

Although RM was (and is) principally seen as a development of, and of particular benefit to, services marketing, its application in the field of consumer goods appears to be growing. In many ways this reflects a recognition by marketers that the boundaries between goods and services (that is, the distinctions between the tangible and the intangible dimensions of the offer) are becoming blurred (Pels, 1999, p. 2). Although services are frequently described as 'intangible' and their central offering as an 'activity' rather than a tangible object, much 'service output' has a tangible component (Johns, 1999, p. 959). Examples of the importance of this tangible component in service industries can be seen when it is recognised that a restaurant's reputation is, in part, built on the provision of food and drink and a retailer's classification based on the type of physical goods supplied.

Products, meanwhile, are more than ever recognised as having intangible attributes. Indeed, many manufactured products are marketed on the basis of these attributes rather than the hard components or features of the offering (e.g. an automobile's prestige status or a beer's macho image). It is indeed a paradox of marketing that these product manufacturers look to promote the intangible element of their offering while service providers frequently look to create tangible features such as physical evidence (e.g. a bank's impressive façade) to establish their credibility.

The traditional view of marketing saw services as the occasion where the producer's production process and the consumer's consuming process intersected (Strandvik and Storbacka 1996, p. 68). In other words, services augmented the product but the product remained the core of the exchange. The RM perspective goes beyond product transactions. Goods and services become part of a holistic, continuously developing service offering (Grönroos, 1999).

Thus the line between products and services and the dominance of the core product is fast fading. Whereas marketers used to talk about the consumption of goods and services they now talk about product experiences (Slater, 1997, pp. 193–4). What once appeared to be a rigid polarity has now become a hybrid (McKenna, 1991, p. 15). Successful marketing is now seen to depend on the capability of firms to add value through different types of service, to the core solution offered to customers (Storbacka et al., 1994, p. 22).

Such is the overlap being witnessed that Strandvik and Storbacka (1996, p. 68) suggest that the goods/services distinction should be removed altogether and that all companies should regard themselves as service companies. In their 'service management' conception physical products (goods) are seen as 'frozen services' where the real quality or benefit of the purchase is not revealed until it is actually used (consumed) by the buyer. Grönroos (1996, p. 11) too notes that successfully executed RM demands that the firm defines its business as a service business and understands how to create and manage a total service offering.

Firms are having to alter their structures to accommodate this sea-change. Some are even re-inventing their businesses. General Motors now makes more profit from lending its customers money than it does from manufacturing cars (McKenna, 1991, p. 15). British Gas has entered the financial services market with its 'Goldfish' credit card, as have Tesco and Marks & Spencer. Unilever, too, sees a more profitable future in domestic cleaning services[4] than in producing the cleaners themselves (see the Case study at the end of this chapter). Movement away from core product towards a total service offering is apparent. When such changes are evident then this re-invention can be seen to be taking place.

Customer service

Customer service is regarded, in the RM literature, as a separate though related concept to service marketing. Whereas service marketing is seen as embracing all aspects relating to services industries, customer service is seen as wider in application (in that it relates to both product and service suppliers) but narrower in focus, being directly and intimately connected to the customer satisfaction process.

Although definitions of customer service vary, what they all have in common is that they are concerned with relationships at the buyer–seller interface (Clark, 2000, p. 213). Customer service is associated with the building of bonds to ensure long-term relationships of mutual advantage to both parties (Christopher et al., 1991, p. 5). The provision of high levels of customer service involves understanding what (and how) a customer buys and determining how additional value can be added to differentiate it from competing offers (Clark 2000, p. 212). According to Buttle (1996, p. 9) relationship marketers must believe that excellent customer service produces improved profitability. The quality of this service, leads (it is suggested) to customer satisfaction that leads in turn to relationship strength and longevity and (ultimately) results in relationship profitability (Storbacka et al., 1994, p. 23). As we have previously discussed (see Chapter 5), this is rather a simplistic model that is unlikely to stand up to close scrutiny across a wide range of industries. It may, however, be used as a starting point in establishing why customer service is regarded, by relationship marketers, as a crucial element in the marketing process and why so much time and money is being spent by practitioners on measuring customer service levels (see Chapter 5).

Customer service and RM

From the earliest days of relationship marketing research, customer service (created at the supplier–customer interface) has been regarded as a core component in the RM process. As Möller and Halinen (2000, p. 33) note, by the late 1970s RM researchers were arguing that a consumer's quality experiences and subsequent satisfaction with the service were primarily an outcome of an interactive relationship between the personnel and the consumer. Christopher et al. (1991, p. 4), more broadly, saw

---

[4] Unilver launched its 'MyHome' cleaning division in the first half of 2000.

relationship marketing as the unifying concept that brought the individual concepts of customer service, quality and marketing together. It was their judgement that one of the biggest challenges to an organisation was to bring these three critical areas into closer alignment (see Figure 6.2)

Christopher *et al.* (1991, p. 4) suggested that customer service, quality and marketing work in harmony, with:

■ Customer service levels being determined by research-based measurement of customer needs and competitor performance, and in recognition of the needs of different market segments.

■ Quality being determined from the perspective of the customer based on regular research and monitoring.

■ The total quality concept influencing the *process* elements (e.g. managing the 'moments of truth' in the customer encounter) associated with the marketing (or more strictly the relationship marketing) concept.

Christopher *et al.* (1991, p. vii) suggest that traditional marketing conceived these three elements as independent 'rather like spotlights shining on a stage and beaming light, often of different intensity at different points on a stage'. The task facing the organisation, they suggest, is to bring about an alignment of the three 'beams' so that the impact upon the customer is more effective. Their conviction was that the point of overlap best describes what RM is all about.

Customer service, therefore, can be seen as playing an important role in the realisation of RM strategies. Its influence at the macro level is complemented by its importance at the micro level of individual relationships and interactions. At this end of the scale customer service may be seen as being concerned with the building of relationships (Clark 2000, p. 213) through the management of an ongoing sequence of episodes. These episodes, it is suggested, require analysis on an episode

Figure 6.2 Relationship marketing orientation
(*Source*: Adapted from Christopher *et al.*, 1991, p. 4)

by episode basis as well as at the long-term relationship level (Storbacka *et al.*, 1994, p. 22) to establish the success or otherwise of customer service strategies. The influence of customer service at the macro and micro levels emphasises that although RM takes a holistic view of relationships it should not ignore the importance of the constituent parts.

Episodes

The concept of a relationship made up of a series of episodes (some of which are 'critical episodes') was introduced briefly in Chapter 5. In terms of customer service it is perhaps the transition from a routine episode to a critical episode that may be seen as determining the adequacy (or otherwise) of customer service performance. As Storbacka *et al.* (1994, p. 30) note:

> Every episode does not carry the same importance or weight in the customer's evaluation of the relationship. Some [are] routine . . . others [are] 'critical episodes'. A 'critical episode' can be defined as an episode that is of great importance for the relationship. The continuation of the relationship is dependent (both in a negative and positive way) on 'critical episodes' . . . The definition of 'critical episode' is customer specific . . . A routine episode can become critical if, according to the customer, the adequate level of performance is not met.

Critical episodes[5] are, therefore, those specific interactions between customers and the firm's employees that are especially satisfying or especially dissatisfying (Bitner *et al.*, 1990, p. 73). According to Strandvik and Storbacka (1996, p. 73) long-term relationships can be defined as being made up of a 'string of episodes'. They emphasise that when analysing relationship benefits and when attempting to calculate relationship costs the configuration of these episodes has to be understood.

Configuration of episodes

Every relationship will have a number of different types of episodes that differ in content, frequency, duration etc. and so be configured differently. During an episode the customer experiences one or several 'interactions' during which the actual service is produced. As SAS president Jan Carlzon points out, 'SAS is created 50 million times a year, fifteen seconds at a time' (quoted in Grossman, 1998, p. 32). These interactions may be said to constitute a 'service chain' that can be analysed from both the customer's and the provider's perspective. The customer's perspective of the service chain may be called the 'customer's service path'. Problems frequently come about because managers rarely have responsibility for, or focus upon, the whole service episode. The customer, meanwhile, sees no such distinction, viewing it all as part of the complete service (Strandvik and Storbacka, 1996, p. 72). The association between interactions, episodes and the service chain/customer service path is illustrated in Figure 6.3.

---

[5] Bitner *et al.* (1990) call these 'critical incidents'.

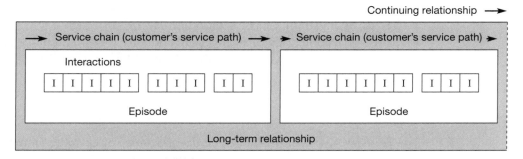

Figure 6.3 Interactions and episodes
(*Source*: Based on Strandvik and Storbacka, 1996, pp. 71–4)

A company that is service orientated has learnt the importance of service elements of the overall transaction and customer service in the development of added value. A service orientation carries with it the need for a shift in managerial thinking from emphasising the value of transactions to developing the value in relationships (Ballantyne, 2000, pp. 3–6).

Building customer relationships

Relationships rarely develop overnight. Relationships evolve, sometimes over a great amount of time. During this period customers may be seen to move through stages of development. Dwyer *et al.* (1987, p. 15) identified five general phases through which relationships evolve with each phase representing a major transition in how parties regard one another (see Figure 6.4).

- Awareness
- Exploration
- Expansion
- Commitment
- Dissolution.

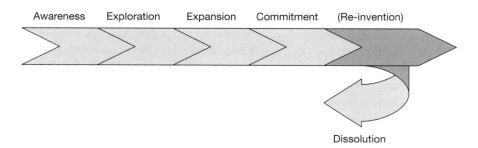

Figure 6.4 Evolution of relationships
(*Source*: Based on Dwyer *et al.*, 1987 pp. 15–20)

Awareness

Awareness refers to one party's recognition that the other party is 'a feasible exchange party'. Interaction has yet to take place but there may be considerable 'positioning' and 'posturing' to enhance each other's attractiveness.

Exploration

This refers to the 'search and trial period' in the relational exchange. It is in this phase that potential relational partners consider the 'obligations, benefits and burdens' of the relationship. Trial purchases may be made but 'the exploratory relationship is very fragile in the sense that minimal investment and interdependence make for simple termination' (Dwyer *et al.*, 1987, p. 16). The exploration phase is conceptualised in five self-explanatory subprocesses:

- Attraction
- Communication and bargaining
- Development and exercise of power
- Norm development (i.e. normalisation of the relationship)
- Expectation development.

Expansion

Expansion refers to the continual increase in benefits obtained by the exchange partners and their increasing interdependence. The critical distinction between this and the previous phase is that 'the rudiments of trust and joint satisfaction established in the exploration stage now lead to increased risk-taking' (Dwyer *et al.*, 1987, p. 18).

Commitment

Commitment refers to the implicit or explicit pledge, made by the partners, to continue the relationship. At this stage the benefits include the 'certainty' developed from mutually anticipated roles and goals, the 'efficiency' established as a result of bargaining and the 'effectiveness' that comes from trust.

Dissolution

The possibility of withdrawal or disengagement, while not being relationship development as such, is integral to the model. Dissolution is always an option and will, ultimately, always take place (see the section on customer/supplier dissolution or exit, p. 127). Reinventing relationships that have passed their sell-by date may thwart dissolution.

As discussed in previous chapters, not all relationships are as complex or as highly motivated as those suggested by the relationship formulation process outlined above. All relationships, however, have some elements that are recognisable in this model.

Customer service failure

Customer service failures test the commitment of an organisation's customers (Bejou and Palmer, 1998, p. 11). When such a situation exists, however, it may not be the problem *per se* that causes a critical episode to develop but the company's response to that problem (Stewart, 1998a, p. 9). Every customer will react differently. Each has a propensity to 'stick to' or 'switch' from the status quo and the magnitude of this propensity will depend on the profile of that individual (Hassan, 1996, p. 4) at any point in time. It is also likely that amounts of tolerance will vary from industry to industry or situation to situation. Tolerating a problem does not mean that a 'negative critical incident' (Stewart, 1998a) is forgotten. Incidents within a relationship are not wholly discrete and further negative incidents may trigger 'memories' of past incidents (Stewart, 1998a, p. 11). Customers are, therefore, seen to engage in a historical evaluation process over time. This evaluation process includes not only the problem itself but also a review of previous problems and how these were handled (Stewart, 1998a, p. 10).

Problems may not necessarily lead to long-term dissatisfaction or desertion. Satisfactory response by the supplier *may* lead to renewed levels of satisfaction, or as is sometimes claimed (e.g. Bejou and Palmer, 1998, p. 11) greater satisfaction than existed prior to the incident. Research by Andreassen (2000, p. 160) suggests that the complainer is usually focused on restoring justice or equity and that a customer's judgement is driven by perceived fairness of the outcome. As Andreassen (2000, p. 167) points out, fairness does not imply that the customer is always right. Even when the customer has received an unsatisfactory response from the supplier this may not immediately lead to 'exit' from, or dissolution of, the relationship (for a definition of 'exit', see p. 127). The negative impact may be compensated by the fact that the overall service quality is perceived to be high enough to sustain the relationship (Odekerken-Schröder *et al.*, 2000, p. 110). There may also be substantial switching costs that are powerful barriers to relationship discontinuation with a particular supplier (Stewart, 1998a, p. 10).

Relationship duration

Relationship duration, as one would intuitively suppose, is a mediating influence on the dissolution and a barrier to 'exit'. The effect of relationship duration may, however, not be as straightforward as it would seem. There would appear to be evidence (Bejou and Palmer, 1998, pp. 15–6) that in the early stages of a relationship there is a 'honeymoon period' when some teething problems or even critical episodes may be tolerated. There is no clear evidence why this aberration should exist. Perhaps it is as simple as a reluctance to admit the failings of a new supplier in whom research resources (time and effort) have been expended. Bejou and Palmer's research suggests that this level of 'toleration' drops to a low point after a short period before building up slowly again over time (see Figure 6.5).

Relationship duration may have another effect. Exiting the relationship may be seen as less complicated at an earlier stage than later when heavy investment in the relationship may result in high switching costs (Boote and Pressey, 1999, p. 8).

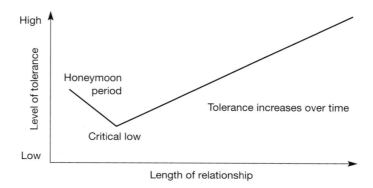

Figure 6.5 Tolerance of critical negative incidents
(*Source*: Based on Bejou and Palmer, 1998, pp. 15–16)

Customer/supplier dissolution or exit

Whereas many RM models imply continual customer development (e.g. 'the ladder of loyalty', Chapter 3) these fail to acknowledge that some relationships (ultimately *all* relationships) will terminate.[6] In the real world there is *always* the possibility of dissolution of, or 'exit' from, a relationship.

If the concept of relationship breakdown is examined more closely it may be seen to include three distinct types:

- Dissolution
- Customer exit
- Supplier withdrawal.

Dissolution

Dissolution suggests some form of agreed separation. This can be either where both parties agree that it would be in their best interests to go their separate ways or that one party (usually the more powerful of the two) forms this view and the other acquiesces. This form of agreed separation is most likely (but not exclusively; for example, in a solicitor–client relationship) to be the case in business-to-business markets where higher levels of relationship are observed to develop rather than in consumer markets where relationships are less likely to be formally acknowledged or contractually arranged. In the case of most day-to-day commercial relationships there would appear to be little driving or compelling either party to formally acknowledge dissolution.

Customer exit

Customer 'exit' has been defined as a 'term used to denote the economic phenomenon of a customer ceasing patronage of a particular supplier' (Stewart, 1998b, p. 235). In

---

[6] Dwyer *et al*.'s (1987, p. 15) five-stage model discussed previously (see Chapter 3) is an example of one that includes the possibility of separation although most RM models appear to (sometimes conveniently) ignore it.

more everyday language it is where the customer decides to end the relationship. Unlike dissolution, the supplier has little input into the final decision although they may use argument or incentives in an attempt prevent it. Exit may be most prevalent where competition is high and many alternative sources of supply exist. What is most important, however, is that the customer is aware of these alternatives. Customers who do not have (or know about) alternatives, even when generally dissatisfied, are likely to remain 'spuriously loyal' (Dick and Basu, 1994, p. 101; see p. 103). In these situations customers may use their 'voice' (i.e. complain) but effectively stay 'loyal'.

Exit is normally seen to be considered when the consumer recognises a (relative or actual) decline in performance although, as we have argued previously (see p. 103), customer dissatisfaction does not necessarily result in exit. This perceived decline does not necessarily mean that quality standards have fallen but may mean that better quality is seen or perceived to be available elsewhere. Stewart (1998b, p. 235) summarises those situations when exit can be expected as

> where competition prevails and alternatives are available to the customer, who is aware of them and alert to any absolute or relative deterioration in performance.

'Exit' and 'voice' have their positive sides (see Box 6.3). They are traditionally seen as the means by which 'wayward businesses and organisations respectively, are made aware of their lapses and can begin to right their affairs' (Stewart, 1998b, p. 236). Customer 'voice' has long been seen as a means of recovering a critical situation (so-called 'problem recovery'). Some writers would even suggest that recovery can lead to even greater levels of satisfaction (e.g. Bejou and Palmer, 1998, p. 11) although research by Levesque and McDougall (1996, p. 14) supports the contention that satisfactory problem recovery, at best, leads to a return to former satisfaction levels. Problem recovery remains a controversial concept as any satisfaction exhibited may be as a result of satisfaction with the 'bribe' (if a bribe such as a refund, discount etc. is used as settlement to a problem) rather than satisfaction with the company *per se*.

A major problem associated with customer exit is how it can be recognised by the supplier as happening or even as having happened. According to Clark (2000, p. 212) 98% of dissatisfied customers never complain about poor service but as a result 90% will not return to the supplier. Except where customers choose to voice their decision to part or where the relationship is particularly close and of high enough volume that desertion is quickly noticed, exit may go unrecognised. To complicate matters further exit may only be temporary, particularly in areas such as FMCG. Customers may choose, in the short-term, to sample from another supplier or they may be temporarily attracted away by the incentives of competitors only to return at a later date.

Supplier withdrawal

As the phrase implies, supplier withdrawal is where the separation is at the instigation of the supplier. In our earlier definition of relationship marketing it was suggested that handling of the termination of relationships should be regarded as

| Box 6.3 | ## The value of complaints |

The story of the customer who held a service engineer hostage for three hours until she could force Currys to replace her new, but defective, washing machine would be amusing if it was not so indicative of something a bit more profound when it comes to company–customer relationships.

Yes, it was illegal, but this woman's actions are an example of how customers are increasingly demanding that companies not only listen to them, but learn. The more fervently companies preach customer care, the more they will be held to account when they fail to deliver.

It's surprising that at a time when just about everything can be copied and improved upon by rivals, so many companies are failing to put into place not only a process, but a culture that encourages listening and learning. This is such a missed opportunity – what better way to collect customer intelligence that is proprietary to each and every company than its complaints?

Most companies have a system to deal with complaints. But too often they are formulaic systems, which deal with complaints efficiently but do little to contribute to learning, and thus improvement.

The problem is that there are complaints, and then there are complaints. Some are doubtless just big whinges, some are because the customer has made a silly mistake – it's a myth that the customer is always right – but others, if intelligently fed back into strategic thinking, could actually make a competitive difference.

This moves well beyond customer satisfaction surveys as a way to gauge customer feeling and hence potential loyalty. Surveys have inherent problems. First, they are too one-directional. They ask customers how they think the company is doing based on its set of criteria. Second, the answers are so aggregated that the level of 'satisfaction' becomes little more than a number on a grid. Meaningless, in other words. And, finally, they talk about satisfaction at a single point in time, which is already in the past. Complaints, on the other hand, are living, breathing focus groups showing what customers don't like, and what they expect, not only today, but also tomorrow. They could also be about to become big business.

A number of web sites are springing up in the US such as eComplaints.com and PlanetFeedback, the latter set up by a Procter & Gamble veteran. The sites provide platforms for consumers to vent their spleen about bad company experiences. Everyone can read the complaints, which are listed anonymously, while they also get redirected to the relevant companies. While eComplaints.com gives the companies a chance to respond, it twists the knife with a constant ranking of the worst offenders. And here's the really clever part: these web ventures also plan to make money through selling back to those companies what could be some very valuable market research.

So it could be that companies will have to listen whether they like it or not. Some won't, if the tale of Dixons and the non-delivery of a dishwasher is true. When the frustrated customer tried to ring the retailer's customer services director, he was told that the customer services director has a policy of not speaking to customers. Dixons vigorously denies this. Maybe it should take advantage of another web site, set up for frustrated businesses. It's called customerssuck.com. Really.

(*Source*: 'Why firms must listen and learn from complaints', Laura Mazur, *Marketing*, July 2000) part of the RM marketing process (see Chapter 1, p. 21–2). Without doubt, some (perhaps in certain industries or companies many) customers are definite 'burdens' (Håkansson and Snohota 1995, p. 522). It is indeed quite possible that a small number of highly profitable customers may subsidise a larger number of customers on which the company actually loses money (Sheth and Sisodia, 1999, p. 83). It may even be the case that increasing customer retention in some firms may actually *decrease* profitability and *destroy* value (Reichheld, 1996, p. 34). For these reasons supplier withdrawal must always remain an option.

Supplier withdrawal or termination, as we noted previously, may be managed in two ways. The first is 'customer de-selection' or 'adverse selection' (Smith, 1998, p. 4), effectively 'dumping' the customer. This may be easier said than done (particularly if the customer believes they are on to a good thing). Withdrawal of certain services and/or discriminatory pricing may be ways that this could be achieved but the danger is that dissatisfaction may spread from the immediate customer to a wider audience. The general outcry in the UK over the closure of Barclays Bank's rural branches in April 2000 was an example of this. The second option is by managing the database (see Chapter 10) in such a way as to either exclude unprofitable customers or, at the very least, minimise losses. Neither is an easy option but may be necessary to protect future prosperity.

Profit chains

Many RM authors have visualised the benefits of RM customer–supplier partnerships through the medium of 'customer relationship life cycles' or 'profit chains' (Gummesson, 1999, p. 184). Probably the simplest model was discussed in Chapter 5 and is shown again in Figure 6.6.

As has been noted, this model may be inherently flawed as it is based on an oversimplification that, in many industries, creates problems (Storbacka *et al.*, 1994, p. 23). Customer satisfaction does not always lead to retention, nor does retention always lead to profitability (see the section on relationship economics, Chapter 3, p. 51)

Gummesson (1999, p. 184) describes a broader model (Figure 6.7) that suggests that building good internal quality operations leads to happy and content employees producing quality products, which in turn results in customer satisfaction, retention and profitability. This model stems from what Gummesson calls the 'indisputable logic' that when everybody is happy the company will do well. Simple logic should, however, always be treated with a degree of scepticism. As Gummesson himself admits, the general validity of such an argument can be questioned as 'market logic' sometimes follows other patterns.

Figure 6.6 Simple return on relationship model

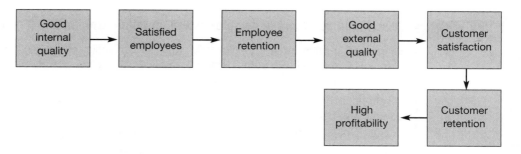

Figure 6.7 Return on relationship model
(*Source*: Gummesson, 1999, p. 184)

Storbacka *et al.* (1994, p. 23) too challenge the basic assumption that improving quality leads directly to customer satisfaction and that this necessarily drives profitability. Instead they put forward their own model (Figure 6.8) that reflects some of the many complexities associated with relational strategy development. This model implies that, although a linkage of sorts can be made between the basic components (highlighted in the model), there are so many intermediary stages that any direct association is tenuous. As the old saying goes, 'there's many a slip twix cup and lip'.

The Storbacka *et al.* model shows a much more complex route to profitability fraught with dangers for the relationship marketer. More in-depth descriptions of the arguments associated with these concepts are shown in Box 6.4.

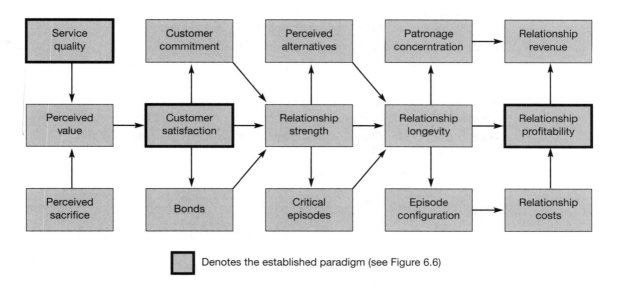

Figure 6.8 Complex return on relationship model
(*Source*: Adapted from Storbacka *et al.*, 1994, p. 23)

| Box 6.4 | **Description of factors in complex return on relationship model (Figure 6.8)** |

Perceived service quality: Customer's cognitive evaluation of the service across episodes compared with some explicit or implicit comparison standard.

Perceived sacrifice: Perceived sacrifices (e.g. price, physical effort etc.) across all service episodes in the relationship compared with some explicit or implicit comparison standard.

Perceived value: Service quality compared with perceived sacrifice.

Customer satisfaction: Customer's cognitive and affective evaluation based on the personal experiences across all service episodes within the relationship.

Commitment: The parties' intentions to act and their attitude towards interacting with each other; high relationship value will affect commitment positively (see Chapter 5).

Relationship strength: Measured both as purchase behaviour and as communication behaviour (word of mouth, complaints). Loyalty (repetitive purchase behaviour), which is based also on positive commitment by the customer, indicates a stronger relationship (see Chapter 2). The bonds between the customer and the service supplier also affect the behaviour.

Bonds: Exit barriers that tie the customer to the service provider and maintain the relationship. These are legal, economic, technological, geographical, time, knowledge, social, cultural, ideological and psychological bonds (see Chapter 3).

Critical episodes: Episodes that are of critical importance for the continuation of the relationship. Episodes can be critical based on the size of the values exchanged during the episode compared with the parties' resources and based on the experiences during the episode (see Chapter 5).

Patronage concentration: The share of a customer's cash-flow in a certain industry in which the customer chooses to concentrate on one provider.

Relationship longevity: The length of the relationship.

Episode configuration: The episode types and number of each type that occur over time in the relationship between a provider and a customer.

Relationship revenue: The total revenue generated from a customer relationship during a fiscal year.

Relationship costs: The total cost incurred from serving a customer relationship – including direct and indirect costs – during a fiscal year.

Relationship profitability: Relationship revenue minus relationship costs.

(*Source*: Based on Storbacka *et al.*, 1994, p. 25)

The lesson that appears to be emerging is that paths to sustained profitability through customer–supplier partnerships are fraught with complexity beyond the scope or control of most companies. While firms continue to strive to outperform their competitors, offering 'legendary service' can be risky (Kotler, 1992, p. 51) as again there is no guarantee that this will translate into retention.

Summary

This chapter looked at the central relationship between a customer and supplier. It discussed the focus of RM as being what you can do *for* or *with* as opposed to what you do to your customer. Service industries were reviewed initially from the perspective of their influence on RM and what effect this has on the customer–supplier strategy. Customer service was discussed extensively, both as a component central to RM and from the perspective of breaking down customer service into episodes and interactions. Relationship formulation was analysed, as was the nature of relationship dissolution and customer satisfaction. Customer service failures and the concepts surrounding dissolution and exit were examined. Finally the ideas surrounding profit chains and the 'return on relationships' were analysed and debated.

Discussion questions

1 How might customers operationalise their 'obsession with the customer'?

2 Why are the boundaries between products and services becoming blurred?

3 Imagine a frequent flyer's relationship with an airline. What situations have the potential to become critical episodes if service failure occurs?

4 What, according to your judgement, are the most important factors in the 'profit chain' illustrated in Figure 6.8?

Case study

Mr. Clean: biography of Toffael Rashid, head of marketing, myhome

On the surface, Toffael Rashid's role as head of marketing for south-west London launderette/home cleaning service, myhome, may not sound like the cutting edge of British marketing.

But myhome isn't any old cleaner. Backed by the might of Unilever, Britain's biggest FMCG marketer, Rashid's company is probably the best bankrolled local business in the UK. And potentially the most significant brand extension in Unilever's 71-year history.

Born of a two-month brainstorming session in mid-1998, and launched in March this year, myhome is Unilever's first excursion into the service sector. The company offers two services: Jif Home Clean, with its promise of a 'brilliantly clean home' and Persil Service, guaranteeing 'beautifully clean clothes'.

'This is not just a bunch of cleaning ladies using our products,' says Rashid. 'The business is about delivering a high quality branded service and that means training, specialist products, specialist equipment and building trust through marketing and performance.'

▶

Rashid is also keen to point out that myhome is not the dotcom venture it was widely reported to be. 'We launched at the same time as the dotcom rush and because we had an Internet site I think we just got caught up in the hype. The Internet is another way of accessing clients for us but a web site won't clean your clothes.'

During its launch, myhome was described by Unilever as an experiment – 'a toe in the water' (*Marketing*, 16 March). The concept is based on three simple principles: people don't want cleaning products, they want clean things; there is a new class of consumer who has more money than time; and a small venture (toe in the water) can afford to make mistakes, take time to learn and be swept under the rug without damaging reputations or bank balances.

Four months on from its launch and that latter scenario is the furthest thing from Rashid's mind. 'We are doing well,' he says. 'This is not an experiment; this is a business with more than 140 employees and more than 1000 customers.'

If Rashid is bullish about myhome's prospects, then it is obvious that others within Unilever share his enthusiasm. Myhome will receive funding toward the end of this year to finance its geographical expansion. Just how big this expansion will be and how quickly it will happen is still being decided. At the moment it remains a relatively low-key service, covering parts of south-west London near its offices on Upper Richmond Road. But it is not listed in the phone book because it is not yet ready to position itself as London-wide. Rashid won't be drawn on a timetable. 'We can either expand in bits or roll the service out rapidly. We are looking at both and haven't ruled out either.' He rules out further discussion of dates and plans, suggesting that myhome is an entrepreneurial enterprise, too fluid to be tied down by such minutiae.

Coming from a Unilever employee, that statement at first seems like a nonsense, and probably would have been five years ago. But under the firm hand of chief executive Niall FitzGerald, Unilever is beginning to show signs of change. The behemoth renowned for its risk adversity is emerging as a competitive business capable of experimentation and quick decision making.

At only 27, Rashid is one of the first generations of senior Unilever marketers whose careers have been forged almost exclusively during the FitzGerald era.

Like so many Unilever employees, he has been with the company since leaving university in 1995. But unlike many, Rashid's career has been punctuated by genuine marketing innovation. While working as brand manager in 1996, on the now defunct Radion brand, Rashid was involved in developing the highly successful scented bus ticket promotion. In 1997, having moved to work on Persil washing up liquid, he worked on the launch of the 'Le Parfum de Persil washing up liquid' ad campaign.

In mid-1998, while still working on Persil, Rashid was seconded to participate as one of four members of a two-month think-tank, code named Project Dazzler.

'We were given a brief to come up with new business ideas for Lever Brothers [Unilever's detergents business]. The brainstorming session threw out some pretty wild suggestions, but in the end we had two potential businesses. One is myhome and the other I don't think we want to talk about yet.'

As the only member of that think-tank who went on to join myhome, Rashid has been instrumental in selling the company's vision to its newer members.

'He is the inspirational member of the team,' says Laura Salasco, head of technology at myhome. 'His great gift is his ability to instil his enthusiasm for the vision in others, and because of that he represents the very idea of myhome to many in the company.'

(*Source*: Paul Whitfield, *Marketing*, 8 June 2000)

Case study questions

1 Why would a consumer goods manufacturer such as Unilever consider setting up such a business as myhome?

2 The article hints at a second 'new business idea'. What might this new business be?

References

Andreassen, T.W. (2000) 'Antecedents to satisfaction with service recovery', *European Journal of Marketing*, 34 (1/2), 156–75.

Ballantyne, D. (2000) 'Interaction, dialogue and knowledge generation: three key concepts in relationship marketing', in 2nd WWW Conference on Relationship Marketing, 15 November 1999–15 February 2000, paper 7 (www.mcb.co.uk/services/conferen/nov99/rm).

Bejou, D. and Palmer, A. (1998) 'Service failure and loyalty: an exploratory empirical study of airline customers', *Journal of Services Marketing*, 12 (1), 7–22.

Bitner, M.J., Booms, B.H. and Tetreault, M.S. (1990) 'The service encounter: diagnosing favorable and unfavorable incidents', *Journal of Marketing*, 54, 71–84.

Boote, J.D. and Pressey, A.D. (1999) 'Integrating relationship marketing and complaining behaviour: a model of conflict and complaining behaviour within buyer–seller relationships', European Academy of Marketing Conference (EMAC), competitive paper, Berlin.

Buttle, F.B. (1996) *Relationship Marketing Theory and Practice*. London: Paul Chapman.

Christopher, M., Payne, A. and Ballantyne, D. (1991) *Relationship Marketing*. London: Butterworth Heinemann.

Clark, M. (2000) 'Customer service, people and processes' in Cranfield School of Management *Marketing Management: A Relationship Marketing Perspective*. Basingstoke: Macmillan, pp. 110–24.

Czepiel, J. (1990) 'Managing relationships with customers: a differentiating philosophy of marketing', in Bowen, D., Chase, R. and Cummings, T. (eds) *Service Management Effectiveness: Balancing Strategy, Organisation and Human Resources*. San Francisco, CA: Jossey-Bass, pp. 299–323.

Dick, A. and Basu, K. (1994) 'Customer loyalty: towards an integrated framework', *Journal of the Academy of Marketing Science*, 22, 99–113.

Dwyer, F.R., Schurr, P.H. and Oh, S. (1987) 'Developing buyer–seller relationships', *Journal of Marketing*, 51, 11–27.

Grönroos, C. (1994) 'From marketing mix to relationship marketing: towards a paradigm shift in marketing' *Management Decisions*, 32 (2), 4–20.

Grönroos, C. (1995) 'Relationship marketing: the strategy continuum', *Journal of Marketing Science*, 23 (4), 252–4.

Grönroos, C. (1999) 'The relationship marketing process: interaction, communication, dialogue, value', in 2nd WWW Conference on Relationship Marketing, 15 November 1999–15 February 2000, paper 2 (www.mcb.co.uk/services/conferen/nov99/rm).

Grossman, R.P. (1998) 'Developing and managing effective customer relationships', *Journal of Product and Brand Management*, 7 (1), 27–40.

Gummesson, E. (1999) *Total Relationship Marketing; Rethinking Marketing Management from 4Ps to 30Rs*. Oxford: Butterworth Heinemann.

Gwinner, K.P., Gremler, D.D. and Bitner, M.J. (1998) 'Relational benefits in services industries: the customer's perspective', *Journal of the Academy of Marketing Science*, 6 (2), 101–4.

Håkansson, H. and Snohota, I. (1995) 'The burden of relationships or who next?', in proceedings of the 11th IMP International Conference, Manchester, UK, pp. 522–36.

Hassan, M. (1996) *Customer Loyalty in the Age of Convergence*. London: Deloitte & Touche Consulting Group (www.dttus.com).

Johns, N. (1999) 'What is this thing called service?', *European Journal of Marketing*, 33 (9/10), 958–73.

Kotler, P. (1992) 'Marketing's new paradigm: what's really happening out there?', *Planning Review*, 20, (5), 50–2.

Levesque, T. and McDougall, G.H.G. (1996) 'Determinants of cost satisfaction in retail banking', *International Journal of Bank Marketing*, 14 (7), 12–20.

McCallum, J. and Harrison, W. (1985) 'Interdependence in the service encounter', in Czepiel, J.A., Solomon, M.R. and Surprenant, C.F. (eds) *The Service Encounter: Managing Employee/Customer Interaction in Service Businesses*. Lexington, MA: Lexington Books, pp. 25–48.

McKenna, R. (1991) *Relationship Marketing*. London: Addison Wesley.

Mitchell, A. (1997) 'Evolution', *Marketing Business*, June, 37.

Möller, K. and Halinen, A. (2000) 'Relationship marketing theory: its roots and direction', *Journal of Marketing Management*, 16, 29–54.

Odekerken-Schröder, G., Van Birgelen, M., Lemmink, J., De Ruyter, K and Wetzels, M. (2000) 'Moments of sorrow and joy', *European Journal of Marketing*, 34 (1/2), 107–25.

Palmer, A.J. (1998) *Principles of Services Marketing*. London: McGraw-Hill.

Pels, J. (1999) 'Exchange relationships in consumer markets?', *European Journal of Marketing*, 33 (1/2), 19–37.

Reichheld, F.F. (1996) *The Loyalty Effect: The Hidden Force behind Growth, Profits and Lasting Value*. Boston. MA: Harvard Business School Press.

Sheth, J.N. and Sisodia, R.S. (1999) 'Revisiting marketing's lawlike generalizations', *Journal of the Academy of Marketing Sciences*, 17 (1), 71–87.

Slater, D. (1997) *Consumer Culture and Modernity*. Cambridge: Polity Press.

Smith, P.R. (1998) *Marketing Communications; An Integrated Approach*, 2nd edn. London: Kogan Page.

Stewart, K. (1998a) 'An exploration of customer exit in retail banking', *International Journal of Bank Marketing*, 16 (1), 6–14.

Stewart, K. (1998b) 'The customer exit process – a review and research agenda', Journal of Marketing Management, 14, 235–50.

Storbacka, K., Strandvik, T. and Grönroos, C. (1994) 'Managing customer relations for profit: the dynamics of relationship quality', *International Journal of Service Industry Management*, 5, 21–38.

Strandvik, T. and Storbacka, K. (1996) 'Managing relationship quality' in Edvardsson, B., Brown, S.W., Johnston, R. and Scheuing, E.E. (eds) *Advancing Service Quality: A Global Perspective*. New York: ISQA, pp. 67–76.

Worthington, S. and Horne, S. (1998) 'A new relationship marketing model and its application in the affinity credit card market', *International Journal of Bank Marketing*, 16 (1), 39–44.

7 Internal partnerships

Introduction

Relationship marketing has, as the concept developed, wholeheartedly embraced the idea of a 'broadened view of marketing' (Christopher *et al.*, p. 1991, p. 21). To this end, aspects of RM theory development have mirrored, and to a certain extent borrowed from, events taking place in other areas of business research, including trends in organisational structure (Gummesson, 1999, p. 7). Whereas traditional marketing focused wholly on the external customer, RM stressed the additional significance of the internal customer (Gummesson, 1991, p. 69). The RM concept calls, therefore, not only for an external marketing orientation but also for an 'internal marketing' (IM) focus on employees (Javalgi and Moberg, 1997, p. 173). A variety of terms, including internal partnerships, internal relationships and internal marketing, have been used to describe the concepts discussed in this chapter. Although authors in some cases imply certain nuances and priorities, the terms are used here (perhaps controversially in some people's eyes) interchangeably to avoid confusion. If a distinction is required *internal marketing* can be seen as the process towards the development of *internal partnerships*.

Customer–employee interface

Recognition of the importance of the employee–customer interface has, in large part, promoted interest in IM. Research suggests that the quality of relationships a company has with its customers is largely determined by how employees at the front line make customers feel (Barnes and Howlett, 1998, p. 21). It was also suggested that where the customer–supplier interface is more immediate, the internal climate had a strong impact upon employee satisfaction and customer retention (Payne, 2000, p. 118) although a direct causal linearity between the two cannot be assumed (Ballantyne, 1997, p. 355). As service firms largely create their offering through human interaction of some kind this suggests that a 'relationship' between employees and customers is almost inevitable (Kandampully and Duddy, 1999, p. 320).

Internal marketing in service organisations in particular can be seen, therefore, as being of the utmost importance. Whereas a service firm's contact with its customers is normally through its own employees, manufacturing firms in contrast may have to rely on intermediaries or (increasingly) technology (e.g. call centres) to develop some type of relationship. Another factor particularly promoting IM in service companies is that these organisations are invariably labour intensive. As such, internal marketing can help these organisations attract, keep and motivate quality personnel, which in turn helps them improve their capability to offer quality services (Berry, 1983, p. 27).

The stimulus for this internal marketing concern was, therefore, the growth in the importance of services marketing. Despite this, there is no insurmountable reason why internal marketing strategies should be limited to this area (Gummesson, 1991, p. 69). Although the importance of the internal dimension is seen to be particularly relevant to service industries, any organisation's final output, be it a good or service, is almost always the product of a series of operations and processes performed by employees (Buttle, 1996, p. 3). The interface between a firm's employees and its customers can be extensive even if the firm is not traditionally thought of as a service firm (Gummesson, 1997, p. 23). As a result, many aspects of internal marketing may have universal appeal.

Theory development

The ideas associated with internal marketing and internal partnerships have had a chequered career. The early views of internal marketing were more akin to the 'persuasion of staff to a management-determined situation' (Varey and Lewis, 1999, p. 929) whereas the concept of the internal customer evolved originally through the idea of 'selling jobs' and making them more attractive for employees (Reynoso, 1996, p. 77). In more recent times internal marketing and internal partnerships have become associated with a wide number of (sometimes overlapping) concepts, among them:

■ The concept of employees as (internal) suppliers and customers (Gummesson, 1991, p. 69; Christopher *et al.*, 1991, p. 79). This assumes chains of internal customers (administrative and manufacturing/processing) within an organisation. An employee who, in the normal course of job, would not deal directly with an external customer would be expected to treat internal customers as if they were external to the organisation.

- The breaking down of functional barriers within the organisation (Doyle, 1995, p. 29).
- Efforts to 'sell' the message of an organisation to its internal audience, using similar techniques to those used in the organisation's relationship with its external audiences (Palmer, 1998, p. 201).
- Marketing that takes place between profit centres inside a decentralised company (Gummesson, 1991, p. 69).
- The orchestration of staff working together and attuned to the company's mission, strategy, goals (Christopher *et al.*, 1991, p. 29) and the wider operations of the company with its environment (Hogg *et al.*, 1998, p. 893).
- Any activity within an organisation that focuses staff attention on the internal activities that need to be changed in order to enhance the external marketplace performance (Ballantyne, 1997, p. 346).
- Activities that improve internal communication and customer consciousness among employees (Hogg *et al.*, 1998, p. 880).
- Meeting the needs of employees so that they can meet the needs of their customers (Shershic, 1990, p. 45).
- The development of a company marketing orientation (Gummesson, 1991, p. 69; Varey and Lewis, 1999, p. 926; Hogg *et al.*, 1998, p. 879).
- How to get and retain customer-conscious employees (Grönroos, 1990, p. 88).

Varey and Lewis (1999, p. 931) while acknowledging the diversity of meanings and usage for the internal marketing concept, see it from a different viewpoint. They conceive that internal marketing can be seen as:

- A metaphor
- A philosophy
- As a set of techniques
- As an approach.

Internal marketing as a metaphor suggests that organisational jobs and employment conditions are 'products' to be marketed with the employee as both buyer and consumer. As a philosophy, internal marketing suggests that human resource management (HRM) requires 'marketing-like' activities to 'sell' the requirement of management. The concept also suggests that HRM should adopt marketing techniques such as research, segmentation, promotional communications and advertising internally to inform *and* persuade. Finally, internal marketing may be regarded as a style of management with key (and perhaps contradictory) objectives of flexibility and commitment.

These ideas converge to suggest the prime constituents of IM. It was this broader concept that Christopher *et al.* (1991, p. 30) were describing when they noted that internal marketing was:

> recognised as an important activity in developing a customer-focused organisation. In practice, internal marketing is concerned with communications, with developing responsiveness, responsibility and unity of purpose. Fundamental aims of internal marketing are to develop internal and external customer awareness and remove functional barriers to organisational effectiveness.

Internal marketing is perceived as a holistic approach to the business in general but to HRM and marketing in particular (Hogg *et al.*, 1998, p. 880). As internal interactions inevitably occur between departments in organisations, organisational dynamics are of particular relevance to both the service products and service delivery (Reynoso, 1996, p. 77; Reynoso and Moores, 1996, p. 55). Indeed, it is perceived as so important to the success of an operation that Gummerson (1991, p. 74) proposes that marketing in the future should be presented and taught from this holistic perspective and be truly integrated with other functions of the firm. In practical terms this would encompass HRM policies designed to attract, select, train, motivate, direct, evaluate and reward personnel (Palmer, 1998, p. 201) and indeed extend this influence to other parts of the organisation by breaking down the traditional functional barriers that exist in many companies. Gummesson (1991, p. 72) sees this as a change from 'marketing management' to 'marketing-orientated company management'.

The internal market[1]

Internal marketing, in the general sense, is seen to describe 'any form of marketing within the organisation which focuses attention on the internal activities that need to be changed in order that marketing plans can be implemented' (Christopher *et al.*, 1991, p. 26) and that enhances external marketplace performance (Ballantyne, 1997, p. 346). Internal marketing is essentially a way of enabling an organisation to recruit, motivate and retain customer-conscious employees in order to boost employee retention and customer satisfaction levels (Clark, 2000, p. 217). It can be broadly interpreted as those activities that improve internal communications and customer consciousness among employees, and the link between those activities and external marketplace performance (Hogg *et al.*, 1998, p. 880). In addition to this general meaning the term can be applied to the concept that every person in an organisation is both a customer and a supplier (Buttle, 1996, pp. 3–4). The essence of internal marketing is not, according to Varey and Lewis (1999, p. 926), a phenomenon of the post-industrial era since there is some evidence of associated attitudes and methods in literature produced early in the 20th century. What is new is the active market-orientated approach.

Internal marketing benefits

Internal marketing focuses on the three core value-adding activities of innovation, effective processes and customer support, and builds networks which design in quality (Doyle, 1995, pp. 26–7). It involves retaining customer-conscious employees (Grönroos, 1990, p. 88) and the development of employee empowerment to better satisfy the needs of the customer. Internal partnerships reflect the belief that

---

[1] There is an obvious danger here of confusing the term 'internal market' with the systems used in some public service organisations and global organisations. No such comparison is suggested.

if management wants its employees to deliver an outstanding level of service to customers, then it must be prepared to do a great deal for its employees (Reynoso, 1996, p. 77).

Internal marketing, therefore, is seen as a requirement for the successful implementation of the internal partnership concept and, ultimately, of RM. According to Buttle (1996, p. 12) the goal is to promote the development of the new culture, to persuade employees that it is sensible to buy into the new vision, and to motivate them to develop and implement RM strategies. In this way internal marketing partnerships become a core business philosophy (Palmer, 1998, p. 201) rather than solely the preserve of the marketing department.

The functional interface

The CIM definition of marketing as 'management process' implies a functional marketing department responsible for a fixed number of responsibilities closely associated with the traditional marketing mix. RM strategies imply breaking down these functional barriers. The oft-repeated maxim (at least in marketing circles) that 'whereas not everything is marketing, marketing is everything' (see McKenna, 1991, p. 18 and Ballantyne, 1997, p. 345) for variations on this theme) suggests that a marketing orientation means more than can possibly be handled by the marketing department alone. Rather, marketing orientation means 'the organisation-wide generation of market intelligence, dissemination of that intelligence across departments and organisation-wide responsiveness to it' (Kohli and Jaworski, 1990, p. 4) According to Doyle (1995, p. 23):

> Marketers have generally made the mistake of seeing the subject [Marketing] as a fundamental discipline rather than an integrated business process. Marketing Directors have sought to make Marketing decisions rather than share responsibility for satisfying customers with cross-functional teams. Unfortunately the only decisions where Marketing has sole responsibility tended to be tactical; promotions, line extension and superficial positioning policies.

Human resources

Over the past few decades, firms have begun to recognise that, more often than not, the limiting factor to their success is far more predicated on the availability of satisfactory skilled people than the availability of other resources such as capital or raw materials (Christopher *et al.*, 1991, p. 26). Recent studies on the major concerns of managers back up the importance of internal resources when they show employee communication and involvement, the redesign of business processes and the importance of the perceived relationship between employees and customer satisfaction as top of their list (Varey and Lewis, 1999, p. 926).

Nowhere is the importance of human assets more evident than in service operations, many of which can no longer be valued on the basis of their physical assets but on the basis of 'intellectual capital'. This intellectual capital, according to Gummesson (1999, p. 190) comes in two types:

- Individual capital
- Structural capital.

Individual capital

Individual capital covers the employees and their qualities, including knowledge, skills, motivation plus the individual's network of relationships inside and outside the company.

Structural capital

Structural capital, as we have noted previously (see Chapter 2), is the embedded knowledge inseparable from its environment and which does not evaporate when an employee leaves. This includes established relationships, the climate and culture, systems, contracts, image and branding. Core competencies, based on specific knowledge, reside in the organisation's staff and the systems that it has developed (Doyle, 1995, p. 28). As the success of 'individual capital' development has the potential to enhance 'structural capital', maintaining the former is crucial. The firm has a responsibility, therefore, to develop company-specific skills and to motivate its staff to harness these skills energetically to deliver superior value to the customer (Doyle, 1995, p. 28).

Teamwork

Research by Reynoso and Moores (1996, p. 58) suggests that one of the key factors contributing to any discrepancy between service quality specifications and the actual service delivered is poor teamwork. It is the existence of 'functional silos' that are seen to act independently and with little coordination that is frequently the major cause both of disagreement and 'non-goal congruence'. For a firm pursuing RM strategies the internal interface between marketing, operations, personnel and other functions is of strategic importance (Grönroos, 1994, p. 12). This acknowledges that all activities in a company are interrelated – what Gummesson (1991, p. 65) calls 'inter-functional dependency'. The interesting issue is whether a holistic marketing orientation calls for more marketing department direct authority over the operating activities of the firm (Ballantyne, 1997, p. 345) or whether the marketing function *per se* has reached its sell-by date and that cross-functional teams are the answer to the functionality problem. It is unlikely that any solution is right in every case. Each company will need to find an organisational form that is both effective and complements its climate and culture.

Part-time marketers

Many companies have centralised marketing and sales staff, who might be called 'full-time marketers'. These employees do not, however, represent all the marketers and salespeople the firm has at its disposal (Grönroos, 1996, p. 8). Gummesson

(1990) has coined the phrase 'part-time marketers' (PTM), in his book of the same name, to describe these non-marketing specialists who, regardless of their position in the company, are crucial to the company's marketing effort. These PTMs include all of those employees who, in any way, influence customer relations, customer satisfaction and the customer's perceived quality (Gummesson, 1991, p. 60). As Grönroos (1996, p. 8) notes, in many situations their impact on customer satisfaction and quality perception is more important to long-term success in the marketplace than that of the full-time marketer.

Christopher *et al.* (1991, p. 17) too recognised the part that both marketers and part-time marketers play in the marketing process. They further subdivide these categories based on the frequency of contact with the company to produce four types, as shown in Figure 7.1:

- *Contractors*: This group have frequent or periodic customer contact and are heavily involved with 'conventional' marketing activities, including sales and customer service roles. They should be well versed in the company's marketing strategy, well trained and motivated to serve the customer on a day-to-day basis. They should be recruited based on their potential to respond to customer needs and evaluated and rewarded on this basis.
- *Modifiers*: Modifiers, while not directly involved with conventional marketing activities, have frequent customer contact. This group includes receptionists, accounting staff, delivery personnel etc. Modifiers should have a clear view of the organisation's marketing strategy and the part they play in it. They should be trained in the development of customer relationship skills and monitored and evaluated on this basis.
- *Influencers*: Influencers are involved with elements of conventional marketing but they have infrequent personal contact. They are, however, very much part of the implementation of the organisation's marketing strategy. Roles include research and development, market research etc. A major skill to be nurtured here is 'customer responsiveness'. Influencers should be evaluated and rewarded according to customer orientated performance standards. Opportunities to meet customers in a programmed way may be also be valuable.

	Involvement with marketing	Not directly involved with marketing
Frequent or periodic customer contact	**Contractors**	**Modifiers**
Infrequent or no customer contact	**Influencers**	**Isolateds**

Figure 7.1 Employee influence on customers
(*Source*: Adapted from Christopher *et al.*, 1991, p. 17)

■ *Isolateds*: Although these employees have neither regular contact with customers nor regular input into conventional marketing activities, their performance could affect successful fulfilment of the company's marketing strategy. Included in this category, for example, are staff from personnel and data processing departments. The appropriate attention should be given to maximising the impact of their activities on marketing strategy and they should be rewarded accordingly.

Climate and culture

Organisations are not tangible objects but rather social constructs made up of people, activities, thoughts, emotions and other intangibles (Gummesson, 1994, p. 10). As Payne *et al.* (1995, p. 95) note, organisational climate and culture have become recognised as the foundation of long-term marketing effectiveness. They define these linked concepts as:

■ *Culture*: the deep-seated, unwritten system of shared values and norms within the organisation (which in turn dictates its climate)
■ *Climate*: the policies and practices that characterise the organisation (and, in turn, reflect its cultural beliefs).

The climate and culture of an organisation are dependent on how the employees view that organisation and its goals (Hogg *et al.*, 1998, p. 881). In particular, they affect both how the individual perceives his or her role within the organisation and how those roles relate to the wider operation of the organisation with its environment (Hogg *et al.*, 1998, p. 893). Internal marketing and the development of internal partnerships suggest the creation of an organisational climate where cross-functional quality improvements can be sponsored and worked upon by the people whose job processes are involved (Christopher *et al.*, 1991, p. 79).

Change within organisations frequently causes concern among employees even if that change will ultimately benefit those employees in some way. With the dramatic change inherent in today's strategy development, a supportive organisational culture is required to successfully implement changes. Dangers are also inherent in change. Climatic problems can quickly develop if issues are not dealt with before extensive change takes place.

Employee retention and loyalty

It must be a truism that the longer an employee stays with a company, the more familiar he or she will become with the business. It may also be generally true that longevity of employment increases learning. According to Reichheld (1993, p. 68) this learning increases the value of the employee to the company based upon how long the worker is expected to stay and grow with the business. This may be somewhat overstating the point in that 'longevity' in itself cannot guarantee 'value', and 'long service' can sometimes be associated with inflexibility. The general point being made, however, is that experience is frequently sacrificed in favour of expediency, particularly in cost-cutting exercises, a situation highlighted recently (April 2000) in a British government report. Although the expression 'our employees are our greatest assets' is often heard, it is frequently no more than a platitude (Christopher *et al.*, 1991, p. 16).

Empowerment

Empowerment was a buzzword of the 1990s. An important driver towards empowerment strategies came from the difficulty of non-homogeneity of delivery in service markets and the need for speedy decision making at the customer interface. Empowerment, however, appears to have been the second-choice solution. In the 1970s, in a bid to overcome the non-homogeneity difficulty, companies (for example McDonalds) took a 'production-line' approach to services (Bowen and Lawler, 1992, p. 31). Through duplication of activities, simplification of tasks and clear divisions of labour, companies were able to keep organisational control and produce efficient, low-cost, high-volume service operations with satisfied customers. This system would appear to work well in highly repetitive and relatively simple operations (e.g. fast food outlets or FMCG retailers).

It is, however, one of the oft-repeated social criticisms of the move from manufacturing economies to service-led economies that skilled jobs are being replaced by low-paid and little-skilled service operations. To an extent (and particularly where there is a production-led approach) this is true. In general, however, it is the rules and lines of authority which most restrict the innate personal skills of employees being fully (and satisfactorily) realised. Empowerment, therefore, according to Tom Peters, is necessary to 'dehumiliate' work by eliminating those policies and procedures of the organisation that demean and belittle human dignity (quoted in Zemke and Schaaf, 1989, p. 68).

In other areas of service (and indeed product) provision there is a need for more complex interactions than suggested by the production-line approach. In some cases these interactions may involve instant decision-making on the part of the employee (e.g. information desk, complaints office etc.). In these cases organisational control cannot be maintained at the point of interaction (although guidance may be involved beforehand and, potentially, censure afterwards). Effectively, the manager must trust the employee to make a decision that will be best from the company's perspective. It is this trust that underlies empowerment.

Empowerment looks to the performer of the tasks for solutions to problems, and looks to these employees to suggest new services and products and to solve problems creatively and effectively. Jan Carlzon, former CEO of SAS (quoted in Bowen and Lawler, 1992, p. 32), sees it as freeing employees from 'rigorous control by instructors, policies and orders, and to give freedom to take responsibility for ideas, decisions and actions'. This, he predicts, will 'release hidden values that would otherwise remain inaccessible to both the individual and the organisation'.

Operationalising empowerment

Bowen and Lawler (1992, p. 32) define 'empowerment' as the sharing with front-line employees of four organisational ingredients that in production-led service and many product industries would be in the hands of senior managers:

■ Information about organisational performance
■ Rewards based on organisational performance
■ Knowledge that enables employees to understand and contribute to organisational performance
■ Power to make decisions that influence organisational direction and performance.

Research by Lindgreen and Crawford (1999, p. 235) suggests that for employee empowerment to work there has to be investment in proper customer-focused staff training to enhance such different skills as industry knowledge, customer service, communications, presentation and teamwork. When managers in organisations establish policies, procedures and behaviour that shows concern for the organisation's customers they are, according to Schneider (1980, p. 53) 'service enthusiasts'. This contrasts strongly with managers interested simply in systems maintenance, and routine adherence to uniform operating guidelines and procedures ('service bureaucrats').

As well as recognising the value of interpersonal relationships and the importance of showing concern for the customer, the difference between the 'service enthusiast' and the 'service bureaucrat' is the former's emphasis on the flexible application of rules, procedures and systems maintenance. This assumes that all employees' workplace objectives are congruent with those of the organisation and that some form of consent must exist between employers and employees (Palmer, 1998, p. 200).

Empowerment benefits and cautions

Empowerment has a number of perceived benefits. According to Bowen and Lawler (1992, pp. 32–3), it results in:

■ Quicker online response to customers' needs during service delivery
■ Quicker online response to dissatisfied customers during service recovery
■ Employees feeling better about their jobs and themselves
■ Employees interacting with customers with more warmth and enthusiasm
■ Empowered employees being a great source of service ideas
■ Great 'word of mouth' advertising and customer retention.

As with most management concepts, empowerment benefits should be considered against the potential downside. To begin with, although the benefits are clear, the implementation is fraught with difficulty. Most commonly problems involve managers who wish to retain authority or employees who have no wish to have such a responsibility. It is also clear that some customers may prefer to be served by non-empowered employees, for example in self-service situations (Bowen and Lawler, 1992, p. 37). Empowerment may not, therefore, always be the preferred strategy. Despite Peter's warnings about the belittling nature of some service jobs, Bowen and Lawler (1992, p. 37) note that the production-line approach makes sense if a company's core mission is to offer high-volume service at the lowest cost because 'industrialising' services can take advantage of economies of scale by leveraging volume throughput. The added value of this may be seen to be cheap, quick and reliable service versus 'TLC',[2] or performing a 'transaction' versus 'managing a relationship'.

There are also (and inevitably) costs associated with empowerment. These are summarised by Bowen and Lawler (1992, pp. 33–4) as:

- Higher investment in selection and training
- Higher labour costs
- Slower/inconsistent service delivery as individual treatment slows down the operation
- Poor reaction of customers who see employees negotiating 'special deals' or terms with other customers
- Too many 'give-aways' and bad and costly decisions.

Empowerment can produce benefits, particularly, but not exclusively, in service industry settings. It must be recognised, however, that it is not a panacea for every internal management problem.

IM implementations

Obtaining and understanding the employee perspective is a critical tool in managing customer satisfaction as it enables managers to exercise internal marketing – in effect meeting the needs of employees so that they can meet the needs of customers (Shershic, 1990, p. 45). Internal marketing, it is claimed, is a relationship development process in which staff autonomy and know-how combine to create and circulate new organisational knowledge that will challenge internal activities that need to be changed to enhance quality in marketplace relationships (Ballantyne, 1997, p. 354). It is built on the premise that employees want to give good service just as customers want to receive it, and managers who make it easier to achieve this will find that both customers and employees are likely to respond positively (Schneider, 1980, p. 54).

At a tactical level internal marketing may include ongoing training and encouragement of formal and informal communications (such as newsletters), whereas at a strategic level internal marketing extends to the adoption of supportive management styles and personnel policies, customer service training and plan-ning procedures (Hogg *et al.*, 1998, p. 880). Doyle (1995, p. 29) suggests that the development of internal strategies requires a three-stage approach:

---

[2] For the unromantic, 'tender loving care'.

1 The organisation has to demonstrate a commitment to the security and development of its employees that ranks at least equal to that of its shareholders.
2 The organisation has to create a structure where functional barriers are torn down. It will have 'flatter' organisational levels, empowerment for front-line staff and will focus efforts on the three core value-adding processes of operations, customer support and innovation.
3 Top management must then provide leadership by reinforcing these values and offering a vision of what the organisation will become.

Reynoso and Moores (1996, p. 57) suggest that implementing an internal customer approach involves a number of processes. These include the creation of internal awareness, the identification of internal customers and suppliers, the identification of the expectations of the former, the communication of those expectations to internal suppliers, and the development of a measure of internal customer satisfaction and feedback mechanisms. The danger inherent in all of these suggestions is that internal marketing may be limited in what it contributes to the wider issues of organisational culture as it all too often defaults to an internal communications exercise (Meldrum, 2000, p. 13).

Staff development

What appears clear is that staff satisfaction is not, in itself, enough. The satisfaction of staff with their work will be positively related to customer satisfaction only when that work is customer orientated. There is no evidence that a broader causality between staff satisfaction and customer satisfaction exists (Ballantyne, 1997, p. 356). Grönroos (1996, p. 10) advocates what he terms a 'process management perspective' (PMP). PMP, he suggests, is very different from the traditional functionalistic management approach based on 'scientific management' principals. A PMP approach would see department boundaries broken down and the work-flow (including sales and marketing activities, productive, administrative and distributive activities and a host of 'part-time' marketing activities) organised and managed as a value-creating process.

Knowledge may be the key driver to staff effectiveness (and indeed satisfaction). As Gummesson (1987, p. 23) notes, all 'contact personnel' must be well attuned to the mission, goals, strategies and systems of the company otherwise they would be unable to handle those crucial 'moments of truth' that occur during the interaction with customers. This is particularly evident in service firms where the interface with the customer is broad and intense but may also be generally true of all companies.

Reward systems too may play a crucial role in internal partnership development. At present, sales and marketing management are widely rewarded with a mix of basic salary and performance-related bonus or commission. As Buttle (1996, p. 13) notes, the common performance criteria include sales volume and customer acquisition data that only reflects the short term. Under an RM strategy employees are more likely to be rewarded by customer profitability, account penetration and customer retention (see Box 7.1).

Box 7.1

Partnership in action

John Lewis Partnership is a retail organisation that has always treated its staff as integral to the business. Staff are not only called 'partners' in practice but are so in reality. They share in all 'partnership benefits', including dividends, and, through their representative, have a say in the strategic and tactical development of the store group. In an age of intense retail competition will John Lewis be forced to restructure more in line with other UK retailers? It would seem not if communiqués from head office are to be believed. There may have to be some rebalancing of priorities, however. According to John Lewis Partnership's administration director, writing in the organisation's internal magazine, the *Gazette*, 22 May 1999, 'the Partnership is a commercial enterprise, and if it is to survive in an increasingly competitive world it must balance the interests of "partners" with the expectations of customers'.

According to Kandampully and Duddy (1999, pp. 321–2) an RM programme should:

> be considered the firm's life-blood – percolating through all ranks, departments, functions and assets of the firm – with the ultimate aim of simultaneously offering and gaining value at all levels. The firm's marketing, management, operations, finance and human resources should constitute nurturing organs assisting the firm to develop, create and nurture the continuous flow of value between the respective stakeholders inside and/or outside the organisation.

Conclusion

RM's environment is not only the market and society in general but also includes the organisation and it is, therefore, dependent on changes in organisational design (Gummesson, 1994, p. 10). Internal marketing is widely seen as a prerequisite for the successful implementation of RM although responsibility for its implementation may not be solely the domain of marketers (Clark, 2000, p. 220). According to Grönroos (1994, p. 13), if internal marketing is neglected then external marketing suffers or fails. Research by Barnes and Howlett (1998, p. 21) suggests that the quality of relationships a company has with its customers is very much determined by how employees make customers feel. Schneider (1980, p. 63) reports research that concludes that if employees perceive a strong service orientation customers report they receive superior service. It works both ways. The success of RM is itself dependent, to a large extent, on the attitudes, commitment and performance of employees. If they are not all committed to their role as marketers (full-time and part-time) and are not motivated to perform in a customer-orientated fashion, RM strategy will fail (Grönroos, 1996, p. 12).

The adoption of RM concepts internally suggest a recognition of the need for a new type of organisation with a new type of management (Gummesson, 1994, p. 10). There is a broad recognition of the failure of conventional 'chimney stack' management with its functional bunkers (including marketing) 'embodying an abstract notion of marketing orientation . . . but a practical unwillingness to get out in the field and deliver on customer service and satisfaction' (O'Driscoll and Murray, 1998, p. 395). Doyle (1995, p. 35), for example, predicts that the changes will lead to smaller marketing departments staffed by a few generalists with big responsibilities for achieving results through teams of internal and external partners. He (1995, p. 38) goes on to suggest that:

> Marketing Managers will have to work more effectively as team players; proactively putting teams together and co-operating with other functions to enhance the core processes of innovation, order fulfilment and customer service. Functional boundaries in the 'professional core' will be seen as irrelevant and general management skills will be much more prized.

Marketing researchers in general strongly endorse these sentiments. Chaston (1998, p. 280) sees internal marketing as requiring priority over any other organisational process when seeking to achieve the goal of customer satisfaction. Grönroos (1996, p. 12) sees RM success as highly dependent on a well-organised and continuous internal marketing process. Buttle (1996, p. 193) cites evidence from the service sector (including the Post Office, banking, hospitality and not-for-profit organisations) that also suggests that organisations are 'likely to be less effective externally if the expectations of internal relational partners are not met'.

Increasing numbers of companies have recognised the need for internal marketing programmes, and the implementation of such programmes has gained momentum in recent years (Clark, 2000, p. 220). On a cautionary note, Varey and Lewis (1999, p. 927), while acknowledging that internal marketing is an evolving subject, note that there is not yet any firm theory or a strong base of empirical evidence to show how and why it is of value to managers. Adoption of internal marketing strategies is, therefore, no guarantee of success. In 1995 Doyle (1995, p. 26) cited three companies, Marks and Spencer, Virgin Airways and the Body Shop, as examples of companies which had eliminated functional boundaries and which had no marketing directors or conventional marketing departments. Over the past few years these three companies have had mixed fortunes. Marks and Spencer, in particular, has faced considerable problems and has recently introduced the position of marketing director. British Airways, cited as the 'most famous' of internal marketing advocates (Clark, 2000, p. 220), has also had continuing difficulties despite the introduction of its 'hearts and minds' employee programme. The argument for internal marketing is strong in theory although, perhaps, less wholly sustainable in practice.

Summary

This chapter looked at internal partnerships (also referred to as internal marketing). It highlighted the importance of the employee–customer interface and the development of an internal marketing approach to the overall success of relational strategies. It reviewed the significance of human resource management in the development of internal marketing and the broader need to remove all functional barriers from the organisational environment. The importance of full-time and part-time marketers was acknowledged and the advantages of teamwork considered. The benefits of employee retention and loyalty were noted and the effect of climate and culture on that employee loyalty discussed. Empowerment was seen as a recognisable feature of internal marketing but it was noted that costs as well as benefits accompany such a policy. Finally, the means of implementing internal marketing was discussed.

Discussion questions

1 What are the basic concepts that underlie internal marketing strategies?

2 Suggest ways in which functional barriers (for example between marketing and human resource management) could be broken down.

3 What are the principal advantages and disadvantages of empowerment?

4 What type of organisational climate and culture might best suit the implementation of relationship marketing?

Case study

Employees hold key to thwarting the competition

In my job I spend a lot of time at various clients' premises, which can tell you a lot about the company you are doing, or set to do, business with.

Take Chelsea Village where I came across an unusually forthright and attention grabbing corporate statement in the reception: 'The Romans didn't build a great empire by having endless meetings – they just killed everybody who got in their way'. Not my preferred method for engaging hearts and minds, but at least you know from the outset where you stand.

The more typical approach is like the one I saw in the reception area of a well-known multinational – a weighty tome delivered in cumbersome corporate vocabulary. I asked the receptionist what one particular piece of jargon meant. 'I've no idea,' she said, 'that was installed on Tuesday and that's my day off.' A woeful example of a communication exercise wasted on someone who plays a key part in any company. Added to this lack of internal involvement, the message's blandness and lack of relevance evoked a cultural picture far removed from the service proposition I know the company offers.

Internal marketing requires the same skill, rigour and discipline devoted to it as consumer marketing. Target audiences need to be segmented and their sophistication in medium and message recognised. Whether the communications task is about corporate beliefs, brand engagement or improving customer service, the principles are the same. You want your target audience ultimately to own the output.

And it's worth the effort. After five years of research, Harvard Business School has established a quantifiable set of relationships that directly link profit and growth not

▶

only with customer loyalty and satisfaction, but also to employee loyalty and involvement. The commitment of employees is an essential part of building customer loyalty to your brand.

Why then are many marketers guilty of paying relative lip service to this area? A lack of evidence linking internal and external measures of engagement, motivation and brand growth may be a reason. But the survey by Cranfield Business School, the Marketing Forum and Added Value, sent to over 200 marketing and communications directors, revealed that while only one-third measure their employees' commitment to their products or services, many have a growing belief that employees hold the key to delivering a competitive advantage.

This may be even more the case in the 'new economy', where it is increasingly difficult to maintain a lead purely in terms of product and service features. In a new era of individualised meetings with the consumer, the burden will fall on people inside the business to deliver the brand experience. That implies investment in communication and training to ensure everyone in the business understands the values and personality of the brand.

I think the most successful companies will be those that invest in building high levels of employee engagement in brand performance. The losers will be those who merely focus on killing the competition and assume the organisation will just march happily behind them. Well, we all know what happened to the Roman Empire.

(*Source*: Article by Peter Bell, global client director at Added Value, *Marketing*, 24th August 2000, p. 24)

Case study questions

1 In your opinion what are the major factors that enhance 'loyalty and satisfaction' among employees in an organisation?

2 From your experience what factors hinder internal communications?

References

Ballantyne, D. (1997) 'Internal networks for internal marketing', *Journal of Marketing Management*, 13 (5), 343–66.

Barnes, J.G. and Howlett, D.M. (1998) 'Predictors of equity in relationships between service providers and retail customers', *International Journal of Bank Marketing*, 16 (1), 5–23.

Berry, L.L. (1983) 'Relationship marketing' in Berry, L.L., Shostack, G.L. and Upsay, G.D. (eds) *Emerging Perspectives on Service Marketing*. Chicago, IL: American Marketing Association, pp 25–8.

Bowen, D.E. and Lawler, E.E. (1992) 'The empowerment of service workers; what, why, how and when', *Sloane Management Review*, 33 (Spring), 31–9.

Buttle, F.B. (1996) *Relationship Marketing: Theory and Practice*. London: Paul Chapman.

Chaston, I. (1998) 'Evolving 'new marketing' philosophies by merging existing concepts: application of process within small high-technology firms', *Journal of Marketing Management*, 14, 273–91.

Christopher, M., Payne, A. and Ballantyne, D. (1991) *Relationship Marketing*. London: Butterworth Heinemann.

Clark, M. (2000) 'Customer service, people and processes' in Cranfield School of Management *Marketing Management: A Relationship Marketing Perspective.* Basingstoke: Macmillan, pp. 110–24.

Doyle, P. (1995) 'Marketing in the new millennium, *European Journal of Marketing*, 29 (12), 23–41.

Grönroos, C. (1990) 'Relationship approach to the marketing function in service contexts; the marketing and organization behaviour interface', *Journal of Business Research*, 20, 3–11.

Grönroos, C. (1994) 'From marketing mix to relationship marketing: towards a paradigm shift in marketing', *Management Decisions*, 32 (2), 4–20.

Grönroos, C. (1996) 'Relationship marketing: strategic and tactical implications', *Management Decisions*, 34 (3), 5–14.

Gummesson, E. (1987) 'Using internal marketing to develop a new culture: the case of Ericsson quality', *Journal of Business and Industrial Marketing*, 2 (3), 23–8.

Gummesson, E. (1990) *The Part-time Marketer.* Karlstad: Centre for Service Research.

Gummesson, E. (1991) 'Marketing orientation revisited: the crucial role of the part-time marketers', *European Journal of Marketing*, 25 (2), 60–7.

Gummesson, E. (1994) 'Making relationship marketing operational', *International Journal of Service Industry Management*, 5, 5–20.

Gummesson, E. (1997) 'In search of marketing equilibrium: relationship marketing versus hypercompetition', *Journal of Marketing Management*, 13 (5), 421–30.

Gummesson, E. (1999) *Total Relationship Marketing: Rethinking Marketing Management from 4Ps to 30Rs.* Oxford: Butterworth Heinemann.

Hogg, G., Carter, S. and Dunne, A. (1998) 'Investing in people: internal marketing and corporate culture', *Journal of Marketing Management*, 14, 879–95.

Javalgi, R. and Moberg, C. (1997) 'Service loyalty: implications for service providers', *Journal of Services Marketing*, 11 (3), 165–79.

Kandampully, J. and Duddy, R. (1999) 'Relationship marketing: a concept beyond the primary relationship', *Marketing Intelligence and Planning*, 17 (7), 315–23.

Kohli, A.K. and Jaworski, B.J. (1990) 'Market orientation: the construct, research propositions and managerial implications', *Journal of Marketing*, 54, 1–18.

Lindgreen, A. and Crawford, I. (1999) 'Implementing, monitoring and measuring a programme of relationship marketing', *Marketing Intelligence and Planning*, 17 (5), 231–9.

McKenna, R. (1991) *Relationship Marketing.* London: Addison-Wesley.

Meldrum, M. (2000) 'A market orientation' in Cranfield School of Management, *Marketing Management: A Relationship Marketing Perspective.* Basingstoke: Macmillan pp. 3–15.

O'Driscoll, A. and Murray, J.A. (1998) 'The changing nature of theory and practice in marketing: on the value of synchrony', *Journal of Marketing Management*, 14 (5), 391–416.

Palmer, A.J. (1998) *Principles of Services Marketing.* London: Kogan Page.

Payne, A. (2000) 'Customer retention' in Cranfield School of Management, *Marketing Management: A Relationship Marketing Perspective.* Basingstoke: Macmillan, pp. 110–24.

Payne, A., Christopher, M. and Peck, H. (eds) (1995) *Relationship Marketing for Competitive Advantage: Winning and Keeping Customers.* Oxford: Butterworth Heinemann.

Reichheld, F.F. (1993) 'Loyalty based management', *Harvard Business Review*, March/April, 1993, 64–73.

Reynoso, J. (1996) 'Internal service operations: how well are they serving each other?' in Edvardsson, B., Brown, S.W., Johnston, R. and Scheuing, E.E. (eds) *Advancing Service Quality: A Global Perspective*. New York: ISQA, pp. 77–86.

Reynoso, J.F. and Moores, B. (1996) 'Internal relationships' in Buttle, F.B. (ed). *Relationship Marketing: Theory and Practice*. London: Paul Chapman, pp. 55–73.

Schneider, B. (1980) 'The service organization: climate is crucial', *Organizational Dynamics*, Autumn, 52–65.

Shershic, S.F. (1990) 'The flip side of customer satisfaction research', *Marketing Research*, December, 45–50.

Varey, R.J. and Lewis, B.R. (1999) 'A broadened conception of internal marketing', *European Journal of Marketing*, 33 (9/10), 926–44.

Zemke, R. and Schaaf, D. (1989) *The Service Edge; 101 Companies That Profit From Company Care*. New York: New American Library.

8 Supplier partnerships

Key issues
➤ Vertical versus horizontal relationships
➤ Partnering
➤ Partnership costs
➤ Partnership benefits

Introduction

An organisation's external relationships can be seen to have a vertical and horizontal dimension (Palmer, 2000, p. 689). These can be described as:

- Vertical relationships representing those that integrate all or part of the supply chain through component suppliers, manufacturers and intermediaries.

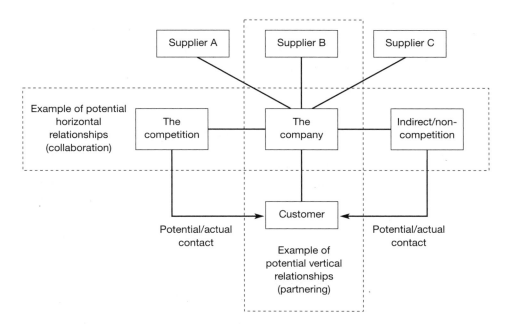

Figure 8.1 Horizontal and vertical relationships

■ Horizontal relationships represented by organisations that are at the same point in the channel of distribution (including competitors) who seek to cooperate and collaborate for mutual benefit.

These horizontal and vertical relationships are not mutually exclusive and it is quite possible for an organisation to have a number of bilateral and multilateral relationships of both sorts. When it comes to relationships of this type, not only is polygamy allowed – it is highly recommended (Gummesson, 1999, p. 129)!

Although many aspects of these relationship types have similar features it may be valuable to investigate them separately. This chapter will, therefore, concentrate on vertical relationships (described as supplier partnerships or partnering) whereas Chapter 9 will look more closely at horizontal relationships. To differentiate the latter, horizontal relationships are termed 'collaborations'.

Supplier partnerships

Partnerships between customers and suppliers come in many forms and under many different guises: for example, Christopher *et al.* (1991, p. 24) note that Phillips calls these 'Vendor Partnerships' and AT&T 'Co-makerships'. Although 'supplier partnerships' is the term used here for these vertical relationships, it refers, more broadly, to any two-way relationship within the vertical chain and is sometimes more simply known as 'partnering'. Supplier partnerships are, evidently, the other side of the 'customer partnerships' coin, so aspects relating to general relationships between 'partners' discussed previously apply. There is, therefore, no need to repeat again those aspects of the supplier–customer relationship outlined in Chapter 6. However, whereas the earlier chapter largely (but not exclusively) looked at the relationships from the consumer goods and services perspective (popularly referred to as business-to-consumer, or B2C) this chapter will concentrate on relationships further back in the supply chain. The most common way of describing these is as 'business-to-business' (B2B) relationships, this term having largely replaced the term 'industrial goods and services marketing'.

We have referred earlier to the concepts of organisational as well as personal relationships. As Häkansson and Snehota (1989, p. 187) note, when it comes to B2B 'no business is an island' thus, by the very nature of the interdependency of most B2B markets, business relationships of one sort or another are inevitable. The problem with discussing B2B relationships is that such is the wide variety of relationship types that the all-encompassing term 'relationship' may be too general to provide wholly constructive insight (Blois, 1999, p. 1). This chapter will, however, attempt as far as possible to overcome this difficulty.

Business-to-business relationship research

It was the pioneering research work of the Industrial Marketing and Purchasing Group (IMP) into the complexities of the B2B markets and the relationships within them (Naudé and Holland, 1996, p. 40) that, in part, led to the development and application of relationship theory in this sector. Indeed, even the earliest development of theory by the group implicitly assumed that relationships enhanced performance (O'Toole and Donaldson, 2000, p. 328) and provided a grounding for what has developed since in relational marketing research. The recognition of the importance of 'relationships' came from real-life evidence that was slowly building up of a movement away from the traditional adversarial relationships between suppliers and their customers towards a new form of relationship based on cooperation (Christopher *et al.*, 1991, p. 24). As Brennan (1997, pp. 759–60) notes:

> In the field of business-to-business marketing researchers associated with the International Marketing and Purchasing (IMP) Group . . . published evidence to support the assertions that inter-firm buying and selling must be seen as related activities, and that the marketing function must be at least as concerned with inter-firm relationship development and management as with conventional marketing mix management.

Webster (1992, p. 10) too saw a 'clear evolution away from arm's length transactions and traditional hierarchical, bureaucratic forms of organisation towards more flexible types of partnerships, alliances and networks' within the B2B sector. IMP researchers suggested that a two-level approach was evident, the first 'including short-term episodes . . . exchange of goods and services, information, financial and social aspects' and the second, and longer-term, 'processes leading to adaptation and institutionalisation of roles and responsibilities' (Grönroos, 2000, p. 7).

Business relationships

Although the importance of IMP research cannot be over-emphasised in the study of industrial relationships, the existence of 'trading partnerships' is not new. In the field of B2B marketing concepts associated with long-term relationships have a long history of acceptance and effective practice (Barnes, 1994, p. 562). For example, personal relationships between the employees and owners/directors of companies have for some time been explicitly recognised by both buyer and seller organisations and individuals within those organisations (Blois, 1997, p. 53). Relational 'bonding' between B2B traders is not even a 20th-century phenomenon. In the pre-industrial revolution world such associations were quite prevalent between traders, partly because of the need, in turbulent, minimally legislated and sometimes dangerous markets, to do business with others you could trust (Sheth and Parvatiyar, 1995, p. 403). Indeed, it may be suggested that it was only with the growth and formalisation of mass-market distribution that traditional relationships between traders in the distribution chain became so strained.

This observable tension in the distribution chain was most evident in relationships between brand suppliers and their retail intermediaries. Both parties had their minds focused on the final consumer but, while their individual objectives overlapped, they frequently differed considerably in strategy implementation. During the so-called 'golden age of marketing' from the mid-

1950s to the mid-1970s, it was the brand supplier who financed the development of individual brands and who dominated and manipulated the means of distribution. Only rarely did brand owners and retailers work together to achieve a result that would satisfy both parties. Most often suppliers used 'pull strategies' with the objective of attracting customers 'over the heads' of the retailer. When 'push strategies' (effectively using trade incentives and promotions to 'push' product through the distribution chain) were used they tended to be one-off tactics rather than strategic cooperative activity. The retailers, on their part, felt no responsibility to any one supplier, being concerned more with overall profit margins rather than specific brands.

The third quarter of the 20th century saw a change in the balance of power between suppliers and retailers, particularly in the FMCG sector, but as yet little movement towards cooperation. As the power of larger supermarket retailers grew, suppliers were often played off against each other. Information regarding production capacity on one side and sales on the other was regarded as commercially sensitive and distrust of one's supplier or customer was the norm.

Only when vertical integration took place through 'acquisition' forward or backward in the supply chain was information seen to flow up and down the chain and, even then, somewhat hesitantly. The commonest justification for acquisition of this sort was protection of either the sources of supply (backward integration) or product markets (forward integration) with the improvement of information flow as a secondary benefit. The problem with these forms of integration was that the capital requirements and lack of flexibility typically led to inter-business subsidisation and transfer pricing as a way of shielding the internal business units from market forces (Sheth and Sisodia, 1999, p. 82). The acquisition route to effective and efficient distribution synergy dominated corporate strategy in the 1970s and 1980s. As the 20th century came to a close there was a growing recognition that the theoretical benefits sought through coordinating elements of the distribution chain might be better achieved in other more effective and efficient ways. Rather than attempting to encompass all or a significant part of the distribution chain, companies were encouraged to concentrate their organisational efforts on their 'core competencies'. This thinking led to consideration of alternative concepts such as outsourcing and partnering.

Outsourcing strategy was again not new. As Gummesson (1999, p. 128) notes, the 'make or buy' choice has always been an issue in manufacturing. Nor was partnering without precedent. Despite the general distrust in the typical distribution chain, there were partnerships which proved to be the exceptions to the rule. Partnering-type relationships existed between companies such as Whirlpool and Sears, and McDonalds and Coca-Cola, the latter of which has lasted for over 50 years (Sheth and Parvatiyar 1995, p. 408). What had before been limited to a few companies was, however, now developing as mainstream strategy.

Partnering

Partnering can take many forms, so a rather generalised definition must suffice:

> Partnering is a relationship between customer and supplier organisations, recognised as such by the parties involved, whose principal objective is a shared increase in the effectiveness and efficiency of joint responsibilities within the remit of their relationship.

The *raison d'être* of a partnership approach is, therefore, to improve the efficiency and effectiveness with which a value-adding system functions (Brennan, 1997, p. 770). Sheth and Sisodia (1999, p. 82) suggest that through partnering buyers and sellers can gain many of the advantages of vertical integration without the drawbacks associated with acquisition. These advantages, they suggest, include:

- Lower transaction costs
- Assurance of supply
- Improved coordination
- Higher entry barriers.

This type of cooperation between buyers and sellers may manifest itself in a number of ways. These include the establishment of long-term contractual commitments, the divulging of personal information,[1] and the adaptation of the production, delivery and buying processes to meet the requirements and needs of both the buyer and the seller (Palmer, 2000, p. 693). This adaptation of processes has become particularly prevalent in the motor vehicle manufacturing and FMCG distribution sectors where strategies for fast-flow replenishment (e.g. 'just-in-time' strategies) are seen as necessary for competitive advantage. In the retail field such replenishment strategies are often referred to as supplier/retailer collaboration (SRC). The GEA Consulting Group (1994) has defined SRC, in a study for Coca-Cola, as where:

> both retailers and suppliers share proprietary internal and external data and/or share policies and processes used in decision making with the clear objective of sharing the benefits.

Technology has driven this information exchange even further than it was envisaged in the past. Systems now exist that allow selected suppliers to monitor sales of any of their products. As a result of changing perceptions and available technology, suppliers and retailers appear to be changing the habits of a lifetime and regarding each other as allies rather than necessary (but combative) elements in the distributive chain.

The development of customer–supplier partnering agreements has grown considerably in the past decade. Margins in the B2B sector are continually tightening, further promoting the requirement for greater efficiency and effectiveness. Rapid technological development has increased the cost of research and development (R&D) and the 'window of opportunity' for getting products and services to market

---

[1] Buttle (1996, p. 194) suggests that B2B marketing is best characterised as management of information.

has shortened, forcing companies to work together in joint research projects and joint product development programmes (Sheth and Parvatiyar 1995, p. 410). Ideas associated with total quality management and efficient and effective management of the channels of distribution have also created a need for the flow of information between customers and suppliers.

Culture gap

Critical to partnering is a good understanding between partner firms. In particular a knowledge and acceptance of each other's organisational cultures would appear critical to successful business relationships (Phan *et al.*, 1999, p. 8). Not only should there be an acceptance of cultures between organisations but the adaptation of cultural styles and organisational mind-sets to allow partnerships to flourish. Brennan (1997, p. 766) notes the scale of the cultural divide to be bridged when he compares the 'old' with the 'desired' inter-organisational cultures that promote relationship development (see Box 8.1).

Box 8.1

Company organisational cultures

Old inter-organisational culture	Desired organisational culture
We are involved in a zero sum game; if we gain then they must lose.	We are involved in a positive sum game: together we must aim to increase our business success.
Information is power; the more we know about them the better. The less they know about us the better.	Information sharing is the key; unless we share information on a large scale then we will be unable to maximise our joint efficiency and effectiveness.
Trust is for mugs. I respect my counterpart as a tough negotiator. I trust him as far as I could throw him.	Trust will emerge naturally: gradually we will learn that each other is trustworthy, and this will improve relationship effectiveness since we will no longer have to keep checking up.
They are out to screw us and we're out to screw them.	This is a valuable relationship: it is very unlikely that my counterpart will risk damaging it to obtain short-term advantage.
Personal success is about winning; if I can consistently negotiate concessions from my counterpart then my career will go from strength to strength.	Personal success is about mutual success: if I can demonstrate that the strength of this relationship has contributed to my company's success my career will go from strength to strength.

(*Source*: Brennan, 1997, p. 767)

Customer and supplier organisations are represented in these partnering arrangements by their employees leading to relationship development on a personal as well as organisational level. These personal bonds can be powerful and enduring inside the relationship although empirical evidence would suggest that they can lessen or break down once one of the participants leaves the organisational relationship. Social bonds have been observed to reduce a buyer's perceived levels of risk and simplify the reordering process (Palmer, 1996, p. 22). They help build up trust between parties in the relationship by creating other situations, outside of formal meetings, by which to observe a partner.

Partnership costs and benefits

According to Brennan (1997, p. 770) the purpose of a partnership approach must be to improve the efficiency with which a value-adding system functions. He candidly notes:

> If there is no improvement in overall systematic efficiency, then the only way one party can gain is at the expense of another, in which case the firms are playing a 'zero-sum game' and are back to old-style adversarial relations. Partnering can only flourish in a 'positive-sum game' where there are real economic advantages associated with this approach to doing business.

Brennan, based on his research in the automobile industry, notes that the primary benefits for the supplier and the customer of the partnership approach are that:

- The supplier gains an in-depth understanding of the customer's requirements and can be proactive in suggesting product improvements.
- The supplier's personnel become familiar with the customer's 'way of doing things', potentially reducing misunderstandings and improving the speed of response.
- Greater supplier involvement (as a 'member of the team') at an early stage in new projects and new product development can increase the 'speed to market'.
- There is a reduction or elimination of the 'cost of sales' for the customer.
- The supplier is not exposed to the hazards of the marketplace, implying greater certainty about future revenues.
- The 'partner–supplier' usually gains privileged access to information about long-term customer plans, enabling a proactive stance to be taken and subsequent reinforcement of its 'preferred supplier' position.
- There is an increased information flow and greater information trustworthiness.
- The ability of both partners to focus on those aspects of the value-added chain that are their 'core competencies' is increased, enabling them to leave other aspects to their trusted partner.

Partnership costs are, however, inevitable. Brennan (1997, p. 771) describes the potential costs to the customer and/or supplier of the partnership approach as:

- The reduction (or dulling) of 'market incentivisation' normally created by vigorous competition (i.e. the risk that the supplier or customer becomes complacent).
- The likelihood that external suppliers will not bother to bid against favoured suppliers.

- The risk of becoming heavily committed to the wrong partner (effectively backing the wrong horse).
- The sunken costs (related to customer-specific or supplier-specific investment in physical or human assets) that are more or less worthless outside of the partnership.

As with any strategy development, the costs and benefits need to be carefully considered before progressing to any partnership agreement.

Power

In organisational relationships the 'balance of power' is rarely symmetrical (Gummesson, 1999, p. 16) with one party usually the stronger of the two. As Gummersson (1994, p. 9) notes, this is acceptable to a degree in an imperfect market but from a welfare perspective it may prove unacceptable over the long term. The balance of power will often affect how partners behave. If, for example, during a dispute the aggrieved party has the upper hand they may adopt a more aggressive complaint resolution strategy than the aggrieved party with less authority over the situation (Boote and Pressey, 1999, p. 9)

Power and dependency in a relationship are very much a function of the relative importance to both parties (Storbacka *et al.*, 1994, p. 29). Imbalance of power, where one partner is seen as dominant and the other dependent – Palmer (1996, p. 20) alternatively calls this 'absence of symmetrical dependence' – creates opportunities for individual parties to pursue short-term advantage, whereas 'balanced or symmetrical dependence represents a mutual safeguard and a collective incentive to maintain a relationship' (Palmer, 1996, pp. 20–1). It will come as no surprise to many small and medium-sized enterprises (SMEs) that relationship power imbalances are most evident when larger companies are involved. There is a strong suggestion, therefore, that the quality of buyer–seller relationships is higher among small-scale businesses operating in 'closed communities' as typified by many less developed economies (Palmer, 2000, p. 700).

An imbalance of power is potentially disruptive to any relationship. Successful partnerships appear to design agreements so that, as far as possible, power/dependence issues are avoided.

The downside of B2B partnerships

As may be expected, other pitfalls (in addition to those related to costs or imbalances of power) exist for potential partners. In all relationships disagreements are probable, indeed inevitable. Complaining behaviour within a buyer–seller context can be seen as different from complaining within a consumer behaviour setting as organisational buying may involve more complexity (Boote and Pressey, 1999, p. 3). In one respect a positive 'spin' can be put on this if parties perceive these disagreements as an effective way of bringing problems out into the open as opposed to bristling with anger and looking for new partners (Hunt and Morgan, 1994, p. 25). Even in the most serious of disagreement situations the opportunity to threaten the ultimate sanction of leaving the relationship may be heavily restricted by barriers to exit, in particular those sunken costs of relationship development. The limited room to manoeuvre within a relationship may be a major negative. Partners trapped in such a situation are reminiscent of the 'spurious loyalists' discussed in Chapter 5.

Another potential downside relates to the length of the relationship. Despite the general perception that the longer the association the more profitable it can be, there is also a darker side to relationships in the longer term. Inherent drawbacks exist in relationships that last any duration (Grayson and Ambler, 1999, p. 132). There is, for example, an intellectually coherent point of view that suggests that there are considerable disadvantages associated with getting 'too cosy' over time with your supplier (or customer) and that in practice these disadvantages outweigh the advantages of partnering (Brennan, 1997, p. 766). Moorman *et al.* (1992, p. 323) observes that long relationships between service providers show evidence of becoming stale or that the partners become too similar in thinking and, therefore, have less value to add. Palmer (2000, p. 696) suggests that a 'dynamic tension' in the buyer–seller relationship may be essential to achieve continuous improvements in value delivery. Long-term relationships settle into predictable patterns and lack the tension of newly formed associations. A lack of such tension, Palmer suggests, is characterised by 'gullible buyers with a low propensity to complain' and 'results in less collective benefit available to the partners'.

There appears, therefore, to be an in-built redundancy factor in relationships that do not re-invent themselves from time to time. Indeed, research suggests (Grayson and Ambler, 1999, p. 132) that many partners reach a stage where they begin to believe it is time for a change. It is interesting to note that it is in those industries where 'fresh ideas' are important currency (e.g. advertising) that the turnover of relationships (e.g. client and agency) is perceived as greatest.

One complaint made against B2B partnering relationships is that, rather than representing a new style of business development, they are often 'old style' transaction marketing under a new guise. It may be perceived in certain industries, for example, that whereas individual companies no longer compete against each other, 'supply chain' now competes against 'supply chain' (Christopher, 1996, p. 62) and 'network' competes against 'network' (Doyle, 1995, p. 24). There is a further serious charge that partnering relationships can have anti-competitive implications where partnering is used as a process by which a seller seeks to restrict the choice set of buyers (Palmer, 1996, p. 22). An additional danger exists when social bonds associated with close inter-organisational relationships become so pervasive they lead to economic inefficiencies and, at the extreme, corrupt networks of buyers and sellers (Palmer, 1996, p. 21). Palmer (1996, p. 22) notes that it is ironic that while western companies seek closer relationships many of those same companies have been applying pressure, through their governments, to have such practices curtailed in Japan.

Summary

This chapter has distinguished between vertical supplier–customer relationships (partnerships) and horizontal (collaborative) relationships within the business-to-business (B2B) sector. It looked at the types of vertical relationships associated with suppler–customer partnerships (or partnering) and established that the generic objectives of these relationships was to improve the efficiency and effectiveness within the value-adding system. The importance of understanding organisational cultures was noted and the likelihood that failure was possible without changes to these cultures proposed. The reasons for the development of partnering were discussed as well as the perceived benefits and costs. The 'darker side' of longer-term relationships was also debated.

Discussion questions

1 Distinguish between vertical and horizontal relationships.

2 What part does the balance of power between the parties play in a relationship?

3 Why are closer ties likely to develop in business-to-business rather than business-to-consumer relationships?

4 Why might partnering relationships lead to 'the reduction (or dulling) of market incentivisation' as suggested on p. 161?

Case study

What to buy

The popularity of the Internet means companies want to connect to it all their systems – from human resources to manufacturing. But that is not always easy. Nor, despite promises of compatibility from the information technology industry, can different systems always be linked to each other.

'Today typical accounts, manufacturing and logistics systems for small and medium-sized companies are mostly standalone,' says Dennis Keeling, chief executive of Basda, the Business and Accounting Software Developers Association.

This is changing, however. Mr Keeling says: 'New software such as Microsoft's Office 2000 will allow users to access the Internet and electronic mail from within applications. There has also been a big breakthrough in getting different accounts packages to work together.'

Mr Keeling says that in the past, the main way of sending data between two company's accounts systems was to use electronic data interchange (EDI). 'But it was incredibly expensive. And at present, it is far more appropriate for large companies such as Tesco, General Motors and Ford than for smaller companies. 'But in the last year, the Internet – and in particular a standard called extensible markup language

(XML) backed by IBM, Microsoft and others – has increasingly been used to allow documents to be exchanged between different systems.'

Basda has developed a set of XML-based rules (the Basda e-BIS Initiative) which enable purchase orders to be sent between accounts packages via the Internet. The system was shown this month at the UK Softworld conference sending purchase orders between several accounts packages, such as Geac and TAS. According to Basda, its schema can easily be added to other accounts packages in four or five days.

It can also be used to send purchase orders via electronic mail to small businesses with no accounts software. All the recipient needs in order to view and print out the purchase order is Microsoft's latest browser Internet Explorer 5.0.

Invoices can then be exchanged using the schema, then delivery notes, order acknowledgements, Bankers Automated Clearing Services (BACS) remittance advices and, eventually, payments. The schema is free for developers to download from www.biztalk.org or www.xml.org.

'Basda is also talking to the UK government about adapting its schema for sending tax documents electronically, starting with self-assessment. We're planning to deliver something before April,' says Mr Keeling.

'An XML-based system for businesses paying national insurance to the Benefits Agency is another possibility as is one for VAT payers. Mr Keeling believes that the schema could also be used to help human resources and manufacturing systems communicate via the Internet.

John Higgins, director general of the Computing Services and Software Association (CSSA), also believes being able to connect to the Internet is important. 'Businesses planning to buy new back-office (behind-the-scenes administration) systems should ask how well they integrate with e-business,' he says. 'This is an area that many back-office suppliers need to pay attention to. So would-be buyers should look for a good interface with the web.'

Mr Higgins believes buyers should also think through the performance implications of connecting their systems to the web. He cites the example of one company which linked its database to the web and found it was far too slow when both in-house and Internet users were searching through it.

As a result, it had to buy a second database to sit in the middle in order to speed things up and is now having to spend time and effort making sure the two databases contain the same version of the data.

Establishing the level of internet performance and connectivity will help businesses avoid becoming isolated. Another tactic is to buy Windows-based software.

'Businesses that don't insist their software conforms to the Wintel (Windows/Intel) standard could have problems,' warns Mr Keeling. 'Even big companies with IT skills in-house are buying Windows-based software, such as enterprise resource planning system SAP/R3. But there are still a lot of packages out there that don't display information in the Windows format.'

Peter Sive, managing director of Catalysis, a specialist IT communications consultancy, says: 'Often the difficulty for a smaller company is not incompatible systems but the sheer complexity of networking them together.' Catalysis networks its PCs using Windows NT on its server system.

Mr Sive says that, even with in-house IT staff, Windows NT features can present difficulties for a small company. 'Incompatible file formats can also be a problem when receiving information over e-mail,' says Mr Sive. 'We have been sent a JPEG graphics file created using an Apple but converted to a PC format that we really need and just can't open.'

The good news is that IT companies such as IBM, Intel and Microsoft are gearing up to help smaller businesses, partly because they represent a growth market. This means simpler solutions and, hopefully, better advice on connecting everything.

(Source: Joia Shillingford, *Financial Times*, 21 October 1999)

Case study question

1 The system described suggests considerable benefits for small businesses. What, in RM terms, might these be?

References

Barnes, J.G. (1994) 'Close to the customer: but is it really a relationship?', *Journal of Marketing Management*, 10, 561–70.

Blois, K.J. (1997) 'When is a relationship a relationship?' in Gemünden, H.G., Rittert, T. and Walter, A. (eds) *Relationships and Networks in International Markets*. Oxford: Elsevier, pp. 53–64.

Blois, K.J. (1999) 'A framework for assessing relationships', competitive paper, European Academy of Marketing Conference (EMAC), Berlin, pp. 1–24.

Boote, J.D. and Pressey, A.D. (1999) 'Integrating relationship marketing and complaining behaviour: a model of conflict and complaining behaviour within buyer–seller relationships', competitive paper, European Academy of Marketing Conference (EMAC), Berlin.

Brennan, R. (1997) 'Buyer/supplier partnering in British industry: the automotive and telecommunications sectors', *Journal of Marketing Management*, 13 (8), 758–76.

Christopher, M. (1996) 'From brand values to customer values', *Journal of Marketing Practice*, 2 (1), 55–66.

Christopher, M., Payne, A. and Ballantyne, D. (1991) *Relationship Marketing*. London: Butterworth Heinemann.

Doyle, P. (1995) 'Marketing in the new millennium', *European Journal of Marketing*, 29 (12), 23–41.

GEA Consulting Group (1994) *Grocery Distribution in the 90s; Strategies for the Fast Flow Replenishment*, GEA/Coca Cola.

Grayson, K. and Ambler, T. (1999) 'The dark side of long-term relationships in marketing', *Journal of Marketing Research*, 36 (1), 132–41.

Grönroos, C. (2000) 'The relationship marketing process: interaction, communication, dialogue, value', in 2nd WWW Conference on Relationship Marketing, 15 November 1999– 15 February 2000, paper 2 (www.mcb.co.uk/services/conferen/nov99/rm)

Gummesson, E. (1994) 'Making relationship marketing operational', *International Journal of Service Industry Management*, 5, 5–20.

Gummesson, E. (1999) *Total Relationship Marketing: Rethinking Marketing Management from 4Ps to 30Rs*. Oxford: Butterworth Heinemann.

Håkansson, H. and Snehota, I (1989) 'No business is an island: the network concept of business strategy', *Scandinavian Journal of Management*, 4 (3), 187–200.

Hunt, S.D. and Morgan, R.M. (1994) 'Relationship marketing in the era of network competition', *Journal of Marketing Management*, 5 (5) 18–28.

Moorman, C., Zaltman, G. and Deshpande, R. (1992) 'Relations between providers and users of market research. The dynamics of trust within and between organisations', *Journal of Marketing Research*, 29, 314–28.

Naudé, P. and Holland, C. (1996) 'Business-to-business marketing', in Buttle, F. (ed.) *Relationship Marketing Theory and Practice*. London: Paul Chapman.

O'Toole, T. & Donaldson, W. (2000) 'Relationship governance structures and performance', *Journal of Marketing Management*, 16, 327–41.

Palmer, A. J. (1996) 'Relationship marketing: a universal paradigm or management fad?', *The Learning Organisation*, 3 (3), 18–25.

Palmer, A. J. (2000) 'Co-operation and competition; a Darwinian synthesis of relationship marketing', *European Journal of Marketing*, 34 (5/6), 687–704.

Phan, M.C.T, Styles, C.W. and Patterson, P.G. (1999) 'An empirical examination of the trust development process linking firm and personal characteristics in an international setting', *European Academy of Marketing Conference* (EMAC), Berlin.

Sheth, J.N. and Parvatiyar, A. (1995) 'The evolution of relationship marketing', *International Business Review*, 4 (4), 397–418.

Sheth, J.N. and Sisodia, R.S. (1999) 'Revisiting marketing's lawlike generalizations', *Journal of the Academy of Marketing Sciences*, 17 (1), 71–87.

Storbacka, K., Strandvik, T. and Grönroos, C. (1994) 'Managing customer relations for profit: the dynamics of relationship quality', *International Journal of Service Industry Management*, 5, 21–38.

Webster Jr, F.E. (1992) 'The changing role of marketing in the corporation', *Journal of Marketing*, 56 (October), 1–17.

9 External partnerships

Introduction

In the previous chapter a distinction was made between vertical relationships (partnering) and horizontal relationships (collaboration).[1] This chapter will concentrate on those horizontal relationships that were earlier described as being represented by organisations at the same point in the channel of distribution[2] (including competitors) who seek to cooperate and collaborate for mutual benefit. In addition, this chapter will look at other relationships (for example with governments) that are, strictly speaking, non-commercial (although every relationship has the potential to affect the commercial viability of an organisation).

Horizontal partnerships

Over the past decade there has been considerable growth in the number of horizontal partnerships between competitors or between complementary players (Sheth and Sisodia, 1999, p. 84). Indeed, it may be claimed that these types of collaborations are significantly changing the competition landscape (Thomas, 2000, p. 530) as well as greatly extending the complexity of inter-firm relationships.

---

[1] It should be noted that the distinction between partnering and collaboration is used here to distinguish, in short-hand form, between the two types of relationship. Other authors use alternative (and sometimes interchangeable) terms.

[2] Strictly speaking, organisations that collaborate *at* the same point in the distribution but not necessarily *from* the same point in the chain. This is particularly relevant when 'complementary relationships' are discussed.

As with the previous chapter, the concentration here is almost wholly on the business-to-business (B2B) sector. Although the beginnings of a growth in consumer networks (particularly via the Internet; see Box 9.1) are apparent, these appear at an early stage of development but may prove to be very significant in the future (see Chapter 10). It is in the B2B sector that collaborations and networks of associations and relationships are currently more obviously developing. It is also more evident that many of the 'higher forms' of relationship discussed in previous chapters are more likely to develop in the B2B sector than in most consumer markets.

Box 9.1

Consumer network developments

Although consumer networks (effectively consumers collaborating to achieve a particular objective) are, in today's economy, rare they do exist and there is some evidence to suggest that they are likely to increase in the future. In the past families and friends have got together to buy in bulk (for example a whole carcass from the butcher) at a much reduced price. Indeed the origins of the Co-operative Movement had the collective spending power of the consumer as its driving force. In more recent years 'share portfolio' clubs have developed where pooled resources cut costs and shared decision making potentially increases efficiency and effectiveness. The limitation with these types of collaboration is usually geographical as extended distribution arrangements add to costs. It is also generally true that the more widespread the membership, the less collaborators have an opportunity to meet. The Internet has the potential to remove this geographical dependence. Already there is the example of the American consumer who, unhappy about the price quoted for her new car, used the Internet to trawl for other potential buyers. As a result she was able to return to the dealership with multiple orders for which she was now quoted a significantly lower price. That consumer networks have potential is evident. Whether they will become widespread is less certain. To succeed they invariably rely on a 'leading partner' who effectively fulfils the function of an intermediary, or 'middleman'. The distinction between the leading partner as the customer or the supplier becomes, therefore, very blurred. Chaffey *et al.* (2000, p. 196) see an alternative in the form of market intermediaries working on behalf of clients. They suggest that 'as customers become aware of the value of information and as technology on the Internet enables them to protect private information relating to site visits and transactions so the opportunity for intermediaries to act as "customer agents" grows'. The sole source of revenue for these new 'infomediaries' will derive from the value they generate for their clients.

Relationship research

According to Blois (1998, p. 256), an observer watching two organisations' behaviour is able to make an assessment of the current state of the relationship between them when:

■ They have knowledge of the contractual terms under which the exchange is being conducted.
■ They can observe the exchange process over an extended period of time.
■ The participants give explanations of the reasons why the observed actions were undertaken.

Subject to some measure of access, research of this type may be seen as relatively straightforward in the B2B sector.[3] Indeed, many researchers (especially from the IMP Group) have taken advantage of the relative visibility in the sector to examine, sometimes in great detail, the interactions between partner companies and their employees. This contrasts with the consumer goods sector (B2C), where most relationships are non-contractual and where consumers' motivations (despite the valiant attempt of researchers) are largely hidden, making assessment of relationships considerably more difficult. Add to this the probability that many consumers have little motivation to explain their actions (if indeed they actually know why these actions took place) and the difficulties of RM researchers in the B2C area are evident.

As a result of the greater openness in B2B marketing a considerable volume of research literature has been produced. While not always consistent (particularly in the language used to describe these relationships), this has provided a wealth of evidence about why networking and collaboration are becoming so widespread.

Networks and collaboration

There is considerable confusion in the usage and meaning of terms such as networks, collaborations and other associations (e.g. alliances). These terms change meaning with different authorship and are frequently used interchangeably depending on the circumstances described. In respect to this chapter the following descriptions are offered:

■ *Networks*: Networks are seen as relationships between individuals (as opposed to organisations). 'Networkers' utilise their 'contacts' in a sometimes systematic, but more often *ad hoc*, way. These 'personal contact networks' are, according to Chaston (1998, p. 276) 'constituted of formal and informal co-operative relationships whereby individual owners/managers seek to build links with each other in their market with the aim of obtaining the necessary information and knowledge to optimise organisational performance'.

■ *Collaborations*: Collaborative relationships are perceived as more formal (in the sense that they are recognised on a company-wide basis) relationships between organisations. These may be contractual, but as Gummesson (1999, p. 130) notes, 'trust cannot be assured through contracts and those that believe that lawyers can prevent the risks and hurdles of collaboration are bound to be disillusioned'. By the very nature of business, however, they are likely to include more formal meetings and involve the establishment of agreements and procedures on the form and nature of the collaboration.

---

[3] I can feel the hackles rising on the necks of my B2B research colleagues. This is not to say that they have any easier time of it; rather, they are more likely to obtain more accurate data than their B2C equivalents.

Networks

Networking was another buzzword of the 1990s and one that continues to hold considerable resonance at the beginning of the new millennium. As networking is more individual than organisational it may be valid to suggest that 'networking' is more effective on a smaller rather than a larger scale. It has been suggested, for example, that personal networks offer opportunities for small firms, in particular, to compete more effectively with larger companies (Chaston, 1998, pp. 275–6).

A network consists of a collection of individuals (see Figure 9.1), albeit individuals who are likely to have organisational affiliations and can use the benefits derived from networking for the good of their individual companies. Certain businesses thrive on networking while others actually depend on the network of contacts developed by their employees (e.g. financial services). In general most companies recognise the value in knowledge terms of their employees developing a networks of contacts with associate and competitive companies, other industries and other influential players (e.g. government) and explicitly encourage it.

Informal and *ad hoc* contact is of considerable importance. Formal relationships between these network players is unlikely and may even be barred by government legislation (for example, if there is any attempt by networkers to manipulate a market). Despite this informality such networks can be both strong and enduring. Social relationships are not discouraged and can indeed sometimes be the 'glue' that holds these networks together.

Networks are not a new phenomenon nor is the blur between acceptable and unacceptable commercial relationships behaviour a new debate. Where, for example, should the line be drawn on corporate entertainment? Is it an unfair advantage that a decision maker and potential supplier see each other socially? Is the membership of organisations that promote kinship ethical? Social membership

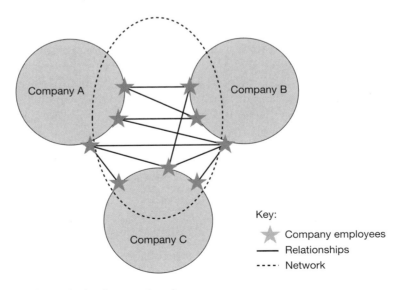

Figure 9.1 Business-to-business networks

of organisations such as the Freemasons, Rotary Clubs and even working men's clubs has always had a self-help element to it that is clear to members, if sometimes less acceptable to those outside.

Collaboration

The paradox of business in the future is, according to Doyle (1995, pp. 33–4), that to be a successful international competitor, the firm also has to be a committed and trusted cooperator. Over the past decade authors have battled to systematically describe the types of cooperation that were apparent in the marketplace. The number and range of such relationships typically defy neat pigeonholing. Brandenburger and Nalebuff (1996), for example, coined the phrase 'coopetition' to describe what at first sight appears to be the anomaly of simultaneous competition and collaboration. Even before the term 'coopetition' was used terms such as alliances, partnerships, joint ventures, joint R&D, minority investments, cross-licensing, sourcing relationships, co-branding, co-marketing and other cooperative descriptions were being used to describe, what were being recognised as a 'key requirement' for successfully competing in the global marketplace (Sheth and Sisodia, 1999, p. 81).

So pervasive is collaboration seen to be that decades-old marketing concepts are being rewritten in the language of cooperative behaviour. Gummesson (1999, p. 127), for example, updates the 1980s 'forces of competition' model (involving present and potential competitors, customers and suppliers; Porter, 1985, p. 5) which he interprets, 'in the spirit of RM', as 'relationships forces giving birth to alliances'. Governments too have noted the spectacular increase in 'collaborative agreements' and are having to reinterpret anti-competitive legislation to take this into account (for example, some partners in the 'Star Alliance' have protection from US government anti-trust legislation; see the Case study at the end of this chapter).

Collaboration should not, however, be mistaken for altruism or an end to competition. Indeed, in some industries competition is more intense than ever as one 'alliance' battles with another in a bid for greater market share (e.g. the airline industry). It is also widely recognised that collaborative relationships can, if restrictions are not observed, have anti-competitive implications (Palmer, 1996, p. 22). They can give birth to 'power networks' which create partly locked markets (Gummesson, 1999, p. 131). So potentially powerful are these collaborations that legislators around the world keep a very close eye on such agreements and have developed powers, where necessary, to prohibit them (see Box 9.1).

Collaboration types

Collaboration can be crudely divided into two types:

■ *Industry collaboration*: where collaborations are with competitors in the same market sector and where objectives may include effectiveness and efficiency of distribution channels, servicing or other support facilities and market sector growth or market sector dominance.

■ *External collaboration*: where collaborators (usually from different industries) bring different skills, competencies and assets to the relationship. The objective of external collaboration is often to take advantage of a new sector or to promote existing sector differentiation.

Industry collaboration

Industry collaboration is becoming a key marketing strategy as firms recognise the possibilities of a 'positive-sum game' where a degree of cooperation results in greater value creation and enlargement of the market for all participants (Sheth and Sisodia, 1999, p. 81). Industry collaboration is not new. Trade associations have existed for centuries to promote particular industry growth. These organisations were set up cooperatively to develop markets through definition of agreed standards and often generic advertising (e.g. British Meat, International Wool Secretariat). The benefits associated with increasing overall market size collectively could be as great or greater than attempts to increase market share individually.

According to Sheth and Sisodia (1999, p. 82) market share will continue to be an important concept but it is fundamentally a 'zero-sum' or 'win–lose' proposition compared with industry collaboration. Most authors agree that collaboration (like partnering) should aim to be a 'win–win' relationship if it is to succeed. Equity is also seen as vital. In this type of relationship parties must treat each other as equals and partners, otherwise there is the likelihood that one party will act covertly to out-manoeuvre the other (Gummesson, 1999, p. 130).

Market-share thinking, therefore, has to be counterbalanced with a 'market-growth orientation' as an industry growing the total market collaboratively is often less costly to its individual firms (Sheth and Sisodia, 1999, p. 82). There is also what Gummesson calls 'tacit alliances', which emerge through such industry consensus and which result in all members acting in the same way. The plus side of these 'tacit alliances' is that they can instil ethical behaviour into an industry. On the negative side they may uphold past bad practices at the expense of the future of the industry.

Alliances

The current growth area in industry collaboration is in so-called alliances. This is where a group or groups of competitors (as opposed to the whole industry) collaborate to achieve cost and efficiency objectives. It is in the airline industry that the development of alliances is most prevalent (see Box 9.2 and Case study). For the airlines involved the objectives of such alliances are improved competitiveness, increased sales, increased revenue and lower cost through coordination of destinations, timetables, reservation systems, ticketing and staffing (Gummesson, 1999, p. 129).

Industry-driven alliances have a history that stretches back across the 20th century. A good example is the Associated Merchandising Corporation (AMC). AMC was formed at the beginning of the 20th century to source merchandise for a number of North American department stores, including Bloomingdales of New York, Filenes of Boston, Bullocks of Los Angeles and other, originally independent,

| Box 9.2 | **The British Airways 'Oneworld Alliance'** |

The complexity of collaboration in the airline industry is illustrated in this extract by Nigel Piercy, which describes British Airways' (BA) 'alliance' negotiations from 1997 to 1999. (For the current list of Oneworld members, see Chapter 3.)

From the base of the proposed BA/AA (American Airlines) alliance, BA is committed to a larger network operating under the new 'Oneworld' umbrella brand. Progress towards this goal has continued while the alliance with AA has been blocked [by the US and European regulators]. Key stages in this building process, leading to the announcement of the 'Oneworld' brand in 1998 have been:

- August 1997 – Richard Branson of Virgin [a long-term objector regarding BA's competitive strategies] makes a surprise press announcement that BA has a 'secret global deal' involving BA/AA with Japan Airlines and KLM, which should be stopped.
- September 1997 – plans to include Iberia of Spain in the alliance fall through, but by January 1998 a looser code-sharing agreement with BA and AA holding equity in Iberia is being discussed with BA and AA each taking a 10% stake.
- October 1997 – BA and Finnair announce a marketing and network alliance in Scandinavia to challenge the Scandinavian Airlines Systems (part of the Star Alliance [see Case Study]) dominance.
- January 1998 – BA and Lot Polish Airlines announce a partnership to counter Lufthansa's strength in Poland.
- May 1998 – news breaks of an imminent end to the dispute between BA and USAir, as a prelude to USAir joining the BA/AA alliance (AA and USAir already have a marketing agreement).
- September 1998 – BA/AA widen their alliance to include Cathay Pacific in Hong Kong, Australia's Quantas and Canadian Airlines.
- September 1998 – the Oneworld alliance branding is announced by BA.
- September 1998 – although designed specifically to avoid regulatory issues, the European Commissioner announces that he is scrutinising the plans and may take action.
- December 1998 – Finnair, the state-controlled Finnish carrier, joins Oneworld.
- January 1999 – Japan Airlines plans to introduce code-sharing flights with BA and Cathay Pacific, seen as a move by Asia's largest carrier towards alliance.

(*Source*: Adapted from Piercy, 1999, pp. 45–6)

stores, each of which held a 'share' of AMC's equity. Although the ownership of these stores is now concentrated in fewer hands, it still operates on the basis of delivering collaborative gains in merchandise cost and distribution efficiency and effectiveness to its 'member' stores. In Japan conglomerate-type industrial groups, known as *Keiretsus*, exist. These *Keiretsus* are made up of a complex web of interacting independent companies which cooperate with each other as 'systems' through which to share skills and resources to achieve competitive advantage (Chaston 1998, p. 275).

It is often the case that a company can belong to numerous collaborative alliances, some of which are in competition with each other. For example, an airline may belong to one group for sales purposes but to another for engine maintenance – even if that means servicing its sales competitor's aircraft (Palmer, 2000, p. 689). Alliances of this type can vary in intensity and duration and can be 'one-shot projects', limited but continuous cooperation or take parties so close that the next step is merger (Gummesson, 1999, p. 127)

External collaboration

Collaboration frequently (and with growing regularity) means arrangements between organisations from different market sectors, each of which bring different skills, competencies and assets to a relationship. These relationships may be for the purposes of improving the total package offering (e.g. the collaboration between British Airways and Hertz) or to create a distinctive advantage in an existing market sector (e.g. Sky Television and Granada Television with a variety of Premier League football teams). Alternatively, they may be developed to take advantage of a new market sector (see Boxes 9.3 and 9.4).

Box 9.3

Handbag.com

Handbag.com is, in Internet parlance, a 'vertical portal' (or 'vortal') aimed at women. Vertical portals are Internet sites which include links to other (often retail) sites and where revenue is largely derived from advertising and sponsorship.[4] Handbag.com was launched in October 1999 as a 50/50 joint venture between the pharmaceutical and beauty product retailer Boots and Hollinger Telegraph New Media. Boots brought to the venture extensive experience of retailing to the site's target female market. Hollinger Telegraph New Media (the media management and investment division of Hollinger International) brought extensive experience of Internet publishing, including the *Electric Telegraph*, one of the UK's best online news web sites.

It is in the area of 'new sector development', particularly those associated with recent technological advances, that collaborations are expected to have the greatest growth potential. As Doyle (1995, p. 38) notes:

> It is in the [area of] external [collaboration[5]] that the major change occurs for the conventional view of marketing . . . Tomorrow's marketing managers will be scanning more broadly and looking at any organisation with capabilities or resources that offer synergies that can be exploited in the market. These external resources might be new products, alternative distribution channels, manufacturing capabilities, or more generally knowledge that can be exploited together.

Developing collaborative relationships

Successful collaboration of any sort is not created overnight but develops over time. The desired level of closeness and/or the complexity of the relationship often determining the length of time it can take. Collaborative relationships mature with interaction, frequency, duration and the diversity of challenge that relationship

---

[4] This is very much a simplification as Handbag.com has a number of ways of generating revenue including through sales commission. The complexity of 'vortals' is, however, beyond the scope of this book.

[5] Doyle uses the word 'networking' but the meaning (within the context of this chapter) does not change.

Box 9.4

Supermarket group in joint venture with US Internet company

Tesco, the supermarket group, has agreed to invest $18m (£12m) over three years in a website aimed at women that it is creating with iVillage, a US web company. The joint venture is the latest in the trend towards content companies, such as iVillage, forming partnerships with traditional retailers. Boots formed a similar alliance last year when it launched Handbag.com, a rival women's portal, with Hollinger International, the media group. Candice Carpenter, founder and chief executive of iVillage, said 'The best way forward for us is a partner with significant brands such as Tesco'.

The new site joins an already crowded market of websites targeting women, including Charlottestreet.com, (circle and Beme.com). iVillage.co.uk will offer a range of content, on issues such as work, relationships, babies and pregnancy. 'iVillage covers the key decisions in women's lives. It is based on the idea that we are not all alike,' said Ms Carpenter. iVillage had been in talks with other potential partners, mainly media companies. Ms Carpenter said: 'I did not know who Tesco was until I came here and realised what an institution they are. There isn't an equivalent in the US.'

Tesco said the additional community content that will be provided by iVillage would be a good way to drive traffic to its website and to get feedback from its customers. 'It improves the content around our e-commerce site and supports our broader objective of moving into non-food areas,' said a Tesco.com executive.

Tesco and iVillage will provide a total of $70m in marketing, branding, cash and resources into iVillage.co.uk. Ms Carpenter said she expected to migrate the 160,000 UK-based users who log-on to the US site to the new version.

The decision by iVillage to move overseas follows a period of turbulence in the US, where its Nasdaq-listed shares have been hit by the negative sentiment towards some business-to-consumer Internet companies. The shares, floated at $24 in March, rose to a high of $114 in April before plunging to about $7.50.

iVillage has also experienced high management turnover and a change in direction. Earlier this month, it said it was selling its assets in iBaby, a baby-products retailer. The sale effectively moved the company away from an e-commerce model towards focusing on content.

Rebecca Ulph, analyst at Forrester Research, an Internet research company said: 'iVillage's target audience fits well with Tesco, in that it attracts the more mature woman, with a family who might be tempted to do her shopping at home.'

(*Source*: *Financial Times*, 20 July 2000)

partners encounter and face together (Lewicki *et al.* 1998, p. 443), ultimately becoming part of the structural capital of the organisation (Gummesson, 1999, p. 5). Tzokas and Saren (2000, p. 8) suggest that this development can be represented by a 'relationship life cycle' that develops through different stages. Each of these stages, they suggest, presents unique requirements and opportunities for those involved. These life cycle stages are shown in Figure 9.2.

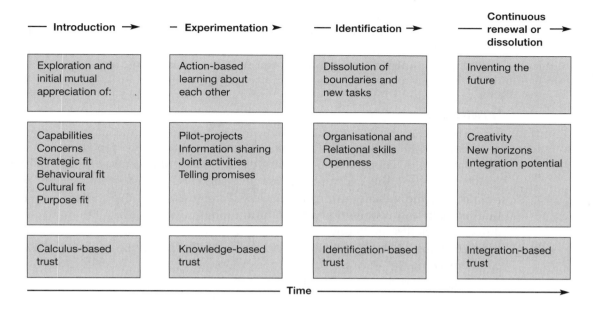

Figure 9.2 Relationship stages
(*Source*: Adapted from Tzokas and Saren, 2000, p. 8)

Tzokas and Saren suggest that specific knowledge requirements are necessity at each stage of the cycle. At the introduction stage partners seek a mutual understanding of each other's capabilities and concerns and their potential for strategic, behavioural, cultural and purpose 'fit'. Trust at this stage is based on rational evaluation. At the experimental stage the first joint tasks are undertaken, testing the effectiveness and efficiency of the relationship and helping develop appreciation by the collaborators of each other's capabilities. Trust is at this stage seen to be based on a working knowledge of the partnership. At the identification stage closer and more ambitious collaboration may be undertaken and the boundaries between the organisations may begin to dissolve. Organisational and relational skills are required at this point to maintain the strategic purpose and direction of the collaboration. Identification-based trust, characterised by a mutual sharing of values, becomes more evident. In the final continuous renewal or dissolution stage two, options are put forward. If the relationship has run its course (for example, if it has become stale) then dissolution may be the end result. Alternatively, renewal may take place if partners identify new tasks to be performed and have the ability to re-invent the relationship. Trust at this stage is integral to the operation.

Tzokas and Saren's model illustrates the potential for collaborative relationships. The existence of such relationships implies a degree of mutual dependency that blunts the ability of either partner to part from the other without some degree of inconvenience (Brennan, 1997, p. 770). The 'usual warnings' must, however, be made concerning models of this type. The movement is not necessarily unidirectional as relationships can be scaled down as well as up depending on perceived needs at a particular point in time. In addition many relationships will never reach the stage where organisational boundaries are seen to dissolve if partners are content to operate at a lower relationship intensity.

Downsides

A variety of environmental factors influence the stability (and indeed the acceptability) of cooperative relationships, including the general values of the society in which the exchanges occur and the specific history of actions and reactions by individuals within that society (Palmer, 2000, p. 690). There is a very fine line between cooperation and collusion (Sheth and Sisodia, 1999, p. 81) and different societies are prone to draw the line according to established national practice. Thus what is acceptable cooperation in Japan may be regarded as anti-competitive in the USA and the European Union. Even within general national parameters countries are prone to 'move the goalposts' in support of their own companies' self-interest. Palmer (1996, p. 22) notes that it is ironic, for example, that while western companies seek closer relationships many of those same companies have been applying pressure, through their governments, to have such practices curtailed in Japan.

Operational defects may also prove damaging. According to Palmer (2000, p. 687) cooperation that is too pervasive may have the effect of reducing efficiency and effectiveness in a market (e.g. the extensive networks of cooperative relationships among Japanese distributors, which can add three levels, and consequent mark-ups, to the distributive system). A further common occurrence in systems where social relationships become intermingled with business relationships is that 'altruism' may be extended by one partner (e.g. accepting goods which fail to meet their expectations of value) to preserve the standing of the other partner (Palmer, 2000, p. 700). Another problem associated with making relationships work is 'culture clash' (see Chapter 8). The potential battle between two corporate cultures can be hazardous. Confrontation between value systems and cultural shock are, according to Gummesson (1999, p. 130), the rule rather than the exception.

The value of replacing one competitive system with another (albeit collaborative) system must also be questioned. As Palmer (2000, p. 700) notes

> The development of co-operative marketing alliances which result in competition between networks of organisations rather than between individual organisations may transfer this selfish instinct to the network rather than the individual firm.

The danger also exists that marketers are mis-reading the partnership and collaboration runes and that relationships of this type are a phase rather than a wholly new direction. Certainly, while the number of collaborative agreements continues to rise, there is evidence of mega-mergers continuing apace with Time-Warner, Carlton-Granada and Seagram's/Universal being but the latest in a long line. There is also evidence of a growing number of equity investments between collaborators that may drive further mergers in the future. Alternatively, this may simply reflect the diversity of the market place and the need for a spectrum of strategies.

Collaborations need to be constantly worked upon if they are to succeed. Gummesson (1999, p. 131) recognises the problems associated with maintaining relationships when he proposes:

> The advice provided by a marriage councillor is surprisingly well suited for the advice needed for a company entering an alliance – choose your partner carefully, invest in a win–win relationship, stay attractive to your partner, develop a sound economy, and search for a division of labour that works for all parties. Good vibrations are needed, even if it is not passionate love. Still we know that decisions on cohabitation are taken under uncertainty with no guarantee whatsoever of the outcome.

Other relationships

Other important external liaisons exist in addition to those so far discussed in this and the previous chapter. These include relationships with:

- Local, national and supra-national legislators
- National and international agencies
- Pressure groups.

Legislators

Companies have long recognised the importance of maintaining good relationships with legislators. After all, legislators have it within their power to considerably benefit or jeopardise the health of commercial organisations. There is, however, a significant difference between the types of relationships permitted with legislators and those between commercial firms. Whereas commercial companies (within the scope of anti-competitive legislation) are free to establish whatever depth of relationship the parties see fit, relationships with legislators at anything less than arm's length are perceived as potentially corrupt practice in most western economies. To suggest it never happens would be naïve. Both parties are, however, aware that there are boundaries (albeit unclear) that they should avoid crossing.

'Lobbying' is the all-embracing term most often used to describe the methodologies applied to influence government. Although the term implies influence though argument, the general meaning is 'to influence or solicit' (politicians) and a wider range of techniques are used in addition to straightforward argument. Thus lobbying may take the form of information transmission (ensuring legislators have the information to make a decision), influence (ensuring that the company's or industry's position is clear), general 'public relations' activities (e.g. social events, trips etc.) and political party funding.

Having the ear of government (or the potential future government) is seen as so important that substantial sums are spent (and sometimes mis-spent) on funding such activities. Companies also see it as useful to bring political appointees into their businesses for advice and lobbying purposes. In the UK, for example, the most common type of interest declared in the House of Common's Register of Members' Interests is payments from organisations that employ them (Filkin, 2000, p. 34). According to Filkin at the time of the 1997 UK election 249 members of the UK Parliament had 'consultancies'. Pressure to publicly declare such appointments, new rules and other pressures meant that by 1999 this had fallen to fewer than 100 and by June 2000 to under 40)). Again, the line between acceptable and unacceptable influence is very blurred.

In addition, it should not be forgotten that governments (local, national and supranational) are large existing and potential customers and that, from the supplier perspective, relationship maintenance will be directed to this end (Zineldin, 2000, p. 20). Given the level of public accountability for this expenditure, however, the development of personal relationships is (technically) severely restricted, although this may not necessarily be the case in all markets.

Agencies

As with legislators, local, national and international agencies can be influential in many industries (e.g. road building and construction) in that they often have the ear of governments and, in many cases, control substantial buying power. There has been a considerable growth in 'agencies' in many countries (e.g. UK, New Zealand), with a growing number of previously directly controlled departmental operations being privatised. As with legislators, the level of relationship will be determined by acceptable practice. The greater freedom of previously government-run businesses (for example the UK Post Office) has meant some easing of the 'rules' (written and unwritten) covering formal and informal relationships between these organisations and those in the private sector. The high public profile of such organisations, however, normally ensures that such relationships rarely reach the levels that may be established between other commercial companies.

Pressure groups

There are a growing number of pressure groups whose actions can affect the commercial success of a company. Direct conflict with such pressure groups can appear inequitable at times with apparently small organisations taking on large, multinational corporations. They can, however, have an influence with consumers and legislators considerably out of proportion to their size, as companies such as Shell and McDonald's can testify. Frequently (but by no means always) commercial organisations find themselves in opposition to such groups. Whereas complete agreement may not always be possible, maintaining a dialogue with such groups can be beneficial.

Conclusion

There is little doubt that horizontal relationships are of current and growing importance in many industries. Gummesson (1999, p. 127) suggests that for companies such as Corning collaboration is so central to their business strategy that the corporation calls itself a 'network of organisations'. He goes on to note (p. 129) that five US corporations together represent 400 formal alliances and countless informal ones. These include IBM (136), AT&T (77), Hewlett-Packard (65), Digital Equipment (63) and Sun Microsystems (45). In those industries driven by new technologies the value of such strategies is also apparent.

There is, however, no guarantee, that such collaborations will always produce results. In a study by McKinsey (quoted in Gummesson, 1999, p. 130) of 49 collaborations studied one-third failed. Whereas collaboration in general is seen as beneficial and can contribute to the effectiveness and efficiency of an operation, such outcomes are far from a foregone conclusion. Important decisions need to be made concerning the validity of all such collaborations, the level of closeness and the probable duration. In addition, companies should not just have 'collaboration' forming strategies but strategies to be implemented when such relationships have run their course.

Summary

This chapter looked at horizontal partnerships and other potential partnerships external to the organisation. It noted the considerable increase of such arrangements between competitors and other complementary players, which may or may not come from a single industry. The chapter differentiated between 'networking' and 'collaborations', subdividing the latter into 'industry collaboration', usually with competitors, and 'external collaboration' with other companies that could offer different skills, competencies and assets to a partnership. The chapter noted that successful collaborations are not created overnight and presented a 'relationship life cycle' describing the factors observed at each stage in the relationship. The importance of other relationships with, for example, governments, agencies and pressure groups was also highlighted.

Discussion questions

1 Distinguish between network and collaborative strategies.

2 Where would you draw the line between collaboration and collusion?

3 Suggest examples of (a) industry collaboration and (b) external collaboration.

4 Why might organisations wish to maintain relationships with consumer or other pressure groups?

Star Alliance saving customers $100 million annually

United Airlines today cited the findings of a recently released University of Illinois study on the benefits of code-sharing and anti-trust immunity as further evidence of the overwhelming customer benefits of alliances between airlines.

The study, based on international fare data compiled by the United States Department of Transportation during the third quarter of 1999, found that customers flying itineraries involving two allied carriers benefited from lower fares. In the specific case of itineraries involving two allied airlines that both code-share and hold US anti-trust immunity, the result was fares that on average were 27% lower than fares where inter-airline (interline) pricing methods were employed. The study also specifically credited Star Alliance airlines with saving customers $100 million annually as a result of the combination of code-sharing and anti-trust immunity that some members of Star Alliance currently hold.

University of Illinois economist Jan K. Brueckner prepared the July 2000 study. Brueckner also predicted that if US anti-trust immunity were extended in the future to airlines within Star Alliance that do not currently have it, an additional $20 million in annual savings would be generated for passengers making two-carrier trips on airlines within Star Alliance.

In the study Professor Brueckner concluded that, 'In addition to enjoying the convenience gains made possible by airline cooperation, interline passengers reap substantial benefits in the realm of pricing, paying substantially lower fares as a result of cooperative behavior.' Brueckner also attributed much of the savings to the anti-trust immunity held by several members of Star Alliance, saying 'The immunity enjoyed by Star Alliance partners generates an aggregate benefit of about $80 million per year for interline passengers. Code-sharing among Star partners yields a further annual benefit of around $20 million. Thus, these two existing forms of cooperation generate a benefit for the alliance's interline passengers of approximately $100 million per year.'

Welcoming the results of the study, United Airlines Vice President for International and Regulatory Affairs Michael Whitaker said, 'These results clearly demonstrate that in addition to all of the seamless service benefits that customers of Star Alliance have enjoyed for the past three years, the anti-trust immunity held by members of Star Alliance is resulting in significantly lower air fares. From its inception, Star Alliance has been about providing customers with access to the world through a travel experience that's as seamless as flying on just one airline. The July 2000 study shows that when the seamless standard is allowed to be extended to pricing, the flying public saves tens of millions of dollars every year.'

The study attributed fare reductions on itineraries involving two allied airlines to three levels of cooperation:

Level of cooperation	Fare reduction
Code-sharing	7%
Alliance membership	4%
Anti-trust immunity	16%
Total	27%

Brueckner's study was based primarily on itineraries that originate or terminate in the United States and involve two allied airlines flying across the Atlantic or between the US and Canada, comparing them to two-carrier itineraries from the same origin to the same destination on carriers that do not hold anti-trust immunity. Star Alliance members Air Canada, Lufthansa German Airlines, SAS Scandinavian Airlines and United Airlines currently hold anti-trust immunity.

A full copy of the report can be obtained at www.brueckner-report.com.

United Airlines offers more than 2,400 flights each day to 134 destinations in 26 countries and two US territories. United Airlines' Internet address is www.united.com.

Current members of Star Alliance are: Air Canada, Air New Zealand, All Nippon Airways, Ansett Australia, Austrian Airlines Group (which comprises Austrian Airlines, Lauda Air and Tyrolean Airways), British Midland, Lufthansa German Airlines, Mexicana, Scandinavian Airlines System (SAS), Singapore Airlines, Thai Airways International, United Airlines and VARIG Brazilian Airlines. The Star Alliance network offers more than 9,200 daily flights to 134 destinations in 130 countries. Star Alliance's Internet address is www.staralliance.com.

(*Source*: PRNewswire, Chicago, 24 August 2000)

Case study questions

1 What are the 'seamless service benefits' that Star Alliance customers receive?

2 What are the advantages to the airlines involved of this relationship?

References

Blois, K.J. (1998) 'Don't all firms have relationships?', *Journal of Business and Industrial Marketing*, 13 (3), 256–70.

Brandenburger, A.M. and Nalebuff, B.J. (1996) *Cooptition*. New York: Doubleday.

Brennan, R. (1997) 'Buyer/supplier partnering in British industry: the automotive and telecommunications sectors', *Journal of Marketing Management*, 13 (8) 758–76.

Chaffey, D., Mayer, R., Johnston, K. and Ellis-Chadwick, F. (2000) Internet Marketing. Harlow: Pearson Education.

Chaston, I. (1998) 'Evolving "new marketing" philosophies by merging existing concepts: application of process within small high-technology firms', *Journal of Marketing Management*, 14, 273–91.

Doyle, P. (1995) 'Marketing in the new millennium', *European Journal of Marketing*, 29 (12) 23–41.

Filkin, E. (2000) 'House rules', *RSA Journal*, 34–5.

Gummesson, E. (1999) *Total Relationship Marketing: Rethinking Marketing Management from 4Ps to 30Rs*. Oxford: Butterworth Heinemann.

Lewicki, R.J., McAllister, D.J. and Bies, R.J. (1998) 'Trust and distrust: new relationships and realities', *Academy of Management Review*, 23 (3), 438–58.

Palmer, A. J. (1996) 'Relationship marketing: a universal paradigm or management fad?', *The Learning Organisation*, 3 (3), 18–25.

Palmer, A. J. (2000) 'Co-operation and competition; a Darwinian synthesis of relationship marketing', *European Journal of Marketing*, 34 (5/6), 687–704.

Piercy, N. (1999) *Tales From the Marketplace; Stories of Revolution, Reinvention and Renewal.* Oxford: Butterworth-Heinemann.

Porter, M.E. (1985) *Competitive Advantage.* New York: Free Press.

Sheth, J.N. and Sisodia, R.S. (1999) 'Revisiting marketing's lawlike generalizations', *Journal of the Academy of Marketing Sciences*, 17 (1), 71–87.

Thomas, M.J. (2000) 'Commentary: princely thoughts on Machiavelli, marketing and management', *European Journal of Marketing*, 34 (5/6), 524–37.

Tzokas, N. and Saren, M. (2000) 'Knowledge and relationship marketing: where, what and how?', in 2nd WWW Conference on Relationship Marketing, 15 November 1999–15 February 2000, paper 4 (www.mcb.co.uk/services/conferen/nov99/rm).

Zineldin, M. (2000) 'Beyond relationship marketing: technologicalship marketing', *Marketing Intelligence and Planning*, 18 (1), 9–23.

Part III

Managing and controlling the relationship

In this third and final part, important aspects of the management and control of relationships are discussed. It should be noted, however, that neither chapter presents a prescriptive approach; rather, they attempt to illustrate the various approaches taken and the opportunities available dependent on a company's individual requirements.

Chapter 10 looks at the enormous impact that new technologies have had, are having and no doubt will continue to have in the future on the management and control of relationships. As is noted in the text some relationship marketers would go so far as to suggest that without these developments RM (under whatever guise) would not have become so prominent.

In Chapter 11 concepts surrounding the planning and control of RM are analysed. The text deliberately avoids the promotion of prescriptive, 'checklist' solutions although some models are generally accepted as valuable from a planning perspective. Instead it suggests a need to design in relational strategies, initially within the current planning process. The chapter also confronts head-on the criticism of RM, in part as a warning against 'prescriptive complacency' and in part to rebalance (if this is needed) the sometimes over-enthusiastic claims made.

10 Relationship technology

Key issues

➤ The language of e-commerce.

➤ Mass customisation

➤ Loyalty schemes and data gathering

➤ One-to-one marketing

➤ Marketing types (RM, DM, DbM, CRM)

➤ The Internet and the changing marketplace.

Introduction

Developments in information technology (IT) and manufacturing technology have had an enormous impact on the theory and practice of marketing in general and relationship marketing in particular. Such is the influence of this new technology that it has been claimed that without these technological advances RM could never hope to be an effective strategy (Zineldin, 2000, p. 9). Certainly, without these developments few companies would be able to handle the growing complexity of their customer and other core relationships. O'Malley and Tynan (2000, p. 799) suggest that this is particularly apparent in business-to-consumer (B2C) marketing. Having been initially ignored by B2C marketers, who considered it conceptually and contextually different, RM was apparently not 'discovered' by these marketers until the advent of available technology.

The pace of technological change is frantic. Developments are unfolding 'so fast, in so unsettling and complex a manner, that it is very easy to see only thousands of different trees and get thoroughly lost in the wood' (Mitchell, 2000, p. 355). The speed of this change makes discussion of new technology difficult as even new technology can become outdated quickly.[1] To avoid potential embarrassment this chapter will concentrate on the actual or potential strategic effects of current technology and its likely successors rather than on the tools themselves.

---

[1] One of the anonymous reviewers of this book graphically described writing about e-commerce as like painting a picture of the Clapham omnibus as it races by.

Buzzwords

A growing problem when discussing the effects of new technology on marketing theory and practice is the myriad of ways these developments are described by different authors. Buzzwords and phrases are created (and subsequently dumped) at a rate that reflects the technocrat's needs to move on to the next best thing. The evident danger is that this form of technological development will lead rather than facilitate the marketing imperative.

The language of electronic commerce is used to convey the strategic priorities of many companies. At the simplest level the prefix 'e-' is seen to imply updated techniques utilising the tools of the technological age (e.g. e-business, e-commerce, e-tail). As Duncan (2000, p. 58) notes, by placing 'e-' in front of it, everyday activities becomes modern, daring and accessible all at one time. The ubiquitous suffix '.com' (or 'dot com'), over and above other suffixes (e.g. .co.uk), is seen to convey the message that businesses wish it to be known that they are competing in this technologically developed marketplace. On a more theoretical level the number of different concepts with the suffix '-marketing' directly resulting from IT and manufacturing technology development is growing fast (e.g. one-to-one, permission, virtual etc). To add to the chaos, it is frequently the case that:

- Many conceptual terms have definitions that appear to overlap.
- Different authors use the same terms to describe different concepts or different terms to describe the same concept.
- Some terms 'evolve' into differently named yet apparently similar concepts.
- Terms are denigrated and ditched as the next 'new' idea (if indeed it is new) comes along (see Box 10.5).

Perhaps the best example of a number of the above-mentioned scenarios is the term 'relationship marketing' itself. At the end of 1999 RM was used by many practitioners (and some academics) to describe what others called direct or database marketing and what others now frequently term customer relationship management' (CRM). The justification for these interpretations would appear to be more cosmetic than substantial although some academics and practitioners (and many consultants) would, no doubt, disagree. They argue that CRM means so much more (or is it less?). Yet the root concepts are so similar as to make little significant difference. This multiplicity of terms would suggest that many marketers no longer wish to be confined by strict definitions and that flexibility of description and title takes precedence over clarity.

Ground rules

The 'rule' followed in this chapter has been to describe the impact of IT developments on marketing relationships using those terms that appear to offer maximum clarity and/or best represent the industry consensus. It is also seen fit to discuss manufacturing as well as IT developments as the former is both driving and being driven by the latter.

Manufacturing technology

Mass manufacturing and mass marketing may have dominated commercial activity in much of the 19th and nearly all of the 20th centuries but this has not always been the case. In earlier times most people traded for basic needs within a confined geographical area. Suppliers knew their customers well and frequently made or supplied to order. It was only with the coming of the industrial revolution that the cost advantages of mass production were fully recognised and the consequent need to market on a mass scale developed. Mass production and mass marketing together drove the enormous increase in consumer spending during the 20th century and were arguably both responsible for the growing wealth (and so-called consumerism) of developed economies.

Mass customisation

The final decade of the 20th century saw the beginnings of a reaction against 'mass production' and 'mass marketing' both prompted by and prompting technological developments of every sort. Although this should not be over-emphasised (most consumers are still happy to benefit from the cost savings of mass-manufactured products or mass-supplied services) the growing wealth (relative to the cost of living) meant more and more consumers were looking for more individual, personally tailored offerings.[2] At the beginning of the 1990s McKenna (1991, p. v) wrote:

> I believe that far from being a homogeneous society that [is] served through mass manufacturing and mass marketing – or to put it another way – through mass manipulation – the next decade, the next century will bring a complexity of products and services that will be, in a very real sense, directly influenced and even designed by customers.

Brookes and Little (1997, p. 98) take the argument further by suggesting that 'in today's fragmented, turbulent marketplace, with its ever shifting demand for innovation and tailor made products and services, the concept of a standard product, a standard service or a standard message no longer makes sense'. While it is perhaps true that these statements are a little over-blown (mass-producers such as Coca-Cola or McDonald's certainly have some life left in them) and that the vision sometimes differs from the reality (see Box 10.1), there is evidence that 'mass customisation', as it has become generally known, is a recognisable, although occasionally faltering, trend.

The term 'mass customisation' has come to refer to 'the notion that, by leveraging certain technologies, companies can provide customers with customised products while retaining the economic advantages of mass production' (Sheth and Sisodia, 1999, p. 80). Mass customisation differs from individually crafted products or services (for which there also appears to be a growing trend) in that it maintains the

---

[2] Although even in highly developed consumer markets there are the 'haves' and 'have-nots'. In addition to those who choose not to 'collaborate' there will always be a percentage of the population who are not in a position to participate in market trends.

Box 10.1 **The vision and reality of mass customisation**

Visionary definition
Mass customisation is the ability to
provide your customers with anything
they want profitably, at any time they
want it, anywhere they want it, and in any
way they want it.

(*Source*: Hart, 1995, p. 36)

Realistic definition
The use of flexible processes and
organisational structures to produce
varied and often individually customised
products and services at the low cost of
a standardised, mass production system.

(*Source*: Hart, 1995, p. 36)

---

economies of scale advantages of mass production. In many industrial sectors,
the capability is becoming available to produce more and more varieties and choices
for the customer although, as Box 10.1 points out, there is still a gap between the
vision and the reality.

The individual tailoring of products suggested by 'mass customisation' has been
described by Ira Matahia (quoted by Chaffey *et al.*, 2000, p. 292), CEO of Brand
Futures Group as 'complicated simplicity'. Matahia goes on to suggest that as
consumers crave individually tailored products there will be a strong demand for
unique items. For businesses this will mean the end of a mass audience orientated
approach and the beginning of an 'audience-of-one' (or 'segment of one') approach
to marketing.

Time to market

In technologically driven industries (i.e. those companies producing, as opposed to
simply using, this new technology) time to market is a key factor. Windows of
opportunity for any new technically innovative product are smaller than before and
product life cycles (PLCs) seen to be getting shorter. The pressure to get a new
product to market means that, in general, there is less time than before to spend on
research. As Gordon (1998, p. 6) notes, 'marketers used to use market research to help
identify issues and assess customer response' but under the more pressurised
conditions that now exist this research can 'take more time than the marketer has
got'. Market conditions are, Gordon notes, changing so fast that a company
addressing current research may quickly find itself dealing with yesterday's issues.
In many instances, instead of pre-launch research, companies are using the marketplace as their testing ground. These firms are using the flexibility of technologically
advanced manufacturing methods to 'roll out' (and at the same time adapt) products
while simultaneously testing their response. This testing (as opposed to research) has
the advantage of producing results based on actual as opposed to forecast sales while
at the same time generating revenue.

Dangers exist in the above strategy, particularly in respect to innovation.
Technologically orientated companies are prone to deceive themselves into thinking
that the extreme novelty of their new invention automatically means there is an

untapped market.[3] This self-deception Palmer (2000, p. 126) calls the 'myth of the big market' and is an example of the potential problems associated with companies reverting to product-driven, as opposed to market-driven, strategies.

Information technology

It is generally acknowledged that IT has enormous potential for relationship building, if used effectively. Developments in IT allow a relationship-orientated management to store and manipulate information about their customers and, ultimately, to provide those customers with a better service. It is, however, very easy to get carried away by the prospects of IT and as a result it is sometimes difficult to tell the genuine from the hype (Gummesson, 1999, p. 89).

In RM terms perhaps the biggest danger is to assume that technology can always effectively replace personal contact. Technology-supported developments aimed at increasing the efficiency of the organisation (e.g. call centres, telephone menus etc.) do not necessarily always increase value or convenience for the customer (see Box 10.2). According to Peppers and Rogers (2000, p. 243) today's 'interactive age' customers

> are accustomed to having their needs met immediately, conveniently and inexpensively. That's why, for many people, contacting customer service representatives can be an excruciating experience. Between navigating lengthy menus of push-button options, waiting on hold for what seems an eternity, never getting a reply to an e.mail, and not having you or your problems remembered the next time you call back, it's no wonder many customers think customer 'service' is a cruel joke.

Loyalty programmes

The most prominent current use of IT is in the management of loyalty (or more strictly usage) programmes, although some would suggest that this has more to do with promotion than relationship development. According to Bejou and Palmer (1998, p. 7), for example, many such loyalty programmes are nothing more than crude attempts to increase short-term sales without adding to the long-term relationship with the customer. Others would argue that 'loyalty technology' has augmented the traditional usage programme (usage programmes, based on stamps or tokens, existed prior to the current card technology). Uncles (1994, p. 339), for example, suggests three reasons why this might be the case:

- The range of organisations involved in promotions and programmes is much wider, extending beyond high street retailers and petrol stations to encompass international travel, financial services and all levels in the distribution chain.
- National borders are no longer a constraint
- Recognition of other usage schemes is widespread, leading to fairly complex offers to retain customers (for example, British Airways and Air Miles, Somerfield, BP and Argos).

---

[3] A good example of this was the first generation 'internet linked' (WAP) mobile telephones, which were difficult to use, with benefits that could more easily be satisfied by simpler technologies.

Box 10.2

Technology is no substitute for thought when it comes to customer care

Why do some companies persist in thinking that technology is the answer to tackling customer care issues? After IKEA became the subject of innumerable consumer-watchdog type television and radio programmes about 'voice-mail-jail' you might think it would have dawned on marketing directors everywhere that technology only improves customer service if it helps to solve customers' problems.

In reality, it is a vain hope that companies will learn from the mistakes of others. If marketing departments take any notice at all, they will at best relate the incident to specific areas of direct functional responsibility. They appear unable to think through the strategic issues and relate lessons learnt to all areas of customer contact.

There is a universal failure to respond to the voice-mail-jail issue. If its inability to manage something as simple as voice mail technology could lead to humiliation for the mighty IKEA, what are the implications for the reputation and brand image of all those companies developing call centres without understanding the role technology plays in customer care?

Alfa Romeo (GB) is a case in point. The company is said to have spent over £1 million building and staffing a call centre. But if my experience is anything to go by, all it has got for its money is a mechanism by which to antagonise even the mildest customer who needs anything more than a brochure.

David Reed, writing in the April issue of *Marketing Business*, outlined how Mercedes-Benz UK has put in place a small customer assistance team whose every member is tasked with resolving any issue brought to them by telephone. Alfa Romeo, by contrast, uses a reference number system.

For anything other than the simplest request they log the enquiry/complaint, give the caller a number and say someone will investigate and respond. Responses come in writing and take the 'don't call us, we'll call you' format. Should the caller phone again they find there is just enough information on file to show that they made an enquiry, but not enough to enable the operator to tell them what has been done about it.

Given, as Mercedes-Benz recognises, the low incidence of one-call complaints resolution, this attitude is disappointing. But from here things go from bad to worse.

Alfa Romeo has fallen into the trap of assuming that investment in technology is a substitute for developing processes that lead to good customer care experiences. It seems to find it easier to spend money than commit the time to think about how to deal effectively with the genuine concerns of its customers.

Senior management is responsible for the way customer care is managed. Alfa Romeo (GB) has a customer service director and a customer relations director. It is hard to imagine two more inappropriate job titles.

It's all right for Jeremy Clarkson to enthuse about the latest Alfa: he can give it back at the end of his test drive.

(*Source*: John Edmund, *Marketing Business*, May 1999)

As previously noted, customer 'data' is considered to have value and the potential to augment a relationship. (Storing data for later retrieval is known as 'data warehousing'; manipulation of 'warehoused' data is known as 'data mining'.) Much of the captured and stored data, however, would appear to be surplus to current requirements, although it holds out the possibility of being utilised at a later date (see Box 10.3).

Box 10.3

Your supermarket knows!

Safeway's brand marketing director Roger Ramsden, in an interview quoted in Whalley (1999, p. 12), claimed that a supermarket could theoretically know a customer was pregnant before she tells her partner. He says that folic acid supplement appearing on the till roll is a dead giveaway that a new baby is on the way. The logic of this is that pre-natal and post-natal offerings can be targeted at the customer at the precise time they are required. According to Ramsden, women starting a family are just the type of customer that Safeway want a relationship with. In 2000, however, Safeway announced the ending of its ABC Loyalty scheme through which most of this 'information' was generated (see the Case study at the end of this chapter). The only assumption that can be drawn is that the cost of this information, useful as it might be, outweighed the benefits of this knowledge. Potential fathers may be glad to know that the pressure is off.

One-to-one marketing

Data collection does offer potential where it improves the information flow and the systems are in place such that knowledge that will be derived from it. Linking suppliers, distributors and customers through electronic data interchange (EDI) in a network of closer relationships potentially provides enormous cost advantages (Zineldin, 2000, p. 20). Used appropriately, technology can help a company learn from every customer interaction and deepen a relationship by advancing ideas and solutions likely to appeal to that customer (Gordon, 1998, p. 168). As Marty Abrams (2000, p. 7) vice president of Experian notes:

> As we move into a new century, manufacturing expertise is a given. If you do not make a great product that you deliver at a great price, you do not have a ticket to play. What will differentiate the winners [from] the losers is their ability to reap the efficiencies that come from understanding the nature of individual demands. Not only will the market make goods better, cheaper and quicker, but it will produce the right goods based on an information driven understanding of individual consumer demand applied at an aggregate level.

However utopian this vision may appear, technology can theoretically make this possible. This individual attention to individual customer needs has been described as 'one-to-one marketing'. One-to-one marketing implies the development of long-term relationships with each customer in order to better understand that customer's needs and better deliver the 'service' that meets that individual's requirements (Chaffey *et al.*, 2000, p. 290). RM theory provides the conceptual underpinning to one-to-one marketing as it emphasises customer service through knowledge of the customer and deals with the markets segmented at the level of the individual (see Box 10.4).

Box 10.4	**Tesco segmentation**

O'Malley *et al.* (1999, p. 84) report that Tesco, via their data analysts Dunn Humby, had by February 1996 identified 12 different customer segments and targeted each with a different version of the Clubcard Magazine. By November 1996 the number had risen to 5,000.

For one-to-one marketing to become a reality there is a need to develop knowledge-based systems, to learn more about individual customers so that firms can really create the value the customer wants and be ready to serve that customer when they are ready (or can be tempted) to buy (Gordon, 1998, p. 6). At the time of writing this is still some way off. According to a recent KPMG Consulting report on knowledge management (reported in *Marketing Business*, April 2000), over two-thirds of companies are overwhelmed by the volume of information held within their systems and are not utilising it to its full advantage.

Marketing types

As noted in Chapter 1, certain types of relational marketing have built a following of their own. It may be valuable to examine these in a little more detail.

Database and direct marketing

The 'database' has been described as the engine that enables RM (Gordon, 1998, p. 194) and as being at the heart of direct marketing. Tapp (1998, p. 6) distinguishes between direct and database marketing by suggesting that:

■ Database marketing (DbM) is using a database to hold and analyse customer information, thereby helping create strategies for marketing. Tapp suggests a big overlap with direct marketing.
■ Direct marketing (DM) focuses on using a database to communicate (and sometimes distribute) directly to customers so as to attract a direct response. Tapp emphasises again the overlap with database marketing.

Möller and Halinen (2000, p. 33) suggest that rapidly developing information technology has created a 'primarily practice based and consultant-driven literature on managing customer relationships through databases'. These programmes (under the auspices of RM) are often criticised for not being 'customer-focused'. Rather, it is suggested, they are designed more to raise switching costs and/or rely on database-driven information to 'market at' customers who may or may not want a relationship (Barnes and Howlett, 1998, p. 15). Caught up in the enthusiasm for technology's information-gathering capabilities, it is possible that companies are forgetting that relationships take (at least) two (Fournier *et al.*, 1998, p. 42).

In some instances RM is used, more or less, as a synonym for direct marketing or database marketing (Tapp, 1998, p. 11) and described in such a way as to imply it is just another instrument in the 'marketing mix toolbox' (Bejou and Palmer, 1998, p. 7). Others suggest that RM, DM and DbM are converging to create a powerful new marketing paradigm (Chaffey *et al.*, 2000, p. 290) where RM provides the conceptual underpinning, DM provides the tactics and DbM is the technical enabler.

Those who consider RM to be little more that the development and maintenance of customer databases have been accused of ignoring the deeper issues related to the nature of relationships (Barnes, 1994, p. 566) for which technology has, as yet, no substitute. The paradox is that as technology develops and more information becomes available through different media, the importance of human contact may actually be increasing. This is the basis for the argument that differentiates RM from DbM, and many of the concepts associated with DM, which (arguably) are primarily associated with data manipulation over and above personal relationships and short-term tactics rather than long-term strategies. Tapp (1998, p. 4) argues that the purest form of DM is capturing individual data so that a relationship can begin and that other techniques such as money-off coupons are not strictly DM. According to Möller and Halinen (2000, p. 38):

> The database marketing and direct marketing tradition is perhaps best characterised as a practice, since it has no clear disciplinary background, no clearly defined methodologies nor a premised theory of markets. It has a strong managerial emphasis aiming at enhancing the efficiency of marketing activities, especially communications – its channels and messages. Competitive markets are implicitly assumed. The organisation–customer relationship perspective is fairly restrained, portraying an image of a relatively loose and distant connection. The focus is on interactive communication, where the seller is the active partner who plans offers and communication on the basis of customer status (profile) and feedback. Relationships are seen as long-term in nature, but conceptual or other efforts to tackle the dynamism of customer relationships have been limited. The main focus is on how to keep the customer loyal and profitable in an efficient way.

Customer relationship management

The latest relational concept to receive 'top billing' is customer relationship management (CRM). The distinction between this and direct or database marketing, however, remains elusive (see Box 10.5). DbM-, DM- and CRM-orientated managers may actually agree with the interpretation of Möller and Halinen, arguing that the problem with RM is that it is too much 'theory based' and not concerned enough with practical and measurable relationship management. This is undoubtedly a valid criticism in many respects. The answer proposed is 'analytical CRM', the explanation of which usually involves the loading of data on individual customers into 'data warehouses' and using business intelligence tools to analyse it (Bray, 2000, p. 1).

Box 10.5 **Customer relationship management**

Customer relationship management (CRM) has been heralded as one of the greatest advances known to man. Ten years ago it was 'total quality management', two years ago it was the 'millennium bug' – the *fin de siècle* mood, not the virus – and most recently 'knowledge management' have kept us humming along to the latest buzz phrase.

Many of these have been bang on the money – with the obvious exception of the millennium bug, which must rank as one of the greatest stings the world has ever seen. However, the problem with buzz phrases is that they begin to take on different meanings to those for which they were originally intended. CRM has for the past three or four years been shortened and transmuted into 'Relationship Marketing', the net result of which is that to many, such activity has become the sole preserve for those campaigns involving the use of databases or lists. This is nonsense.

So why has it happened? Over the past ten years, the power of computing has soared while costs have plummeted, which means that customer databases, if set up and managed well, are the most potent tool a business can have. Companies can truly become 'knowledge-rich' and exploit that knowledge profitably. It is the tool by which current customer relationships can be managed and the learning tool for acquiring yet more of the valuable customer types.

However just because these databases are powerful tools for managing relationships doesn't mean database marketing – usually meaning personalised communications – is relationship marketing.

Tony O'Reilly once said 'I'll take the brands, you take the factories. We'll get back together in five years and see who's doing best.' He was, of course, proposing the brand–consumer relationship as a company's most valuable asset and their factories as their most dangerous liability. He wasn't talking about databases, he was talking about bonding. Brands have been successfully building relationships with consumers long before anyone knew how to spell the word database, let alone build one.

Aren't we all, therefore, relationship marketers? Client side, agency side, design, sales promotion, new business development, research, ads – you name it, we're all playing the dating game. If whatever you're doing isn't aimed at developing or maintaining brand relationships, I suggest you are in the wrong business. But, of course, this wasn't what CRM was originally meant to be about.

Ultimately it was such a lack of understanding that led to the petering out of integrated marketing – another buzzwagon of bygone days. At it's heart was a great idea, that the brand–consumer relationship was sacrosanct. Unfortunately it too became misunderstood as a term meaning 'co-ordinated' campaigns, if you wanted to 'do relationship marketing', best get a DM agency in.

So next time you see a buzz phrase coming along, take care that it's in its original form and not in the agency-modified version.

Anyone want to buy some Totally Knowledgeable Quality Customer Management for de-Bugged Millennium Relationships?

(*Source*: Julian Dodds, 'Look out for the bastardisation of buzz phrases', *Marketing*, 29 June 2000).

Even here, however, there appears no agreement. Definitions of CRM, according to McDonald (2000, p. 28) include:

- 'a continuous performance initiative to increase a company's knowledge of its customers'
- 'consistent high quality customer support access across all communications channels and business functions and business partners'
- (tongue in cheek) 'ERP[4] is from Mars, CRM is from Venus'

CRM is usually associated with the use of IT in managing commercial relationships (Ryals, 2000, p. 259). Depending on your source of reference, a number of different aspects are associated with CRM. These include data warehousing, customer service systems, call centres, e-commerce, and web marketing together with operational and sales systems (McDonald, 2000, pp. 28–9). According to Kelly (2000, pp. 264–5) key analytical CRM applications include:

- *Sales analysis*: offering the organisation an integrated perspective on sales and enabling the sales function to understand the underlying trends and patterns in the sales data.
- *Customer profile analysis*: allowing the organisation to distinguish, from the mass of customer data, the individuals as well as the micro-segments.
- *Campaign analysis*: providing the ability to measure the effectiveness of individual campaigns and different media.
- *Loyalty analysis*: measuring customer loyalty with reference to the duration of the customer relationship.
- *Customer contact analysis*: analysis of the customer contact history of any individual.
- *Profitability analysis*: measuring and analysing the many different dimensions of profitability.

Supporters suggest that CRM seeks to systematically resolve the problems associated with the collection and interpretation of customer data although even advocates will admit that progress has been slow with data not being harnessed with anything like the degree of sophistication that technology allows (Kelly, 2000, p. 262). McDonald (2000, p. 29) suggests that the simple truth is that CRM projects will produce enormous amounts of data. Again doubts must be raised as to whether an organisation will be able to turn this into 'information' and then 'knowledge'.

Nothing so far has differentiated the objectives of CRM from those of RM (or indeed DM and DbM) other than the confidence of its promoters to deliver the results (see Box 10.6). Duncan (2000, p. 58) perhaps hits the nail on the head when he suggests that 'today's CRM fever is rather odd'. He goes on to comment that:

> Unless I missed something, the only genuinely new concept added to the 'old' database marketing mix is a new communications channel (in the absence of a suitable acronym, this is called the Internet) and a desire to apply differentiation to all customer contacts.

---

[4] Enterprise resource planning (ERP), according to Price-Waterhouse Coopers, are systems software packages designed to increase efficiency, identify shortcomings in your business processes and resolve complex problems. For further details see www.pwcglobal.com/ca/eng/about/svcs/techs_erp.html.

Box 10.6

Fact, fiction or fad?

Step along there, don't push – there is room for all. The all-new, glitzy, razzmatazz bandwagon is waiting to explode on your senses. Be the first to experience the latest special effects (corporate self-mutilation in full colour) and gloat over your friends and competitors. For the very latest, state-of-the-art, must-have management fad is coming your way, and customer relationship management (CRM) is too good to miss. But what about the previous, now forgotten fads? Remember 'in search of excellence'? Of 43 excellent companies, only six were considered excellent only eight years later! Remember 'TMQ [sic]'? For most it turned out to be an exercise in getting a certificate to prove that they could make 'rubbish' perfectly every time ('rubbish' being goods and services that customers don't buy). Remember 'BPR' [business process reengineering]? For most it brought merely cosmetic savings. Remember 'relationship marketing'? The domain quickly became occupied by happy-clappy, touchy-feely, weepy-creepy, born-again zealots without any underpinning process. Apart from which, 'delighting' or 'exciting' all customers is the quickest way to bankruptcy! There are others, of course. The reality is that most fads were merely the clever packaging of long-standing, sound concepts that have always worked – providing certain fundamental conditions are fulfilled.

(*Source*: McDonald, 'On the right track', *Marketing Business*, April 2000, p. 28)

The application of new technology, as proposed by CRM programmes, can greatly assist in relational development and despite the mixed usage of terms the objectives of RM, CRM, DM and even DbM seem almost indistinguishable. The similarity between RM and CRM is highlighted in an article posted on the Microsoft Business Technology web site in June 2000 by Bray (2000). In this he describes CRM as:

> learning as much as you can about each of your customers in order to serve them better and keep their custom in an increasingly fickle world.

The only argument that appears substantial would seem to be what level of automation (as a substitution for personal contact) is appropriate to manage these relationships. Industry and product or service type may well play a part, and reference to the relational–transactional spectrum (see Chapter 4) may prove an effective indicator as to the appropriate level of automation

The changing marketplace

Although the importance of database technology cannot be overstated perhaps the greatest change now and in the future will be in the market itself. As McKenna (1991, p. 1) notes, 'technology is transforming choice and choice is transforming the marketplace'.

For the past 100 years marketing has been about helping sellers sell. The information age is opening up a completely new dimension in marketing – helping buyers buy (Mitchell, 2000, p. 360).

Nowhere is this change more evident than in the area of Internet marketing. The Internet is affecting every facet of business life, obliterating current business models (Zineldin, 2000, p. 9). By 1999 there were 14.1 million adult users of the Internet in the UK, a healthy 30.7% of the population. Regardless of the effect on sales (which may or may not grow into something substantial) an argument rages as to the effect of online marketing on the customer retention and/or relationship building process. To some (e.g. Zineldin, 2000, p. 14) the Internet is the very encapsulation of 'one-to-one marketing' and, as such, gives companies the ability to establish enduring relationships with individual customers. On the other hand a recent study of retailing services carried out by the Canadian-based Bristol Group, reported in *Marketing Business*, April 2000, p. 4, dramatically contradicts this by suggesting that encouraging customers to go online could lead to desertion in the long term. Irvin (2000, p. 9), commenting on the results of this research, outlines the problems:

> 'Everything online' may be the most recent marketing mantra, but it seems that Net is not always best. Encouraging customers to go online can, in some instances, lead to a decline in customer loyalty, referrals to friends and, over the long-term, a decline in profits. This, of course, is when the need for whizzy technology over-takes the customer's needs. Price, access to inventory, speed of shipping and other distribution factors are important, but customers also need to feel that the retailer will provide a human touch where necessary.

That the Internet will encourage disloyalty is evident when comparability with the competition's offering is often 'just a click away'. It is, however, the sites that manage to make themselves indispensable to the consumer that will be the ones that suffer least from this phenomenon.

On the positive side, the Internet as a marketing vehicle does take the concept of targeting to new levels as the user's every movement becomes a piece of marketing information (Prabhaker, 2000, p. 158). Companies can gather information on users in various ways, including (Prabhaker, 2000, p. 162):

- Registration
- Electronic address capture
- Cookies (data written to the user's hard disk, allowing web preferences to be tracked and stored on a file that can be accessed by the cookie owner).

This information can be used to good effect. Rather than rely on demographic information (although this too can be captured) Internet data capture (particularly cookies and related technology) gives the marketer the opportunity to establish actual as opposed to predicted behaviour as the customer moves from site to site (this has data protection implications that will be covered in Chapter 11).

'Virtual exchange' is bringing buyers and sellers together electronically rather than having to go to a physical marketplace (Mitchell, 2000, p. 359), offering the promise of substantial cost savings and considerable upheaval in the traditional distribution chain. Adaptations of established associations (e.g. customer/supplier) are appearing as Internet technology holds out the potential of new types of relationships. Mitchell, (2000, pp. 356–9) predicts substantial changes, as illustrated in Figure 10.1.

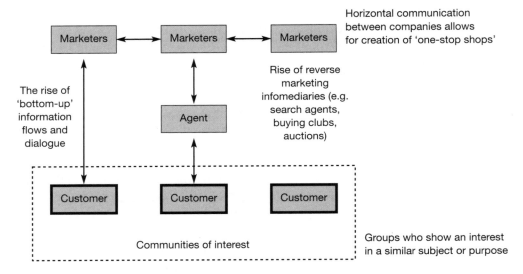

Figure 10.1 Virtual exchange: potential new types of relationships
(*Source*: Adapted from Mitchell, 2000, pp. 356–9)

Mitchell considers that these new and adapted relationships include:

■ Marketer – customer
■ Agent – customer
■ Marketer – marketer
■ Customer – customer.

Marketer – customer

The traditional market relationship will see changes with the rise of 'bottom-up' information flows' and 'dialogues' between the marketer and his or her customer. As Mitchell notes (2000, p. 356), 'the faster the cost of information falls the more it is democratised. Whereas information processing was once the exclusive preserve of giant institutions with gargantuan budgets, more and more ordinary people can afford to do information processing of their own'.

Agent – customer

The 'death of the intermediary' suggested by some sources is almost certainly premature. Indeed, the rise in the number of 'cybermediaries', such as Amazon and Lastminute.com, continues apace. One area that will undoubtedly develop is that of 'reverse marketing'. This includes 'infomediaries' such as search agents, buying clubs and 'reverse auctions'. The principal difference will be that 'infomediaries' will (theoretically) be working on behalf of the consumer rather than as an agent for the supplier.

Marketer – marketer

The growth of 'alliances' was discussed in Chapter 9 and it is likely that the Internet will further promote this trend. The Internet relies heavily on customers actively approaching the company. The importance of 'visibility' is, therefore, of considerable importance. Collaboration between companies, whether through links, vertical portals (e.g. handbag.com) or online communities (e.g. Barclay Square), will undoubtedly increase.

Customer – customer

As noted in Chapter 9 (see Box 9.1) the rise of consumer groups (or communities of interest) is likely to be a feature of the new marketplace. These will comprise of groups of individuals who share an interest in a similar subject or purpose. It stands to reason that marketers will find these communities very valuable for targeting purposes and it may be in the interest of marketers to sponsor or otherwise support such ventures.

Summary

This chapter discussed the effects of developments in manufacturing and information technologies. It noted the confusion of terms, particularly when describing relational strategies and tactics. It noted that there is some evidence to suggest that consumers are reacting against mass production and mass marketing, both promoted by and itself promoting technological development. As a result of this trend and the creation of technologies to support it, 'mass customisation' (the customisation of products while retaining economies of scale) may be an important future development. There still appears, however, to be a gap between the vision and the reality of this concept. In technology-driven industries, time to market is now a major priority. This is affecting companies' ability to undertake market research as it can take more time than marketers have available.

Information technology development has enormous potential for building one-to-one relationships although developments in this area may not always meet with customers' wholehearted approval. Loyalty programmes were highlighted as a prominent utilisation of technology although, in general, they are perceived to be more akin to short-term promotions than longer-term relationship building.

The concepts of direct marketing, database marketing and customer relationship management were discussed and the danger of substituting technology for 'relationship proximity' highlighted. The chapter concluded that DM, DbM and CRM were more tactical than strategic. Although RM has been accused of being too much 'theory based' and not concerned enough with practical and measurable relationship management, it serves to underpin the principles associated with these tactics. The suggestion is that the objectives of all of these 'relational concepts' appear indistinguishable.

The changing marketplace, particularly as a result of developments in Internet technology, was highlighted. The requirement for the customer to be proactive and the 'democratising' of information processing is adapting current, and developing new, relationships.

1 Why is marketing research expenditure perceived to be difficult to justify?

2 What do you understand by the term 'one-to-one marketing'?

3 Distinguish between the terms 'relationship marketing', 'direct marketing', 'database marketing' and 'customer relationship management'.

4 How is the Internet changing the marketplace?

Case study

End of the line for loyalty?

It's official: loyalty schemes are a gimmick and consumers are tired of them. This is according to Carlos Criado-Perez, chief executive of Safeway, who rocked the world of grocery marketing by announcing that Britain's third biggest supermarket chain was all but scrapping its five-year-old ABC customer loyalty programme.

Safeway will keep ABC going for select groups of valuable and tied in customers – such as its teleorder client base – but is transferring £50 million from the scheme's marketing budget to new sales promotion scheme's for its entire customer base.

Understandably, the move has caused a major stir, representing as it does the first big set back for customer loyalty – which was arguably the biggest driver of grocery marketing in the 1990s. But how significant is this development? Is it just an isolated strategic withdrawal, or is it the beginning of the end for loyalty programmes as a force in the UK? And does it mean that sales promotion is about to enter a new era, largely taking over from loyalty?

Safeway claims it has taken the controversial step because ABC was simply not working as a means of rewarding customers, or gathering data on its main targets. 'It was not only our core customers that were using it,' says Safeway spokesperson Suzanne Withers, who claims vast quantities of data on more casual shoppers was also being gathered. She says this random data is worth very little, and that as a result the decision was made to limit the scheme to customers of the 'shop and go' and 'collect and go' services and the crèche.

Significantly, says Withers, ABC was also proving ineffectual in customer recruitment. 'Loyalty schemes are good for rewarding existing customers, but not for getting new ones,' she says. Sales promotion, on the other hand, is a key tool in attracting new customers.

She further denies that the switch to sales promotion is in any way an attempt to ape the Wal-Mart strategy of massive discounting.

However, Safeway has been dismissed by much of the grocery industry for failing to fully embrace the loyalty concept, and to maximise the benefits in terms of data gathering and profiling.

'Loyalty is not something you can dabble with,' says Edwina Dunn of Dunn Humby, the consultants that were instrumental in developing Tesco's ground-breaking loyalty programme. She implies that Safeway has never been serious with loyalty, viewing it primarily as a means of rewarding customers, something which Tesco – for example – regards as purely secondary. Dunn says this is devaluing loyalty programmes and making consumers see them as gimmicky. 'They are losing interest,' she says.

Sue Short of the ISP offers a similar perspective, pointing out that the proliferation of loyalty programmes always had the potential to undermine consumers' respect for them. 'It has actually created disloyalty,' she says.

So while the downscaling of ABC looks unlikely to spell the end of the road for customer loyalty schemes in the wider sense, it will undoubtedly be good news for sales promotion. 'With such a big budget available Safeway will be able to do some really innovative things,' says Catherine Shuttleworth, director of sales promotion.

However, any expansion in sales promotion will not occur in isolation and will inevitably run alongside loyalty programmes – regardless of whether they are comprehensive like Tesco's Clubcard, or more selective like ABC.

'It is all about striking a balance,' agrees Russell Craig, spokesperson for Tesco.

As with any marketing initiative, it is horses for courses.

At the end of the day, Tesco has used its Clubcard data as a springboard for launch into other areas, such as its financial services operation. With Safeway's intention to stick to its core grocery business – particularly once loyalty cards were ten a penny and becoming devalued – continuing to gather this kind of data on a mass level is less important.

And in the long run, if Safeway can manage to reverse the recent decline in its profits, this strategy will be vindicated. If, however, things start going pear shaped we will truly know the benefit of loyalty.

Postscript: rivals seek to profit

Both Tesco and Sainsbury's have sought to profit from Safeway's rapid retreat from the loyalty market, offering 250 or 500 points respectively for any ABC member in return for their card.

It was a clear signal of intent from the two leading supermarket chains that they have no intention of getting out of the loyalty game. 'We know from experience that once customers start using the Reward Card scheme, and its many third party offers, it becomes an indispensable part of their shopping trip,' comments Sir Peter Davis, CEO of Sainsbury's.

Tesco marketing director, Richard Brasher, adds, 'Customers tell us that they want points and price cuts. We believe Safeway has dropped a clanger. To compensate shoppers who feel they've been let down, we will give them a golden hello of 250 points.'

(*Source:* Adapted from Joel Harrison, *Incentives Today*, June 2000, p. 16)

Case study questions

1 Who, in your opinion, has made the right decision: Safeway or the stores that are maintaining the scheme?

2 If Tesco sees rewarding customers as 'purely secondary' what are the principal reasons for it continuing the programme?.

References

Abrams, M. (2000) 'Contribution to debate paper', *Interactive Marketing*, 2 (1), 6–11.

Barnes, J.G. (1994) 'Close to the customer: but is it really a relationship?', *Journal of Marketing Management*, 10, 561–70.

Barnes, J.G. and Howlett, D.M. (1998) 'Predictors of equity in relationships between service providers and retail customers', *International Journal of Bank Marketing*, 16 (1), 5–23.

Bejou, D. and Palmer, A. (1998) 'Service failure and loyalty: an exploratory empirical study of airline customers', *Journal of Services Marketing*, 12 (1), 7–22.

Bray, P. (2000) 'Analytical customer relationship management', *Microsoft Business Technology*, June (microsoft.com/uk/business_technology/dw/798.htm).

Brookes, R. and Little, V. (1997) 'The new marketing: what does 'customer focus' mean?', *Marketing and Research Today*, May, 96–105.

Chaffey, D., Mayer, R., Johnston, K. and Ellis-Chadwick, F. (2000) *Internet Marketing*. Harlow: Pearson Education.

Duncan, C. (2000) 'Customer evolution', *Marketing Business*, 58.

Fournier, S., Dobscha, S. and Mick, D.G. (1998) 'Preventing the premature death of relationship marketing', *Harvard Business Review*, 76 (1), 42–9.

Gordon, I.H. (1998) *Relationship Marketing*. Etobicoke, Ontario: John Wiley and Sons.

Gummesson, E. (1999) *Total Relationship Marketing: Rethinking Marketing Management from 4Ps to 30Rs*. Oxford: Butterworth Heinemann.

Hart, C.W.L. (1995) 'Mass customisation: conceptual underpinning opportunities and limits', *International Journal of Service Industry Management*, 8 (3), 193–205.

Irvin, C. (2000) 'Testing time for technology', *Marketing Business*, April, 9.

Kelly, S. (2000) 'Analytical CRM: the fusion of data and intelligence', *Interactive Marketing*, (3), 262–7.

McDonald, M. (2000) 'On the right track', *Marketing Business*, April, 28–31.

McKenna, R. (1991) *Relationship Marketing*. London: Addison Wesley.

Mitchell, A. (2000) 'In one-to-one marketing, which one comes first?', *Interactive Marketing*, 1 (4), 354–67.

Möller, K. and Halinen, A. (2000) 'Relationship marketing theory: its roots and direction', *Journal of Marketing Management*, 16, 29–54.

O'Malley, L. and Tynan, C. (2000) 'Relationship marketing in consumer markets: rhetoric or reality?', *European Journal of Marketing*, 34 (7).

O'Malley, L., Patterson, M. and Evans, M. (1999) *Exploring Direct Marketing*. London: International Thompson Business Press.

Palmer, A. J. (2000) 'Co-operation and competition: a Darwinian synthesis of relationship marketing', *European Journal of Marketing*, 34 (5/6), 687–704.

Peppers, D. and Rogers, M. (2000) 'Build a one-to-one learning relationship with your customers', *Interactive Marketing*, 1 (3), 243–50.

Prabhaker, P.R. (2000) 'Who owns the on-line consumer?', *Journal of Consumer Marketing*, 17 (2), 158–71.

Ryals, L. (2000) 'Organising for relationship marketing' in Cranfield School of Management *Marketing Management: A Relationship Marketing Perspective*. Basingstoke: Macmillan, pp. 249–64.

Sheth, J.N. and Sisodia, R.S. (1999) 'Revisiting marketing's lawlike generalizations', *Journal of the Academy of Marketing Sciences*, 17 (1), 71–87.

Tapp, A. (1998) *Principles of Direct and Database Marketing.* London: Financial Times Management/Pitman.

Uncles, M. (1994) 'Do you or your customer need a loyalty scheme?', *Journal of Targeting, Measurement and Analysis*, 2 (4), 335–50.

Whalley, S. (1999) 'ABC of relationship marketing', *SuperMarketing*, 12 March, 12–13.

Zineldin, M. (2000) 'Beyond relationship marketing: technologicalship marketing', *Marketing Intelligence and Planning*, 18 (1), 9–23.

11 Relationship management

Key issues
➤ The management of relationships
➤ The marketing plan
➤ High/low involvement management
➤ Managing personal information
➤ Criticism of RM.

Introduction

How do you manage relationships of the type discussed in previous chapters? Perhaps the idea of managing relationships is itself illusory as it implies controlling, or attempting to control, a notoriously fickle and increasingly independent customer base. Management planning and decision making are, however, necessary to coordinate the direction and resource allocation of any organisation and important factors in creating the organisational climate in which relationships can flourish. What RM management does not imply is a formula or prescriptive solution that can guarantee success. Both the decision to apply relational strategies and the ways in which these are designed and implemented are, if they are to be successful, situation specific.

Undoubtedly this lack of specific guidelines has led to criticism. RM has been accused of failure to be systematic and relationship marketers as 'happy-clappy, touchy-feely, weepy-creepy, born-again zealots without any underpinning process' (McDonald, 2000, p. 8). This criticism is perhaps partly dependent upon whether you view marketing as an art or a science. A scientific view of marketing demands systematic solutions. The view of marketing as an art, however, suggests creating the 'best-fit' unique solution to an individual situation that may not be replicated elsewhere. The science versus art debate has continued for some time with little hope of resolution. Perhaps the worst outcome here has been the polarisation of opinion that takes place when marketers reject alternative perspectives and (at the extreme) claim that success is only achievable by adopting their particular prescriptive solution. There is room for alternate opinions and approaches of both a scientific and artistic nature. To paraphrase Voltaire, those who are certain they are right should be certified.

Advocates of direct marketing, database marketing and customer relationship management, in particular, are prone to advance generalised solutions, often with too little consideration as to appropriateness to particular situations. Not that all RM supporters are innocent of such overstatement. Relationship marketing, however, and whatever its faults, is conceptually distinct from direct marketing, database marketing, customer relationship management, loyalty marketing etc. in so much as these are tactical methodologies, by definition short-term, although they can contribute in various ways to longer-term relational development.

There is no claim (at least in this book) that RM is right for every, or even the majority of, situations. This one standpoint has no credible right to be dominant or superior (Littler, 1998, p. 1) over any other. As Micklethwaite and Wooldridge (1996, p. 22) somewhat sarcastically note:

> Dig into virtually any area of management theory and you will find, eventually, a coherent position of sorts. The problem is that in order to extract that nugget you have to dig through an enormous amount of waffle.

The application of relational strategies should be a response to a need and they imply an element of flexibility and cunning. Neither are relational strategies mutually exclusive. Rather than single, narrow, one-concept strategies, companies need a 'portfolio of strategy types' (see Chapter 4) of which relational strategies can play an important part. Ideas ebb and flow, concepts come and go. The company needs to examine the ideas and adopt or reject as appropriate. After all, observation of 'real world' marketing practice suggests that a hybrid managerial approach is the most appropriate response to prevailing marketing circumstances (Chaston, 1998, p. 273). It is even possible to envisage a company using a relational approach for some customers who need or require this, or in situations where it is profitable for the company. Other customers may not seek such services, or may contribute nothing to profit. The skill (or art) of the marketer is not in the application of RM or TM strategies *per se* but in applying the strategies to appropriate customers in given situations.

Relationship management

None of the foregoing should suggest that management has no role. Neither is there any pretence that managing relational strategies is easy. Indeed, making RM work in practice, by means of a system within the company, is one of the most difficult of marketing tasks (Ryals, 2000, p. 231). What should be avoided is 'throwing the baby out with the bath water'. In our headlong rush for instant results (prompted by prophets of doom) there is the danger of applying inappropriate relational strategies to a given situation. The biggest risk of all is creating relationships without considering how value will be created (Ballantyne, 2000, p. 4); Ballantyne calls this the 'lobsterpot approach' to RM, characterised by an over-enthusiastic rush into the unknown. If we accept (as it is suggested) that every customer is uniquely individual we must accept that every company is unique too. So beware following the herd too far and too fast. As Damarest (1997, p. 375) notes, not 'what is right' but 'what works' or even 'what works better'.

Marketing, perhaps more than any other discipline, is prone to the 'new broom' syndrome (Mazur, 2000, p. 33). Attempting to restructure everything overnight is more than chancing fate. Flexible adaptation over time is the key. Using a scalpel not a hatchet (Micklethwaite and Wooldridge, 1996, p. 21) is the appropriate metaphor; reviewing and adapting current strategies the most appropriate solution. According to Grönroos (2000, p. 11)

> We know too little about how relationship marketing should be best integrated into the planning of a company. The only way to find out is through trial and error in our companies and through research. Under these circumstances it seems reasonable to start by adding RM dimensions to the marketing plan in use, retaining its basic format.

The advantage of using the 'current format' and 'adding RM dimensions' is direct comparability: the ability to establish what works and why. Although most marketing plans tend towards being overly systematic and to be applied prescriptively it is better to adapt than replace one system for another, as yet untried. There is, however, a downside. The language of strategy, tactics, power and intelligence gathering coexists rather uncomfortably with that of trust, harmony and commitment (O'Malley and Tynan, 1999, p. 595). Where practical, 'new' language might be adopted that recognises the value of cooperation over confrontation.

Marketing plan

The traditional marketing plan usually follows the pattern of analysis, design, implementation and control. Various formats exist so no generic form is proposed as necessarily better than any other. The plan presented in Figure 11.1, for example, is represented by the acronym SOSTAC (Situation, Objectives, Strategies, Tactics, Action, Control) and, approximately, follows the 'standard' format. One difference from most is that, rather than a linear approach, the model recognises that marketing plans are not 'one-off' but need to be continually revisited. Rather than a list, the model is seen as a continuous circle of activities.

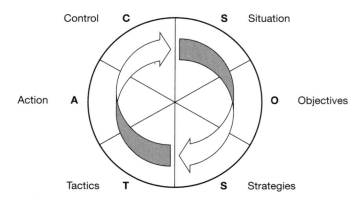

Figure 11.1 Basic SOSTAC planning model

Alternatively, other, perhaps more traditional, marketing plan formats exist. In Figure 11.2, for example, Brassington and Pettitt's (1997, p. 882) 'stages in the planning process' and McDonald's (1999) '10-step strategic marketing planning' model are shown for comparison. It may be noted that they are similar although different authors give different prominence to different parts of the plan. In any marketing plan, although they appear sequential, several stages may happen simultaneously and information is being constantly updated. As systematic as they appear, flexibility is again the key.

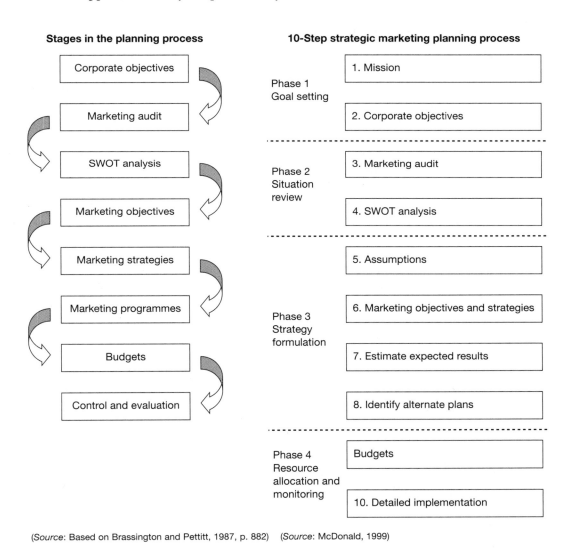

(*Source*: Based on Brassington and Pettitt, 1987, p. 882)   (*Source*: McDonald, 1999)

Figure 11.2 Alternative marketing plans

Developing a marketing plan

It is not the purpose of this book to go into the minutiae of a marketing plan. Other authors (including those represented in Figure 11.2) have covered this extensively. What follows is a series of observations concerning the development of a marketing plan particularly as it relates to the incorporation of relational strategy development. The structure is based on the SOSTAC model in Figure 11.1 but might well apply to any chosen plan.

Situation (situational analysis)

The old adage rings true: how can you know which direction to go when you do not know where you are coming from? Most companies begin (or resume) the planning process by establishing (or reiterating or adapting) their *mission* and *scope*. The mission and scope relate to the 'attitudes and expectations within the organisation with regard to the business that the organisation is in, how the organisation rates against competition and how it fits into its environment' (O'Malley *et al.*, 1999, p. 37). Corporate and/or business objectives need to be known so that the priorities (often financial) of the organisation can be attended to and incorporated into the plan.

The situational analysis, upon which decisions will be based, is a comprehensive assessment of the organisation and its competitive and macro environment. Analysts have commonly used versions (both simple and complex) of PEST(L), SWOT and competitive market models to develop such analyses.[1] As RM emphasises the importance of customer retention and the existing customer base, a 'customer analysis' is considered vital. Conceptualising where the company, and the individual customer types, are on the strategy continuum could provide useful insight. Review of the drivers towards relational and/or traditional may help in this process. Buyer–seller relationships rarely exist in pure types. Understanding when to utilise RM strategies requires distinguishing between the discrete transaction, which has a distinct beginning, short duration and sharp ending, and relational exchange, which traces to previous agreements and is longer in duration, reflecting an ongoing process (Morgan and Hunt, 1994, p. 21).

Although much has been said about the advantages of the 'segment-of-one', current capabilities are such that aggregation of customer types is likely to be the most practical. The identification and profiling of target markets is, therefore, important. For 'customer acquisition' purposes this may still require the use of socio-demographic, geodemographic and/or lifestyle (including propensity to buy) data, whether exercised through rented 'lists' or communications media audience classifications. The internet may, however, offer new means of tracking actual behaviour (see Chapter 10) that may revolutionise this, at least in part. Not all

---

[1] PEST (or STEP) stands for elements of the macro environment: political, economic, sociological and technological, to which legal is frequently added; SWOT stands for strengths, weaknesses, opportunities and threats.

customers are equal and part of the 'skill' of the relational marketer is targeting the 'right' customer, not necessarily the easiest to attract or the most profitable in the short term (Reichheld, 1993, p. 65).

From the customer retention and development perspective the company database is of paramount importance as it should indicate customer preferences and profitability. Direct marketers, for example, use recency, frequency and monetary value (RFV) models that incorporate data on a customer's most recent purchases and the frequency and value of previous purchases to target offerings (including 'cross-selling' and 'up-selling'). In addition to establishing customer traits, an RM perspective implies segmentation by type of relationship that can profitably be engaged (Smith and Higgins 2000, p. 87).

Objectives

Objectives are what drive an organisation. They are the 'where we want to be' of any business. They should be SMART (strategic, measurable, actionable, realistic and timely), communicable and aspirational. Traditionally marketing objectives were derived (or cascaded down from) business objectives. The development of technologies that can interrogate databases and establish objectives from this information has led to the incorporation of this 'bottom-up' approach to objective setting into the existing model.

To ensure that everyone in the company is working to the same agenda there is a need to ensure that all employees are aware of top-level and marketing objectives. The RM approach further suggests that this information should be available to all other core relationship partners.

Strategies

If the objectives are 'where we want to be' then the strategies are 'how we are going to get there'. Marketing strategies may include sub-strategies (e.g. media strategy, creative strategy). Box 11.1 indicates a number of different strategic options that may prove useful in strategy development dependent on whether the aim is transactional or relational.

Tactics

Tactics are the operational element and, by necessity, short term. The choice may be between different media (including the internet) or techniques (e.g. direct marketing). The danger here is confusing the tactical with the strategic. For all its influence on business habits in general, the internet is a tactical tool. It is part (certainly not all) of a company's armoury. It may promote different approaches but it is, in strict terms, another media channel. In the same way database marketing, direct marketing and CRM are, within a RM strategy, tactical tools rather than strategic approaches to company development.

Box 11.1	**Transactional versus relationship marketing**	
	Transactional marketing	**Relationship marketing**

- Do the deal and disappear
  - Negotiate a 'win–win' sale situation and stay around being a resource for better results

- Push price
  - Promote value
- Short-term thinking and acting
  - Long-term thinking and acting
- Build the business on deals
  - Build the business on relationships
- Getting new customers
  - Keeping customers
- No structure for on-going business
  - Structure created to support relationships

- Selling focused
  - Relationship focused
- Short-term empathy
  - Long-term empathy and rapport
- Incentive for 'doing the deal'
  - Incentive for long-term relationship and revenue

- Foundation of sale telling and selling
  - Foundation of revenue trust
- After-sales service at additional cost
  - After-sales service as investment in relationship

- Product service focused
  - People expectations and perception focused

- Rewards incentives for 'doing deals'
  - Rewards incentives for maintaining and growing relationships and revenue
- The deal is the end
  - The sale is the beginning

(*Source*: Adapted from Thomas 2000, p. 531)

Action

Action plans provide the means by which the organisation's ideas are turned into reality by being given a structure and format through which they can be implemented (O'Malley *et al.*, 1999, p. 59). The action plan is the blueprint through which the objectives are realised. As with the objectives, there is a need to disseminate information to employees and, increasingly, to suppliers, customers and strategic partners.

Control

The control element involves setting clear evaluation criteria (e.g. target response levels). It may also involve testing prior to full execution. Testing differs from research in that it is actual response (albeit on a smaller scale) as opposed to forecast response. In this regard technology has a considerable part to play in the control element of any marketing plan.

Managing relationships

When an RM dimension is incorporated into a company's marketing plan this should be done in the knowledge that certain additional factors will need to be incorporated and subsequently managed.

Handing relationships

While there is nothing new in the desire of businesses to develop ongoing relationships with their customers, recent developments in information technology offer new opportunities for creating individual relationships between a seller and each of its customers (Bejou and Palmer, 1998, p. 7). Ultimately it may lead to a greater ability to attend to individual customer's concerns (or one-to-one marketing). If the RM concept that each customer is an individual regardless of the number of customers to be addressed (Kunøe, 1998, p. 1125) is accepted then 'one-to-one marketing' is the ultimate aim. It emphasises that every customer requires a different form of communication and (in an ideal world) individual attention. The danger is that replacing personal contact with the technology that may permit 'one-to-one marketing' needs to be done in the realisation that it may not always be appropriate to every situation.

The management of customer relationships will, therefore, differ from industry to industry. In 'low involvement' consumer markets the relationship with the customer is likely to be managed through technology such as a database and/or the World Wide Web (O'Malley and Tynan, 1999, p. 589). Databases can be used to target customers with customers having little or no knowledge of the company in question or the existence of the database (Barnes and Howlett, 1998, p. 15). This database view of RM, according to Copulsky and Wolf (1990, pp. 16–17) incorporates three key elements:

- Identifying and building a database of current and potential customers
- Delivering differentiated messages
- Tracking each relationship

The 'low involvement' customer may be quite happy with technology-based RM where technology substitutes for physical proximity (Zineldin, 2000, p. 16). This may contrast with the 'high involvement' consumer who may need a more personal, less mechanised and individually tailored approach that technology (currently) finds difficult to duplicate.

The management of relationships is prone to pitfalls. The problem is that many marketers have taken their eye off the ball. Rather than viewing a database as simply an 'enabling technology' too many firms have focused their energies on 'database building' rather than 'relationship building' (O'Malley et al., 1997, p. 553). In addition, now that it is possible to manipulate a database in such a way that relationship development is feasible does not mean that all customers want or need such a relationship. As Pels (1999, p. 33) points out, this 'technology-allows-me-to-do' approach has more in common with a production type orientation than a marketing orientation.

Managing personal information

The management of customer information through advanced technology can create doubts over privacy. Although these privacy concerns are not peculiar to RM, CRM, DbM etc. – medical records being another example – what differs is the depth and variety of information that is collected and used (Smith and Higgins, 2000, p. 83). The three major concerns would appear to be that:

- The handing over or collection of personal information is an infringement of personal liberty.
- The handing over of information will result in unwanted attention being paid to that customer.
- If companies are permitted to hold such information that they should utilise the information wisely.

Infringement of personal liberty

The commercial incentive to collect, merge, warehouse and sell customer information is enormous while the safeguards tend to be weak and easily ignored (Prabhaker, 2000, p. 158). In the UK, which has data protection legislation, there is continued pressure from the regulator for tighter control. Currently the legislation provides customers with the opportunity to opt out of future 'offers' and, theoretically, from having their details passed to other suppliers. Opting out, however, requires the customer to act to avoid their details from being captured, stored and, potentially, sold on to other suppliers. This is usually achieved by ticking a 'privacy box'.[2] There is little doubt that the UK (and European) legislation will get tougher and that rather than opting out customers may have to 'opt in' to such arrangements. In the knowledge that legislation will soon be introduced practitioners are developing techniques for encouraging customers to 'opt in' or 'join' them. This may include the provision of information or services (e.g. online news) in exchange for data. This range of customer authorised data collection strategies has been called 'permission marketing'.

There is also some suggestion that customers react badly when they believe their personal details are being indiscriminately passed on. The covert acquisition of information, rather than representing a phase in relationship building, may actually undermine the relationship building process (O'Malley et al., 1997, p. 552). On the other side of the coin there is the irony that strictly regulating the collection of personal information could ultimately limit the quality and level of service that a business can deliver (Prabhaker, 2000, p. 160).

Nowhere is this privacy debate more pertinent than with the internet.[3] As Prabhaker (2000, p. 159) notes:

---

[2] A typical statement would be 'we may use the details we have about you to provide you with information about products and/or services offered by us or other persons. If you do not wish to receive this please tick this box'.

[3] It is not within the scope of this chapter to distinguish between terms such as World Wide Web, internet, intranet etc. For a full explanation see Chaffey et al., 2000, pp. 11–18.

Every time an individual interacts with the web she leaves behind a trail of extraordinary detailed information about who she is, her buying habits, financial status, maybe her medical records and other intimate personal details. She has very little control over who can have access to this information and what they will do with it. It is unrealistic to expect profit driven businesses not to infringe on consumer privacy in an environment that makes it increasingly profitable and a technology that makes it easier than ever to collect and share personal information.

Undoubtedly what some marketers imagine as a means of developing the relationship through information exchange some customers will see as intrusion into their private lives. Finding an acceptable balance may become marketing's greatest challenge.

Unwanted attention

O'Malley *et al.* (1997, p. 553) quote one respondent in their recent research into consumer's views on data management as commenting that 'handing over personal details just means more rubbish coming through the letterbox'. This is not an isolated perception and it is easy to see why. Direct mail, for example, while being described as a more targeted and flexible medium, has a response rate of around 4%, a return generally seen as satisfactory in the industry. This means that for every one customer evidently interested enough in the offer to respond 24 are not. Although many consumers will, as a consequence of modern life, take this in their stride a percentage will be annoyed about what they regard as untargeted junk mail. Whether the direct marketing industry likes it or not, the ever-growing number of postal[4] and electronic mailshots will ensure that this will become an even greater cause for concern in the future.

Utilising information

The poor utilisation of information is surprisingly commonplace. Another customer in the O'Malley *et al.* study (p. 551) showed her frustration with companies that have the information (they suppose) but do not use it (see also Box 5.2). She explains:

> I go overdrawn at the end of every month and have trouble making the repayments but my bank are constantly making me loan offers. They should know that I can't afford to take out another loan. They, of all people, should know because they have all my details and I often deal with them person-to-person.

Fournier *et al.* (1998, p. 47) note what they call 'the forgotten rule': that intimacy and vulnerability are intertwined. If a company routinely asks its customers for sensitive information, but does not put that information to good use, it should stop asking those questions. Marketers must use the information they already have more effectively and develop appropriate processes to initiate and maintain meaningful dialogue with customers (O'Malley *et al.*, 1997, p. 553). Today's 'interactive age customers' are accustomed to having their needs met immediately, conveniently and inexpensively (Peppers and Rogers, 2000, p. 243) by companies utilising the

---

[4] According to the Royal Mail web site (www.royalmail.co.uk) between 1987 and 1997 mailshots increased by 126%.

information they already have at their disposal. Nothing can be more frustrating than having to repeat the details of problems over and over again to assorted customer service personnel.

Appropriateness

Used appropriately, technology can help the company learn from every customer interaction and deepen the relationship by advancing ideas and solutions likely to suit the customer (Gordon, 1998, p. 168). Used inappropriately, the backlash is likely to ensure restrictive controls. Ultimately the evolution of any technical advances in information gathering is dependent on its acceptance by the public (Prabhaker, 2000, p. 161). The compromise is likely to settle around what is becoming known as 'permission marketing' (Chaffey et al., 2000, p. 233) where consumers actively cooperate in the supply of data.

Criticism of RM

An important aspect of management is knowledge of the (actual or perceived) weaknesses of any strategy Although this book chronicles and generally supports the development of relational strategies in marketing, it would be inappropriate to ignore any perceived weaknesses or criticism of the RM concept or indeed the dangers inherent in the introduction of any new management ideas. Although some of these criticisms have emerged earlier in the text it is valuable, at this stage, to consolidate these criticisms. It is only by acknowledging the weaknesses that the strengths of relational strategies can be fully appreciated.

Management fads

Is RM a fad? Will companies ten years from now regret adopting RM strategies, as has happened with other fads in the past (see Micklethwait and Wooldridge, 1996, for an excellent discussion of this phenomena). In their introduction to a collection of writings on RM Payne et al. (1995, p. vii) include this warning:

> There is a tendency when new ideas in management emerge to embrace them keenly for a while and to see them as the ultimate solution to whatever problems we currently perceive to exist. Equally there is a tendency to put them aside after the initial novelty has worn off, and they are found to be not quite the panacea that we once thought. Marketing particularly has been prone to this 'flavour of the month' syndrome . . . Already there are some who would claim that 'relationship marketing' is another of these short-lifecycle management phenomena.

Brennan (1997, p. 768) too has noted that fashionable management expressions are prone to over-use, abuse and consequently devaluation. RM has not proved immune to this effect.

RM, like all successful ideas, has initial intuitive appeal (Blois, 1997, p. 53) and there have been a number of successful implementations that have helped to promote the concept. It would, however, also be true to suggest that with the rapid development of RM the boundaries have often been stretched and claims made which could never be universally justified. As East (2000, p. 1) notes, some of these propositions have little evidence to support them and/or rest on invalid or over-simplified reasoning. As is often the case with radical change there is a tendency to over-correct (Baker, 1999, p. 212) and consequently over-hype a concept. Care should be taken, therefore, when implementing relational strategies, to clarify that the concept is right for particular industries or individual situations. This involves seeing through the rhetoric to the core of what RM purports to be all about.

RM as a new marketing concept

There is a certain justifiable criticism regarding RM's novelty (as there is with CRM). The question raised is whether RM is a 'new' concept or simply an old concept given a new lease of life by marketing's spin doctors; a new paradigm or an old idea in new clothes (Palmer, 1998, p. 106) possibly 'the emperor's new clothes' (Gummesson, 1997, p. 53). Brown (1998, p. 173) is particularly scathing. RM, he suggests is not new and was already anticipated as part of the original marketing concept. His view is that to regard RM as something novel is 'arrant nonsense'. The concept of 'relationships in marketing' is, indeed, not new as traders have been practising it for centuries. Cynics might suggest, therefore, that RM is nothing but a marketing makeover, the latter-day version of changing the sign on the departmental door from 'sales' to 'marketing' (Brown, 1998, p. 173).

In RM's favour it is frequently suggested that its biggest achievement is that it has brought back 'relationships' into the mainstream of marketing. That it is really a rebirth of marketing practices of the pre-industrial age (Sheth and Parvatiyar, 1995, p. 399). This may be largely true; however, while relationships may have been 'rediscovered in western corporate markets' they have remained a fundamental part of exchange in many eastern cultures (Palmer, 1996, p. 19). Perhaps, even in our own culture, the concept may have also been kept alive in 'less sophisticated' village and suburban communities or small companies previously largely ignored by marketing academics. According to Gummesson (1999, p. 6):

> The renewed interest in RM may imply that marketing theorists are getting closer to reality; that we are beginning to discern the marketing content of Japanese *Keiretsus*, Chinese *Quanxies*, global ethnic networks, the British school tie, trade between friends, loyalty to the local pub and so on. Marketing has not invented these phenomena, practice has!

In these terms RM is merely re-emphasising certain neglected areas of marketing (Brown, 1998, pp. 173–4) rather than creating something wholly new – the equivalent of 'going back (or forward) to basics' (Gummesson, 1999, p. 13).

Selective research

Another valid criticism of RM is that the universal success implied in case studies is frequently based on selective organisations in a limited number of industries. These claims are usually implied rather than directly stated when, in promoting RM (or indeed DM, DbM or CRM) strategies, writers frequently omit industries where relational strategies may be of marginal, if any, importance. A potential hazard is where this selective research leads to a polarisation of opinions. This in turn causes some marketers to reject alternative perspectives and, at the extreme, begin to claim that firms can only succeed by adapting their particular prescriptive solutions (Chaston, 1998, p. 277).

These prescriptive solutions are of particular concern when it comes to dealing with consultant agencies that promote the RM (or any other) concept. Any search of the internet using the phrase 'relationship marketing' (or more recently 'customer relationship management') will produce a host of these consultants each extolling the virtues of their vision. As Mitchell (1997, p. 37) cynically notes, consultants 'peddling relationship marketing solutions' are growing at a rate of 30–40% per year, whereas their clients are growing at a more modest 3–4%. Marketers should, therefore, take care, when examining the evidence supporting RM that the factors which led to its successful implementation in one industry or in other contexts are comparable to their own.

O'Malley and Tynan (2000, p. 12) also point out that, although marketers have appropriated the technology, it remains unclear whether they have internalised the philosophy, particularly in consumer markets. They note that, in many markets, all that is apparent is a resource shift from above (i.e. advertising) to below the line (other marketing communications tools; e.g. sales promotion), indicating that RM may, on occasion, be more rhetoric than reality.

One-sided communication

It is suggested that, despite suggestions of co-producing value, the voice of the customer is often missing from much of RM (Buttle, 1996, p. 13), most particularly in consumer goods marketing. Caught up in the enthusiasm for the rapid increase in information gathering techniques and for the benefits that long-term engagement with customers may hold, many companies that claim to have adopted RM techniques and concepts have forgotten that relationships take two (Fournier *et al.*, 1998, p. 42). The term 'relationship' has often been used by practitioners to underpin a supplier's marketing activities without the customer necessarily being conscious that they are even participating in an RM campaign (Blois, 1997, p. 53).

This viewpoint raises the question (discussed in Chapter 2) of whether it is legitimate to use the term 'relationship' for the interaction between an end consumer and a large company. Perhaps predictably, much RM research is designed not for the benefit of the consumer but in the interest of the selling firm (Mattsson, 1997, pp. 43–4). This has meant a focus on suppliers' needs overlooking the perspective of whether or not the buyer wants to develop an ongoing relationship (Palmer, 1998, p. 118). There is also concern over pseudo-relationships (Barnes,

1994, p. 565), where what passes for a relationship is one-sided, with customers locked-in and, effectively, kept in the relationship against their will because the costs of leaving the relationship are seen to be too high.

Corruption

Social bonds (particularly in business-to-business situations) can, without doubt, become pervasive to the point where they allow economic inefficiencies to develop. In extreme cases networks of corrupt buyers and sellers may acquire sufficient market power to result in an overall loss of economic welfare (Palmer, 1998, p. 118). Indeed, anti-competitive legislation has been introduced in most developed markets of which some cooperating companies may fall foul. Gummesson's (1999, p. 6) reference to the 'British school tie' and 'trade between friends' also raises possible moral issues into cooperative trade.

Outmoded marketing

It has been said that marketing in general is going through a 'mid-life crisis'. Perhaps it is just that it has not yet matured. Certainly the heat generated by the RM debate suggests less rationality than juvenile pride. Micklethwait and Wooldridge (1996, pp. 15–17) in their critique of management theory list four grounds which link to a description of a management discipline as adolescent:

- It is constitutionally incapable of self-criticism
- Its terminology usually confuses rather than educates
- It hardly rises above basic common sense
- It is faddish and bedevilled by contradiction that would not be allowed in more rigorous disciplines.

RM could be accused of all four – but again so could many of the alternate theories, many of which are put forward as solutions. It is hoped that this text has avoided all four!

Postscript

Whereas many would argue that the 'classical approach' to marketing is coming to an end and that we are in the process of an orderly transition to a 'new marketing paradigm', there are powerful voices that suggest that marketing is in a state of chaos and going nowhere (Brookes and Little, 1997, p. 96). Indeed, it may also be said of RM, with some justification, that although it is powerful in theory it may be decidedly troubled in practice (Fournier et al., 1998, p. 42). On this basis it has some way to go before fully justifying the faith and resources that academics and practitioners have put behind it.

While none of the criticisms or potential dangers noted earlier can be ignored or swept under the carpet they should not be allowed to wholly devalue RM as a valuable marketing concept. Without doubt overly simple arguments have been put forward under the guise of RM that ignore the full complexity of relationships and have the potential to mislead. Even simple arguments, such as those put forward for RM, by the originators of a theory, give no guarantee against misuse (Holland, 1990, p. 24). The role of true marketing scholars is to eliminate as far as possible misuse and abuse, uncover myths and present reality in innovative ways, thus providing improved road maps (Gummesson, 1997, p. 58). Most of all, marketers must learn that, if we are to prevent the premature death of RM, we must separate the rhetoric from the reality (Fournier *et al.*, 1998, p. 42)

Summary

This final chapter looked at the management of RM. It noted the criticism that RM was not systematic enough for some although this may be more to do with whether marketing is viewed as an art or a science. The chapter suggested 'using a scalpel not a hatchet' by introducing RM strategies into an existing marketing plan. This allows for comparability with existing strategies. A number of aspects, specific to RM, were discussed within the context of the marketing plan.

The chapter looked specifically at how relationships might be managed, particularly in relation to available technology. It reviewed the concerns relating to information handling, notably the infringement of personal liberty, unwanted attention and poor utilisation of information.

The chapter concluded with a review of some of the criticisms of RM as it was proposed that knowledge of RM's actual or perceived failings may contribute to the development of successful relational strategies. Specifically, it challenged and clarified claims that RM is a 'management fad', a re-worked (and therefore not new) concept, based on selective research and one-sided communication, and prone to corruption.

In a postscript it was proposed that while none of the criticisms or potential dangers could be ignored they should not be allowed to wholly devalue RM as a valuable marketing concept. Most importantly, marketers must distinguish the rhetoric from the reality.

Discussion questions

1 What factors distinguish a marketing plan that incorporates relational strategies from a more traditional plan?

2 Why might the management of customer information become even more important in the future?

3 What, in your judgement, are the most sustainable and least sustainable criticisms of RM?

A difficult age

Not long after the turn of the last century, car legend Henry Ford told an interviewer at the *Chicago Tribune* that 'History is more or less bunk'. His point? Radical innovation comes not from gazing at the past but taking a leap into the unknown.

And in a sense he was right. Too many companies, stifled and smothered by both attitudes and systems that promote what worked before, do very little real innovation – the sort of innovation so desperately needed to promote enduring growth.

John Kearon, founding partner of innovation agency Brand Genetics, argues that marketing has little reason to be proud of its first century. He has cited as evidence statistics showing that only 4% of those 50 biggest fmcg brands which were the foundation of the category in which they operate – Coca-Cola, Pampers, Persil *et al.* – have been developed in the last 50 years.

So no stars for category innovation. But there is another, less publicised but more fundamental problem which affects companies of all shades and hues. And that is, after a decade or so of corporate slash and burn, as well as a merry-go-round of mergers and acquisitions, too many companies try and create their future having lost their sense of history of what made them special. Now too often they are just another collection of insecure people scared of the future and so constantly looking for salvation by reinventing themselves.

This isn't about the history of the company being preserved in aspic in adulatory books written to show the company in its best historical light. This is the real history of a company, the stuff of reality, the collection of triumphs and disasters that saw a group of people conquer or be conquered in the battlefield of the market. It's the corporate memory.

Unfortunately, marketers, charged with helping to ensure the futures of their organisations, too often deliberately ignore the past because it is just that – the past. Marketing, probably more than any other function, is prone to the 'new broom' syndrome which sees the eager new marketing manager ready to make a clean sweep of all that went on before. Get rid of the old campaigns, no matter how well they worked. Extend the brand, despite hind-sight telling them that few extensions survive in the long term. And get away with it – since for many, in other parts of the company, marketing is regarded as a black hole.

To be fair, in too many cases that history has been lost anyway. Some of the first victims in the great re-engineering boom were those with a sense of the corporate story. A lot of big companies even had corporate archivists who recorded the company over time. But that went in the pursuit of shareholder value as a wasteful overhead. Hence the current desperate bid to install knowledge management systems, as companies belatedly realise that losing the knowledge of seasoned, experienced staff can put a big dent in their competitive position.

Take the trap so many retailers have locked themselves into with loyalty cards. History should have told them there is a difference between real loyalty, based on the right offering, as opposed to the false loyalty engendered by investment-draining schemes.

▶

It's no surprise the chairman of Sainsbury's, Sir George Bull, told the *FT* the retailer has to rebuild its core business to achieve regeneration, 'getting it back to being where it belongs as the best of the supermarkets in the country'. So Sainsbury's, along with other great but ailing brands, has to remind itself of the qualities that gave it its past success and build on them.

It could be argued these are revolutionary times in business where history has no place – where, indeed, when it comes to business models, success will go to those who start from Ground Zero and don't let the weight of the past stifle innovative thinking. And there is some truth to that. But only some. Because it ignores the fact that the ingredients of any successful business contain the same elements: an enticing proposition, good quality and follow-through, and commercial acumen. And that applies as much to the local car repair shop as to the flashiest of dot coms

Marketing has always been comfortable with the new. This isn't surprising. In the scale of things, it's a relatively new profession. But it shouldn't be obsessed with the new: there are lots marketers can learn from the past. You could say it's time for grown-up marketing – because those who ignore history, to paraphrase a famous saying, are condemned to repeat it.

(*Source*: Laura Mazur, *Marketing Business*, December 1999/January 2000)

Case study questions

1 Is marketing obsessed with the new?

2 Why, as suggested in the article, might 'losing the knowledge of seasoned, experienced staff' affect the competitive position of the company?

References

Baker, M.J. (1999) 'Editorial', *Journal of Marketing Management*, 15, 211–14.

Ballantyne, D. (2000) 'Interaction, dialogue and knowledge generation: three key concepts in relationship marketing', in 2nd WWW Conference on Relationship Marketing, 15 November 1999–15 February 2000, paper 7 (www.mcb.co.uk/services/conferen/nov99/rm).

Barnes, J.G. (1994) 'Close to the customer: but is it really a relationship?', *Journal of Marketing Management*, 10, 561–70.

Barnes, J.G. and Howlett, D.M. (1998) 'Predictors of equity in relationships between service providers and retail customers', *International Journal of Bank Marketing*, 16 (1), 5–23.

Bejou, D. and Palmer, A. (1998) 'Service failure and loyalty: an exploratory empirical study of airline customers', *Journal of Services Marketing*, 12 (1), 7–22.

Blois, K.J. (1997) 'When is a relationship a relationship?', in Gemünden, H.G., Rittert, T. and Walter, A. (eds) *Relationships and Networks in International Markets*. Oxford: Elsevier, pp. 53–64.

Brassington, F. and Pettitt, S. (1997) *The Principles of Marketing*. London: Pitman.

Brennan, R. (1997) 'Buyer/supplier partnering in British industry: the automotive and telecommunications sectors', *Journal of Marketing Management*, 13 (8), 758–76.

Brookes, R. and Little, V. (1997) 'The new marketing. What does 'customer focus' mean?', *Marketing and Research Today*, May, 96–105.

Brown, S. (1998) *Postmodern Marketing II*. London: International Thompson Business Press.

Buttle, F.B. (1996) *Relationship Marketing Theory and Practice*. London: Paul Chapman.

Chaffey, D., Mayer, R., Johnston, K. and Ellis-Chadwick, F. (2000) *Internet Marketing*. Harlow: Pearson Education.

Chaston, I. (1998) 'Evolving "new marketing" philosophies by merging existing concepts: application of process within small high-technology firms', *Journal of Marketing Management*, 14, 273–91.

Copulsky, J.R. and Wolf, M.J. (1990) 'Relationship marketing: positioning for the future', *Journal of Business Strategy*, 11 (4), 16–20.

Damerest, M. (1997) 'Understanding knowledge management', *Long Range Planning*, 30 (3), 374–84.

East, R. (2000) 'Fact and fallacy in retention marketing', Professorial Inaugural Lecture, 1 March, Kingston University Business School, UK.

Fournier, S., Dobscha, S. and Mick, D.G. (1998) 'Preventing the premature death of relationship marketing', *Harvard Business Review*, 76 (1), 42–9.

Gordon, I.H. (1998) *Relationship Marketing*. Etobicoke, Ontario: John Wiley & Sons.

Grönroos, C. (2000) 'The relationship marketing process: interaction, communication, dialogue, value', in 2nd WWW Conference on Relationship Marketing, 15 November 1999–15 February 2000, paper 2 (www.mcb.co.uk/services/conferen/nov99/rm).

Gummesson, E. (1997) 'Relationship marketing – the emperor's new clothes or a paradigm shift?', *Marketing and Research Today*, February, 53–60.

Gummesson, E. (1999) *Total Relationship Marketing: Rethinking Marketing Management from 4Ps to 30Rs*. Oxford: Butterworth Heinemann.

Holland R. (1990) 'The paradigm plague: prevention, cure and inoculation', *Tavistock Institute of Human Relations*, 43 (1), 23–48.

Kunøe, G. (1998) 'On the ability of ad agencies to assist in developing one-to-one communication: measuring "the core of dialogue"', *European Journal of Marketing*, 32 (11/12), 1124–37.

Littler, D. (1998) 'Editorial; Perspective on consumer behaviour', *Journal of Marketing Management*, 14, 1–2.

Mattsson, L.G. (1997) 'Relationships in a network perspective' in Gemünden, H.G., Rittert, T. and Walter, A. (eds) *Relationships and Networks in International Markets*. Oxford: Elsevier, pp. 37–47.

Mazur, L. (2000) 'A difficult age', *Marketing Business*, December 1999/January 2000, 33.

McDonald, M. (1999) 'Strategic marketing planning: theory and practice' in Baker, M. (ed.) *The CIM Marketing Book*, 4th edn. Oxford: Butterworth Heinemann, pp. 50–77.

McDonald, M. (2000) 'On the right track', *Marketing Business*, April, 28–31, 28.

Micklethwait, J. and Wooldridge, A. (1996) *The Witch Doctors: What the Management Gurus are Saying*. London: Heinemann.

Mitchell, A. (1997) 'Evolution', *Marketing Business*, June, 37.

Morgan, R.M. and Hunt, S.D. (1994) 'The commitment–trust theory of relationship marketing', *Journal of Marketing*, 58 (3), 20–38.

O'Malley, L. and Tynan, C. (1999) 'The utility of the relationship metaphor in consumer markets: a critical evaluation', *Journal of Marketing Management*, 15, 587–602.

O'Malley, L. and Tynan, C. (2000) 'Relationship marketing in consumer markets; rhetoric or reality?', *European Journal of Marketing*, 34 (7).

O'Malley, L., Patterson, M. and Evans, M. (1997) 'Intimacy or intrusion? The privacy dilemma for relationship marketing in consumer markets', *Journal of Marketing Management*, 13 (6), 541–59.

O'Malley, L., Patterson, M. and Evans, M. (1999) *Exploring Direct Marketing*. London: International Thompson Business Press.

Palmer, A.J. (1996) 'Relationship marketing: a universal paradigm or management fad?', *The Learning Organisation*, 3 (3), 18–25.

Palmer, A.J. (1998) *Principles of Services Marketing*. London: Kogan Page.

Payne, A., Christopher, M. and Peck, H. (eds) (1995) *Relationship Marketing for Competitive Advantage: Winning and Keeping Customers*. Oxford: Butterworth Heinemann.

Pels, J. (1999) 'Exchange relationships in consumer markets?', *European Journal of Marketing*, 33 (1/2), 19–37.

Peppers, D. and Rogers, M. (2000) 'Build a one-to-one learning relationship with your customers', *Interactive Marketing*, 1 (3), 243–50.

Prabhaker, P.R. (2000) 'Who owns the on-line consumer?', *Journal of Consumer Marketing*, 17 (2), 158–71.

Reichheld, F.F. (1993) 'Loyalty based management', *Harvard Business Review*, March/April, 64–73.

Ryals, L. (2000) 'Planning for relationship marketing' in Cranfield School of Management *Marketing Management: A Relationship Marketing Perspective*. Basingstoke: Macmillan, pp. 231–48.

Sheth, J.N. and Parvatiyar, A. (1995) 'The evolution of relationship marketing', *International Business Review*, 4 (4), 397–418.

Smith, W. and Higgins, M. (2000) 'Reconsidering the relationship analogy', *Journal of Marketing Management*, 16, 81–94.

Thomas, M.J. (2000) 'Commentary: princely thoughts on Machiavelli, marketing and management', *European Journal of Marketing*, 34 (5/6), 524–37.

Zineldin, M. (2000) 'Beyond relationship marketing: technologicalship marketing', *Marketing Intelligence and Planning*, 18 (1), 9–23.

Index

Relationship Marketing

Exploring relational strategies in marketing

John Egan

Relationship Marketing: Exploring relational strategies in marketing comprehensively examines relationships in marketing and how these influence modern marketing strategy and practice. Based principally on the concepts and theories surrounding relationship marketing, John Egan critically reviews and analyses what has been described as 'marketing's new paradigm'.

Key features:

- written in a clear, easy-to-read, informal style
- real-life examples and cases throughout, to bring the subject alive
- learning objectives and chapter summaries put each chapter in context
- annotated reading lists for further study

Relationship Marketing: Exploring relational strategies in marketing should be of particular interest to both undergraduate and postgraduate students studying for a general marketing qualification as well as those specialising in Service Marketing, Marketing Communications and Relationship Marketing. It will also be of benefit to marketing practitioners.

For tutors: There is an Instructor's Manual to accompany this text, available to adopters at www.booksites.net/Egan.

John Egan is Principal Lecturer at Middlesex University Business School and a Chartered Marketer. He has twenty-four years' experience working in the retail marketing sector with companies such as Bloomingdales (New York), Hudson Bay Company (Canada), Harrods (UK), Chinacraft, Mappin & Webb and Garrard (the Crown Jewellers). He is a fellow of the Royal Society of Arts and Commerce and a member of the Chartered Institute of Marketing, Institute of Direct Marketing and the Academy of Marketing.

ISBN 0-273-64612-5

9 780273 646129 >

www.pearsoneduc.com

FT Prentice Hall
FINANCIAL TIMES

an imprint of PEARSON Education